도서관과
경제성 분석

연구논집

도서관과
경제성 분석

정혜경 지음

▋서문

18년 전, 대학원 첫 수업 시간의 기억이 생생하다.

10여 개의 다양한 도서관 주제를 다루는 세미나 형식의 전공필수 과목이었다. 이 과목에서 학생들은 개별적으로 주어진 특정 주제에 대해 문헌을 읽고 발표하게 되어 있었다. 나에게 할당된 주제는 "도서관과 경제성 분석"이었다.

"도서관의 경제성을 굳이 입증해야 하는가?

도서관은 존재 그 자체로 가치 있는 건 아닌가?

내가 아니라도 내 가족이, 우리의 후대가, 그리고 지금이 아니라도 언제든지 필요할 때 갈 수 있는 곳이 도서관 아닌가?"

그 당시 내 머릿속을 스친 생각은 그 이상도, 그 이하도 아니었다.

그러나 이러한 의구심은 선행문헌을 읽고 분석해 나가면서 서서히 걷히기 시작했다.

IT 기술의 발달은 삶의 질을 바꾸었다.

누구나 다양한 플랫폼을 통해 곳곳에 편재된 여러 형태의 정보에 손쉽게 접근할 수 있게 되었다. 이제 도서관 존재 자체를 막연한 경쟁력으로 주장하던 시대는 지났다. 도서관이란 공간은 필요한 정보를 얻기 위한 수많은 알고리즘 중 하나일 뿐이다. 도서관의 미래에 대한 고민이 필요한 시점이 되었다.

　이러한 시대적인 요구에 따라 국내·외 도서관계에도 변화의 조짐이 나타나게 되었다. 도서관계는 정보서비스 분야에서의 무한한 활용 가능성을 찾는 능동적인 움직임으로 그 가치를 최대한 부각해야 할 필요성을 인지하게 되었다. 고객이 원하는 바를 쫓아가기에 급급한 수동적인 서비스로 도서관의 경쟁력을 보여주긴 역부족이기 때문이다. 2000년대 초에 들어오면서 도서관이 예산의 설정·배분 등 주요한 의사결정 과정에서 선(先) 순위를 확보해야 한다는 데 대한 합의와 함께 해외 학자들(Aabø, Svanhild 등)을 중심으로 도서관의 경제적 가치측정 연구의 물꼬가 트이기 시작하였다.

　이와 같은 맥락에서, 본 연구논집은 도서관에 관한 가치측정의 필요성을 공유하고 경제성 분석모형을 체계화하기 위한 목적으로 저자가 지난 20년간 국내외 학술지에 발표한 논문들을 엮어서 출간하게 되었다. 크게 세 개의 범주로 구분할 수 있다. 제1장, 국내 디지털 사업 초기 대표사업인 디지털 아카이빙의 타당성 분석모형; 제2장, 지역사회와 주민들에게 제공하는 다양한 도서관 서비스의 가치에 관한 경제적 분석모형; 그리고 제3장은 도서관에 적용된 '가상가치평가법(Contingent Valuation Method, CVM)'의 편의(bias) 검토 및 경제적 가치평가 모형을 제시한다.

도서관 정보서비스와 같은 공공재는 시장에서 거래되는 민간재와 달리 시장가격이 형성되어 있지 않아 그 가치를 입증하기 위해서는 시장가격으로 환산할 필요가 있다. 제1, 2장은 도서관 서비스에 포함된 무형편익의 파악과 이를 포함한 경제적 가치측정 모형을 제시한다. 제3장은 생태계나 환경 서비스 등 공공재의 가치추정을 위하여 거의 유일하게 사용되어 온 가상가치평가법(CVM)을 적용할 때 평가결과를 왜곡시키는 주요 편의들을 완화하는 여러 가지 방안들을 제시하고 있다.

필자는 본 연구논집이 후속 연구 및 교육에 적극적으로 활용되어 도서관의 경제성 분석연구를 선도해 가는 밑거름이 되기를 기대한다. 아울러, 후속 연구를 통해 도서관의 가치측정에 사용되는 가상가치평가법(CVM)의 결과를 왜곡시키는 다양한 편의의 원인을 메타분석을 통해 통계적으로 검증함으로써 CVM의 신뢰성을 확보하는 근본적인 대안을 제시할 수 있기를 바란다. 다만, 제한된 지면으로 인하여 모든 논문의 전문을 싣지 못하는 부분에 대하여 독자 여러분의 양해를 구하는 바이다.

　이 책이 세상에 나올 수 있도록 함께 연구했던 동료, 제자, 그리고 결과 활용에 도움을 준 한국무역정보통신 최동준 박사, 출판을 가능케 해 준 한국학술정보 채종준 대표님께 감사드린다. 끝으로 지나온 60년간의 삶을 함께 나누며 회갑 기념으로 이러한 저술을 하도록 격려해준 가족 모두에게 무한한 고마움과 사랑을 표한다.

2020년 7월
정혜경

▌목차

제3장 도서관과 가상가치평가법(CVM)

디지털 아카이빙의
경제성 분석

2000년대 초 정보통신기술의 발달로 인해 행정의 효율성 증대 및 대국민 서비스 활성화를 위한 전자정부의 구현을 위한 노력이 선진국을 중심으로 앞다투어 이루어지고 있었다. 국내에서도 국가 행정기관을 중심으로 초기 정보화 사업의 마련을 위한 핵심과제 중 하나인 디지털 아카이빙 사업 및 DB 구축사업이 추진되기 시작했다. 디지털 아카이빙은 디지털 형태로 생산된 문서와 본래 인쇄 매체로 생산되었으나 이후에 디지털로 매체 변환된 전자문서의 관리를 지원하는 활동으로 정의된다.

'디지털 아카이빙의 경제성 분석 연구(2004)'는 디지털 아카이빙의 무형편익을 파악하고, 이를 정량적인 가치로 환산하기 위한 모형을 제시하는 것이 목적이다. 초기 연구들은 디지털 아카이빙 사업의 공간 절약, 교통비용 절감 등의 가시적인(유형) 편익 연구에만 초점을 두고, 무형편익인 행정 효율성(의사소통 향상 등)을 정량화하려는 노력은 거의 전무한 상태였다. 즉, 선행연구에서는 디지털 아카이빙 사업에 드는 막대한 초기 비용(스캐닝, 인코딩, 저장등록, 시스템 구축, 콘텐츠 유지 등)과 유형편익만을 고려하여 경제적 가치를 평가하였으므로 디지털 아카이빙 사업 추진의 타당성에 의문이 제기될 수

밖에 없었다. 그런데도 이를 해소할 수 있는 종합적 연구는 거의 찾아볼 수 없었다. 우리에게 적합한 전자정부의 방향과 개념을 확립하기 위하여, 디지털 아카이빙 사업에 대한 수요와 경제성 파악을 통한 타당성 입증이 선행되어야 할 필요성이 제기되었다.

본 연구는 기존 연구와 달리 유형편익뿐만 아니라 무형편익을 포함하여 디지털 아카이빙의 타당성을 구체적으로 측정하고자 하는 시도를 하였다. 무형편익에 디지털 아카이빙의 가치가속과 가치연결로 인한 가치를 설정하였다. 가치가속으로 인한 편익은 기존 인쇄문서보다 디지털 매체에 신속하게 접근할 수 있어 절감되는 접근시간의 효과로, 가치연결 효과는 디지털 매체로 인한 업무의 효율성 향상, 즉 기관 내 의사소통의 향상(타 부서 방문 빈도, 전화통화 빈도, 메시지 보내는 빈도, 회의 빈도 감소횟수의 합)으로 절감되는 근로자의 기회비용을 적용하였다. 유형편익은 디지털 아카이빙 사업 도입으로 인해 절감 또는 회피할 수 있는 공간비, 시설비, 복사비의 합이며, 비용은 공간비, 인건비, 시설·장비비, 전산장비비, 유지보수비 등이 포함되었다.

이 모형을 기존에 디지털 아카이빙을 도입하여 활용하고 있는 국내 9개 공공기관을 대상으로 한 사례분석을 통해서 디지털 아카이빙 사업으로 인한 부가가치를 정량적으로 파악하였다. 사례분석 결과, 유형편익만을 포함하였을 때 디지털 아카이빙의 경제성은 거의 없으나, 가치연결 효과 및 가치가속의 무형편익을 단계적으로 추가하게 되면서 경제성이 큰 폭으로 증가하면서 8개 기관에서 투자한 비용대비 경제성이 있는 것으로 나타났다. 다만, 시도교육청 등 대부분의 사례분석 대상기관이 시범 운영하는 단계라 설문지 회수율이 저조하였다는 한계가 있음에도 불구하고, 디지털 아카이빙의 도입은 궁극적으로 기관 운영의 효율성 향상에 이바지하였음을 입증하였으므로 국내 전자정부의 방향성 구축을 위한 전략적 근거를 제시하였다는 점에서 의의가 있다고 하겠다.

'디지털 보존의 비용요소에 관한 연구 (2005)'[1]는 디지털 자료에의 정기적인 접근을 보장하기 위한 디지털 보존비용의 산출식을 제시하고 있다. 본 연구는 디지털화 사업을 대규모로 진행하고 있는 국내 두 대형 도서관(국립대학도서관, 공공도서관)을 대상으로 사례 분석하여 보존현황 체계와 이에 따른 보존비용을 분석하였다. 디지털 보존은 "디지털 콘텐츠의 무결성(integrity)을 유지하면서 디지털 매체의 손상 및 하드웨어, 소프트웨어의 문제로 인한 기술적 퇴화의 위협으로부터 디지털 객체를 안전하게 보호하는 일련의 관리 활동"으로 정의한다.

연구 결과, 두 도서관의 디지털 아카이빙 사업에 드는 보존비용은 초기 원문 DB 구축비용의 8.6%와 11.8%로 나타났다. 한편 이들 보존비용은 초기 단계의 필수적인 보존 활동에만 제한되어 있다는 점을 고려할 때, 실제로 디지털 아카이빙 사업을 도입하기 위해서는 그 이상의 보존비용을 확보해야 할 것으로 생각한다.

---

1) 이 논문은 제한된 지면으로 본문에 포함하지 못함. 2005년 정보관리학회지 22권 1호(47~64쪽)를 참조하기 바람

디지털 아카이빙의 경제성 분석연구[2]

한 기관이 디지털 아카이빙을 도입하기 위해서는 경제성 분석이 선행된다. 기존의 경제성 분석은 유형적 편익만을 고려하여 무형적 편익은 간과됐으나, 디지털 아카이빙의 무형적 가치를 반영하여 분석하는 모형이 필요하다. 본 연구는 정보경제학 측면의 가치사슬 개념을 적용하여 종합적인 경제성 분석 모형을 제시하였다. 가치가속과 가치연결 개념을 도입하여 디지털 아카이빙의 경제성을 사례분석하고, 민감도 분석을 통하여 경제성의 요인들을 추출한다. 연구 결과는 국내 기관들에 디지털 아카이빙의 도입이 효율성 향상에 이바지한다는 인식을 확산시킬 것으로 기대된다.

---

2) 이 논문은 2004년 한국문헌정보학회지 38권 4호(251~270쪽)에 게재되었음.

1. 서 론

우리 사회가 디지털 중심의 정보사회로 진전함에 따라 디지털 기록물에 대한 비중과 의존도가 현저히 높아지는 만큼 이에 대한 구체적이고 체계적인 관리 방안의 필요성이 대두되고 있다. 인쇄 매체에 담긴 정보보다 보존 기간이 짧은 디지털 정보를 관리하고 진본성을 유지하기 위해 디지털 아카이빙[3]을 도입하는 기관들이 나타나고 있는 것이 좋은 예이다. 이들은 디지털 정보의 보존 관리뿐만 아니라 이로 인해 발생하는 공간 절약 등의 유형편익 그리고 시간 절약, 유용성, 의사소통 향상 등의 무형편익에 대해 막연한 기대를 하고 있다. 그러나 디지털 아카이빙의 도입에는 스캐닝, 인코딩, 저장등록 및 시스템 구축 등에 대규모의 초기 투자비용이 요구되기 때문에, 이들의 기대는 단기간 내에 충족되기 어렵다.

한편 기관들은(특히 영리 기관) 사업투자 평가 시 타당성 입증을 요구하여 경제성이 높은 것으로 판명된 사업에 우선순위를 두는 것이 일반적이다. 따라서 국내에서는 디지털 아카이빙으로 인해 발생하는 여러 가지 편익에도 불구하고 이의 도입을 적극적으로 추진하지 못하고 실정이다. 이에 비해 선진국에서는 디지털 아카이빙의 도입이 활발하게 진행되고 있는데, 이는 기록물 관리의 중요성에 대한 인식이 확산해 있기 때문이다. 따라서 국내에 디지털 아카이빙의 도입을 활성화하기 위해서는 디지털 아카이빙의 도입에 대한 타당성 입증이 선행되어야 하며, 궁극적으로 기록관리의 중요성과 디지털화

---

3) 디지털 아카이빙(Digital Archiving)은 "디지털 형태로 생산된 기록물과 본래 인쇄 매체로 생산되었으나 이후에 디지털로 매체 변환된 자료관 기록물의 장기(또는 영구) 보존을 지원하는 활동"으로 정의함.

의 효율성에 대한 인식이 확산할 필요가 있다. 그러나 이 분야의 기존 경제성 분석은 기록물의 처리에 드는 비용이나, 유형편익만을 포함하여 평가되기 때문에 그 가치를 과소평가하는 경향이 있다.

　디지털 아카이빙의 경제적인 가치를 종합적으로 분석할 수 있는 기본모형의 개발이 시급한 시점이다. 이 모형은 기존의 모형과 달리 디지털 아카이빙의 무형적인 가치를 포함하며, 이를 정량적으로 분석할 수 있는 구체적인 측정 방법을 제시할 수 있어야 한다. 이러한 모형을 바탕으로 평가된 디지털 아카이빙의 경제성은 각 기관의 의사결정자들이 이 사업이 투자자금의 단기 회수를 위한 것이 아니라 업무의 효율성 증대를 통한 기관의 중장기적 목표를 달성하기 위한 것임을 입증할 수 있는 근거가 될 수 있다. 디지털 아카이빙의 경제성 분석 사례는 기존 연구에서는 찾아보기 어려우므로 관련 분야인 기록관리, 정보시스템 및 디지털화의 경제성에 관한 여러 이론과 모형을 근거로 경제성 분석의 기본모형을 도출하는 것이 필요하다. 이러한 필요성에 따라 본 연구에서 수행하고자 하는 연구의 목적은 다음과 같다.

　첫째, 무형편익을 포함하여 종합적으로 디지털 아카이빙의 경제성을 분석할 수 있는 모형을 도출한다.

　둘째, 이 모형을 현재 디지털 아카이빙을 도입하여 활용하고 있는 국내의 기관들에 적용하여 정량적인 경제성을 파악한다.

　셋째, 분석대상 기관들의 디지털 아카이빙 담당자 또는 책임자를 대상으로 한 심층 면담을 통하여 디지털 아카이빙의 경제성에 영향을 미치는 요인들을 파악한다.

2. 연구 방법

2.1 연구의 설계 및 절차

본 연구는 디지털 아카이빙의 종합적 가치를 평가할 수 있는 기본 틀을 구축함으로써 유형편익의 측정에만 주안점을 두는 기존의 경제성 분석모형으로 인한 문제점을 해결하고자 하였다. 데이터 수집은 정량적 조사 방법과 정성적 조사 방법을 병용하여 이루어졌다. 정량적 조사를 위한 데이터 수집은 디지털 아카이빙 사용자 대상의 설문 조사를 통하여 이루어졌다. 정성적 조사는 경제성에 미치는 요인을 분석하기 위한 것으로서 디지털 아카이빙 담당자 및 책임자와의 심층 면담을 통하여 자료를 수집하였다.

경제성 분석에 사용되는 가정들에 대한 불확실성과 이로 인하여 발생하는 결과에 대한 신뢰도 문제를 해결하기 위하여 미래의 상황 변화에 따른 경제성 변화 내역을 민감도 분석을 통하여 추정하였다. 또한, 디지털 아카이빙의 경제성 분석에 영향을 미칠 수 있는 요인들(기관의 유형, 도입 목적, 구축 방법)에 따라 나타나는 경제성의 차이가 통계적으로 유의한지를 검증함으로써 디지털 아카이빙의 도입 계획 및 전략에 근거를 제시하고자 하였다. 본 연구의 절차는 크게 네 부분으로 구성된다.

첫 번째, 관련 분야의 경제성에 관한 여러 이론과 모형으로부터 디지털 아카이빙의 경제성 분석에 적용할 수 있는 모형을 도출한다.

두 번째, 도출된 디지털 아카이빙의 경제성 분석모형을 현재 국내에서 디지털 아카이빙을 구축하여 활용하고 있는 기

관들을 대상으로 사례분석을 시행한다. 사례분석은 심
층 면접과 설문 조사를 통해 수행되며 분석대상은 국내
광역지자체 3개 기관, 시도교육청 3개 기관, 그리고 일
반 기업체 3개 기관으로 총 9개 기관이다.
세 번째, 할인율과 공사비의 변화에 따른 분석 결과의 오차를 최
소화하기 위하여 경제성의 변화 내역에 대한 민감도 분
석을 시행한다.
네 번째, 디지털 아카이빙의 경제성에 영향을 미치는 요인을 파
악하고 이들이 통계적으로 유의한 차이를 주는지 검증
하기 위해서 요인 비교분석을 시행한다.

2.2 경제성 분석모형 도출방법

디지털 아카이빙의 경제성 분석모형은 관련 분야인 기록관리, 정
보시스템 및 디지털화의 경제성에 관한 선행연구로부터 비용편익분
석의 요소인 비용, 유형편익 및 무형편익을 기준으로 삼아 추출하
였다. 추출된 이론과 모형을 토대로 실시된 적합성 평가는 보편타
당성과 정량적 측정 가능성 유무를 기준으로 이루어졌다. 이때 보
편타당성의 기준은 제시된 분석모형이 타 연구에서 적용된 사례가
있는지다. (그림 2-1 참조)

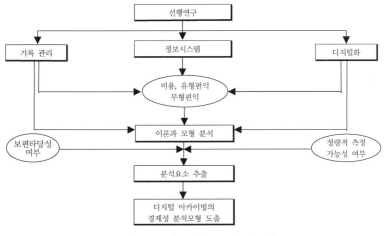

<그림 2-1> 경제성 분석모형 도출방법

2.3 경제성 분석방법

2003년 8월부터 11월까지 4개월간 디지털 아카이빙 사용자 대상의 설문 조사와 담당자들과의 심층 면담을 통한 자료 수집이 이루어졌다. 설문대상자의 수는 총 630명으로 각 기관에서 70명씩을 할당 추출하였다. 설문지의 문항은 인구통계학적 요인들, 가치가속에 의한 효과, 그리고 가치연결에 의한 효과를 측정하기 위한 항목 및 기타 항목으로 구성하였다. 심층 면담에는 디지털 아카이빙의 도입목적, 구축 방법, 소요된 비용 등의 문항이 포함되어 있다. 이를 토대로 디지털 아카이빙의 편익을 직접편익, 가치가속 그리고 가치연결의 효과로 구분한 다음, 이들 각각의 효과를 단계적으로 추가하는 분석방법을 실시하였다. 이는 직접편익을 통한 유형적인 가치만으로 경제성을 평가하는 방법에 비해 가치가속, 가치연결의 무형적 효과가 추가되었을 때 디지털 아카이빙의 가치가 얼마나 향상되는

지를 비교·분석하기 위한 것이다.

경제성 분석에서 최소 분석 기간은 10년이라는 것이 전문가의 견해이며, 디지털 아카이빙이 국내에서는 초기 단계여서 예측 불허한 부분이 많이 발생할 수 있어서 본 연구에서는 사례분석 기간을 10년으로 설정하였다.[4] 분석대상으로는 디지털 아카이빙을 도입하여 이를 업무에 활용하고 있는 기관만을 포함하였다. 이는 잠재 사용자 수를 추정하는 데 있어서 실제치(도입 후 현재까지의 활용빈도)를 근거로 함으로써 추정 오차를 최대한 줄이기 위한 것이다. 선정된 분석대상은 크게 공공기관과 민간기관으로 구분되며, 공공기관은 광역지자체와 시도교육청으로 나누어진다.

2.3.1 분석 도구

분석 도구로는 투자 대안을 평가할 때 자주 사용되는 순 편익, 순 현재가치와 편익비용비율을 사용하였다(그림 2-2 참조). 순 편익과 순 현재가치의 한계점을 보완하기 위해 편익비용비율을 측정지표에 추가함으로써 규모와 관계없이 기관 간의 객관적인 평가가 가능하도록 하였다. 순 현재가치 추정 시 각 기관의 디지털 아카이빙 도입연도에 해당하는 국고채 평균 수익률을 할인율로 적용하였다.[5] 또한, 편익비용비율을 측정지표로 함께 선정함으로써 순 현재가치만을 기준으로 했을 때 대규모 사업에 통상 유리하게 나타나는 사업의 규모에 따른 문제점을 보완하며 경제성 분석 결과에 대한 비

---

4) 한국개발연구원 공공투자관리센터

5) 국고채 수익률은 정부가 발행하는 국공채에 부과된 이자율로서 정부가 민간 부분으로부터 차입하는 차입금에 대하여 지불하는 이자율로 무위험 수익률(risk-free rate)임. 국고채 평균 수익률: 1999년(9.03%), 2000년(6.70%), 2001년(5.91%), 2003년(4.23%).

교가 가능하도록 하였다.

* 순 편익(net benefit) = 편익(benefit) - 비용(cost)

* 순 현재가치(Net Present Value: NPV)

$$\sum_{n=0}^{n} PVn = \frac{(B-C)_0}{(1+r)^0} + \frac{(B-C)_1}{(1+r)^1} + \frac{(B-C)_2}{(1+r)^2} +$$

$$\frac{(B-C)_3}{(1+r)^3} + \ldots + \frac{(B-C)_n}{(1+r)^n}$$

(PVn: n 해의 순 편익의 현재가치, r: 할인율, B: 편익, C: 비용)

* 편익비용비율(ratio of benefit to cost)=편익(benefit)/비용(cost)

$$\frac{B}{C} = \sum_{n=0}^{n} \frac{B_n}{(1+r)^n} \div \sum_{n=0}^{n} \frac{C_n}{(1+r)^n}$$

(r: 할인율, B: 편익, C: 비용)

<그림 2-2> 디지털 아카이빙의 경제성 분석 도구

2.3.2 민감도 분석

일반적으로 경제성 분석을 하는 데는 여러 가지 상황을 가정하여 경제성을 분석하는 것이기 때문에 불확실성이 존재하며, 이로 인해 추정결과에 대한 신뢰도의 문제가 제기될 수 있다. 따라서 민감도 분석을 함으로써 이 사업의 미래 불확실성이 얼마나 큰가를 가늠해 보고자 하였다. 민감도 분석을 시행한 내용은 크게 두 가지로 구분 된다. 첫째는 할인율, 둘째는 공사비의 차이에 대한 경제성 변화 내 역이다. 민감도 분석에서는 국고채 수익률을 중위 수준으로 놓고 고위수준은 7.5% 사회적 할인율[6]을, 저위수준은 기준연도의 물가 상승률을 적용하여 경제성이 어떻게 변화하는지 살펴보았다. 물가

6) 사회적 할인율 7.5%는 한국개발연구원(2000년도)의 예비타당성조사 연구보고서에서 제안한 수치임.

상승률은 디지털 아카이빙이 도입된 기준연도의 수치를 연구기간 동안 일정하게 적용하였다.

할인율에 대한 민감도 분석에서는 가정한 변수들의 변화 정도를 저위수준, 중위 수준, 고위수준의 세 단계로 구분한 다음, 각 단계에서의 경제성을 분석하였다. 이때 중위수준은 본 연구의 경제성 분석에서 사용한 가정치이다. 저위수준은 본 연구의 가정치보다 낮아졌을 경우이며, 고위수준은 본 연구에서의 가정치보다 높아졌을 경우의 가정치이다. 한편 공사비에 대한 민감도 분석에서는 변화의 내역을 고위수준과 저위수준의 두 단계로 구분하였다. 고위수준은 본 연구의 경제성 분석에서, 저위수준은 단순히 구조를 재배치함으로써 자료관을 설립한 경우의 가정치이다. 민감도 분석에서 효과로 본 내용은 직접편익, 가치가속, 가치연결을 포함한 내용이다.

2.3.3 요인 비교분석

요인 비교분석은 디지털 아카이빙의 경제성에 영향을 미치는 주요 요인들을 파악하여 디지털 아카이빙에 대한 도입 여부를 판단하는 데 유용한 기준을 제공하기 위한 것이다. 기관의 유형, 도입 목적, 구축 방법을 디지털 아카이빙의 경제성에 영향을 미칠 수 있는 요인으로 설정하고 이에 초점을 맞추어 심층 면담을 수행하였다. 심층 면담 분석은 면담내용을 모두 간략 기록의 형태로 옮긴 뒤, Lincoln and Guba(1985)의 자료 분석방법인 단위화와 범주화의 단계를 거쳐 이루어졌다.[7] 이러한 요인(독립변인)을 토대로 다음과 같이 가설을

---

7) 단위화란 데이터가 독자적인 의미를 가질 수 있는 최소한의 단위로 나누는 방법임. 범주화란 단위화 된 데이터를 각 단위의 전체 상황에서의 특성과 의미를 고려하여 범주를 정하는 방법임.

설정하여 통계적으로 유의한지를 검증하였다.

가설 1) 기관의 유형(광역지자체 對 시도교육청 對 일반 기업체)에
따라 디지털 아카이빙의 경제성에 미치는 영향에는 차이
가 있을 것이다.

가설 2) 도입 목적(활용 對 보존)에 따라 디지털 아카이빙의 경
제성에 미치는 영향에는 차이가 있을 것이다.

가설 3) 구축 방법(외부용역 對 자체작업)에 따라 디지털 아카이
빙의 경제성에 미치는 영향에는 차이가 있을 것이다.

독립변인인 기관의 유형, 도입 목적, 구축 방법이 실제로 경제성에 유
의한 차이를 가져오는지를 검증하기 위하여 수집한 9개 기관의 데이터를
정량적인 방법을 이용하여 항목별 비교 요인분석을 시행하였다. 유의도
검증은 p-값 0.05를 기준으로 하였으며, 검증방법으로는 Kruskal-Wallis
test와 Wilcoxon Two-Sample test를 사용하였다.

3. 경제성 분석모형의 도출

3.1 경제성 분석이론과 모형분석

(1) 경제성 분석방법 모형

1990년대에 들어서면서 비용에 국한된 기존의 처리비용 연구와는
달리 투입된 비용과 이로 인해 발생하는 편익을 함께 고려하여 경제
성을 추정해야 한다고 주장하는 기록관리 분야에서의 연구들이 발표
되었다. Brumm(1993)은 기록관리의 효과를 파악하기 위하여 비용편

익분석을 사용하여 사례분석을 수행하였으며 Dmytrenko (1997)는 비용편익분석이 기록관리의 경제성 분석을 위하여 가장 전략적인 방법이라고 주장하였다. Saffady(1999)는 기록관리의 경제성 분석에 사용될 수 있는 방법-비용편익분석, 비용효과분석, 투자액회수기간, 투자수익률-을 비교·설명하였다. 이 연구 중 편익을 고려하여 정량적으로 경제성을 평가하고 후속 연구에 따라 그 타당성이 입증된 모형은 비용편익분석이다.

(2) 비용분석 모형

비용분석 모형은 크게 처리비용 분석과 분석비용의 범주화에 관한 연구로 나뉜다. Maher(1982)와 Wilstead(1989)는 기록물 처리에 소요되는 평균 단가를 인건비, 자재비 및 서가비를 고려하여 산출하였는데, 이 결과는 타 기관에 적용하는 데에는 한계가 있는 것으로 나타났다. 한편 Ericksen and Shuster(1995)는 저장비, 보존비, 행정비를 추가하여 처리비용의 단가를 산출하였으며 결과의 객관성을 보완하기 위해 비율로 산출하는 방법을 제시하였다. 이 분석모형은 Saffady(1999)의 연구에서 기록관리의 경제성 분석을 위해서 적용된 바 있다. 경제성 분석비용의 범주화 방법으로는 디지털 아카이빙 관련 분야의 여러 이론과 모형 중 Saffady(1999)와 Kingma(2000)에 의하여 제시된 고정비용과 가변비용의 범주화 방법이 채택되었으며, 이는 초기에 고정비용이 크게 투입되는 반면, 가변비용이 거의 없는 디지털 아카이빙의 특성을 고려한 것이다. 디지털 아카이빙의 관련 분야에서 추출된 비용 범주화 모형을 보편타당성과 정량적 측정 가능성 측면에서 분석하면 <표 3-1>과 같다.

<표 3-1> 비용모형 분석표

모형		보편 타당성	정량적 측정 가능성
연구	내용		
마허(1982), 월스테드(1989)	인건비, 자재비, 서가비	X	O
에릭슨과 슈스터(1995)	인건비, 자재비, 서가비, 저장비, 보존비, 행정비	O	O
이국희(1992)	직접비용과 간접비용	X	O
브럼(1993)	직접비용과 간접비용	X	O
김효석(1996)	하드웨어 비용, 통신비, 인건비, 기타	X	O
새퍼디(1999)	직접 vs. 간접비용, 고정 vs. 가변비용 통제 vs. 비 통제비용, 초기 구축비용 vs. 유지비용	O	O
킹마(2000)	고정, 가변비용	O	O

(3) 편익분석 모형

편익분석 모형은 크게 유형편익과 무형편익 분석모형으로 구분된다. 유형편익 분석모형으로는 Brumm(1993)이 제시한 비용 절감과 비용회피의 유형편익이 Dmytrenko(1997)의 연구에 적용됨으로써 보편타당성이 있고 정량적 측정이 가능한 요소로 적합성이 인정되었다. 한편 무형편익에 대한 경제성 분석은 Schement(1990), Skupsky(1991), Silver(1998)를 비롯한 몇몇 연구에서 나타나기 시작하였으며, Cisco(1999)와 Saffady(1999)는 이러한 무형의 편익을 계량화하여 측정할 필요가 있음을 주장하였다. 그러나 이 연구들은 단지 이론에 그침으로써 보편타당성이 입증되지 못하였으며 정량적으로 측정할 수 있는 근거와 방법을 제시하지 못하였다. 정보시스템 분야에서는 Porter(1985)의 가치사슬 개념이 무형편익을 측정할 수 있는 근거 이론으로 경제성 분석에 적용되어왔다. 이를 바탕으로 Parker(1988)는 정보시스템의 무형편익을 가치가속, 가치연결, 가치재구성, 그리고 혁신으로 인한 가치로 범주화한 모형을 제시하여 무형편익을 정량화하는 데 직접적인 영향을 주었다. 그러나 가치재구성과 혁신으로 인한 가치는 Parker 자신과 후속 연구에 의하면 정량적으로 측정하기에 난해한 요소로 평가되었다. 따라서 Parker의 모형 중 부분요소만이 보편타당성과 정량적 측정 기준을 모두 만족시킨 무형편익의 요소로 채택되었다.

가치가속 효과와 관련된 무형편익 분석으로는 Kingma(2000)와 김동석 등(2001)에 의하여 제시된 접근 편익을 들 수 있다. Kingma는 시스템의 도입으로 발생하는 접근 속도의 향상을, 김동석은 여러 곳에서 디지털 자료에 접근할 수 있으므로 나타나는 편익을 접근 편익으로 정의하였다. 이들 연구는 접근 편익이 디지털 매체의 경제성에 가장 큰 영향을 미치는 무형편익이라는 사실에 동의하고 있으며 정량적 측정 방법을 제시하고 있다. 가치연결 효과와 관련된 유일한 무형편익 분석으로는 Anselstetter(1986)의 모형을 들 수 있다. 그는 가치연결의 편익 체계를 분석하면서 정보시스템의 도입으로 나타나는 의사소통의 향상이 파급 효과-회의횟수 및 부서 간 이동 감소, 작업의 신속성 증가, 전화통화 수 감소, 문서 메시지 또는 편지 사용의 감소, 개선된 문서의 질, 그리고 신속한 문서작성 및 전달로 이어져 기관의 전략적인 목표를 달성하게 한다고 설명하였다. Anselstetter의 분석모형은 Parker의 연구에서 인용되었으며 부분적으로 정량적 측정이 가능한 것으로 평가되었다. 이들의 편익 범주화 모형을 보편 타당성과 정량적 측정 가능성 측면에서 분석하면 <표 3-2>와 같다.

<표 3-2> 편익모형 분석표

모형		보편 타당성	정량적 측정 가능성	비고
연구	내용			
브럼(1993)	유형편익: 비용절감과 비용회피	O	O	유형 편익
드미트렌코(1997)	유형편익: 비용절감(직접편익)	O	O	
포터(1985)	가치사슬 개념 제시	O	O	무형 편익
쉬멘트(1990) 스콥스키(1991)	기록관리의 무형편익: 신속한 경쟁 정보, 필요한 자료의 적시 제공, 정확한 자료제공	X	X	
실버(1998)	무형편익의 중요성을 사례로 입증 (푸르덴셜)	X	X	
씨스코(1999) 새퍼디(1999)	무형편익의 정량적 분석 필요성 주장	X	X	
포터(1985)	가치사슬 개념	O	O	
파커(1988)	정보시스템의 무형편익: 가치가속, 가치연결, 가치재구성, 혁신으로 인한 가치	O	O	
킹마(2000)	디지털화의 무형편익: 접근 편익	O	O	
김동석 외(2001)	디지털화의 무형편익: 접근 편익	O	O	
안셀스테터(1998)	가치연결 효과 체계 확립	O	O	

(4) 경제성 분석 기본모형 및 분석요소

디지털 아카이빙의 경제성 분석에 관한 제 이론과 모형 및 분석 요소에 대한 분석을 토대로 도출된 본 연구의 기본모형은 <그림 3-1>과 같다. 디지털 아카이빙의 경제성 분석의 비용요소는 고정비용과 가변비용을, 편익요소는 유형편익과 무형편익을 포함한다. 고정비용은 공간비, 인건비, 시설·장비구매비, 전산 장비 구매비, 유지보수비로 측정되며, 가변비용은 인건비, 소모품비, 관리비 및 예비비로 측정된다.8) 유형편익은 비용(고정비용과 가변비용)의 절감으로 측정되며, 무형편익의 가치가속 효과는 접근 편익으로, 가치

---

8) 고정비용의 인건비는 정규직원의 급여, 가변비용의 인건비는 시간당 봉급자의 급여임.

연결 효과는 의사소통 향상의 정도(타 부서 방문횟수, 전화통화 횟수, 이메일 횟수, 미팅 횟수의 감소로 인한 비용절감)로 측정된다.

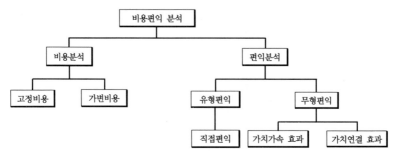

<그림 3-1> 디지털 아카이빙의 경제성 분석 기본모형

3.2 비용의 측정

디지털 아카이빙 사업에 투입되는 비용은 고정비용과 가변비용으로 범주화하며, 이들의 합으로 산출된다. 고정비용은 디지털 아카이빙을 구축하기 위해서 기본적으로 투입되어야 하는 불변의 비용으로 공간비, 인건비, 시설·장비비, 전산 장비비, 전산 장비의 유지보수비로 구분된다. 가변비용에는 기록물 한 단위를 생산하는데 투입되는 인건비, 소모품비 및 기타 비용이 포함된다. 본 연구의 경제성 분석에 매몰 비용은 포함되지 않는다.9) 또한, 경제성 분석은 재무 분석과는 달리 세금 등의 비용은 포함하지 않으므로 모든 세금은 분석대상에서 제외한다.

---

9) 매몰 비용은 디지털 아카이빙에 사용되는 장비 및 소모품이라 하더라도 이미 기존에 다른 목적을 위 한 구입에 드는 비용이며, 이는 경제성 분석에 포함하지 않는다는 일반 경제성 이론을 근거로 함.

(1) 공간비

고정비용에 포함되는 공간비는 자료관의 신축공사에 드는 추정 공사비이며, 해당 자료관의 면적에 면적당 신축 공사비를 곱하여 산출하였다. 자료관의 신축 공사비의 추정은 한국감정원의 건물신축 단가표를 근거로 하였으며, 이는 기관의 유형, 건축자재 및 등급 등 공사비 내역에 영향을 미치는 제 요인을 통제하기 위한 것이다.10) 공공기관에는 2,000평 이하의 공공청사 건물, 일반 기업체에는 6층~15층 이하의 사무실 건물에 해당하는 단가표를 적용하였다. 건축자재는 철근 콘크리트 슬래브를, 등급은 3급을 일괄적으로 모든 기관에 적용하였다. 단, 본 연구의 경제성 분석에서는 부대설비 보정단가와 내용 연수는 고려되지 않는다. 또한, 자료관 공간의 토지 매입 및 보상비 등의 비용 역시 사업평가 이전에 이미 발생한 매몰 비용으로서 비용 항목에서 배제되었다.

(2) 인건비

디지털 아카이빙 구축에 참여하고 있는 정규직의 급여가 고정비용에, 임시직의 급여가 가변비용에 포함되었다. 정규직은 사업 동안 계속 고용될 것으로 가정되는 반면, 임시직은 스캐닝 작업을 하거나 데이터 입력을 위해서 임시로 고용된다. 임시직의 급여는 취업상태에 있을 때 실제로 지불된 인건비를 기준으로 하며, 여기에 실업 수당 등은 고려하지 않았다.

---

10) 한국감정원. 2002. 「건물신축단가표」.
　　공공청사: 1998년(627,000원), 2000년(591,000원), 2002년(667,000원)
　　사무실: 1998년(680,000원), 2000년(643,000원), 2002년(692,000원)

(3) 시설·장비비

시설·장비비는 디지털 아카이빙을 구축하고 보존하는 데 필요한 항온 항습기, 소화기, 공기 청정기, 서가 캐비닛 등의 시설·장비 구입비용이다. 공공기관의 기록물 관련 법률 시행령에 의하면, 자료관에는 기본적으로 면적 $99m^2$당 항온 항습기 1대(패키지형 1대, 500만 원)와 소화기 1대(1대, 약 100만 원)가 구비되어야 한다.[11][12] 이를 근거로 시설·장비비를 산출하였다.[13] 단, 분석대상 기관이 실제로 투입한 시설·장비가 법률 시행령에서 요구하는 기준보다 많으면 실제 구입비용을 적용하는 반면, 그렇지 못할 때는 시행령에 따르는 시설·장비비를 추정하였다. 시설·장비 및 전산 장비의 생애주기인 5년마다 재투자가 발생하는 것으로 가정하였다. 재투자할 때 발생하는 비용은 초기 비용과 동일한 것으로 가정하는데, 이는 시간이 흐르면서 장비의 질이 향상되어 동일한 비용으로 향상된 품질의 장비 구입이 가능해지기 때문이다.

(4) 전산 장비비

전산 장비비는 디지털 아카이빙의 구축을 위한 소프트웨어(프로그램), 주크박스, 스캐너, 프린터 등의 장비와 서버 장비, 저장장치, 네트워크 등의 하드웨어 구입비용을 의미한다. 공공기관은 행정부에서 제안하는 자료관리시스템(ERMS)을 2004년까지 의무적으로 도입하도록 법률로 제정하고 있으며 이미 구축된 전자문서관리시스템(EDMS)과의 연계 연동의 정도에 따라 비용의 차이가 크게 날

---

11) 기록물관리기관의 보존시설 장비의 기준(제38조 기준)

12) 2003년도 12월 구입 기준으로 국가기록원 행정지원과 연구원의 자문을 토대로 한 것임.

13) 시설·장비비 = 【(자료관 면적 ÷ $99m^2$) x 500만 원】 +(자료관 면적 ÷ $99m^2$) x 100만 원】

수 있다. 예상 구축비용을 평균 3억으로 가정하였다.[14] 디지털 자료의 장기보존 및 원격접근 환경을 계속 유지 강화하기 위한 관리에 투입되는 매체 재생, 매체변환, 기술이전 등의 관리비용은 일반적으로 전산 장비의 업그레이드에서 발생하기 때문에 전산 장비의 재투자비용에 포함하였다.

(5) 유지보수비

유지보수비는 투입된 전산 장비를 생애주기 동안 유지 관리하기 위해서 매년 투입하는 비용을 말한다. 전산 장비의 유지보수비는 구입비용의 8%로 설정하였으며, 이는 일반적으로 경제성 분석에서 이용되고 있는 기준치이다. 유지보수비는 구입 후 1년간은 무상 하자보수 기간이므로 그다음 해부터 적용한다.

(6) 관리비 및 예비비

사업을 진행하는 과정에서 예기치 못한 일들이 무수하게 발생하게 될 문제들에 대한 사전 예방조치로 관리비 및 예비비로 가변비용에 포함된다. 관리비는 자료관의 지속적인 관리를 위한 것이며, 예비비는 전산 및 시설·장비 등 각 비용 항목에 책정된 예산 이외에 추가로 비용이 투입되어야 하는 불가피한 경우를 대비하기 위한 것이다. 그러나 기존 대부분의 경제성 분석들이 예비비를 반영하고 있지 않기 때문에, 타당성 조사를 위한 관리비 및 예비비의 일관성 있는 기준은 아직 없다. 예비비를 산정한 국내의 연구로는 수자원 개발사업과[15] 교통사업의 경우를 들 수 있고 이들이 적용하는 국

---

14) 국가기록원 보존관리과 연구원의 자문을 토대로 한 것임.

15) 한국수자원공사. 1998. 「감포댐 예비타당성 조사보고서」

제적 관례 등을 참조하여 관리비와 예비비를 각각 자료관 공사비의
0.5%, 10%로 산정하였다.

(7) 기타 소모품비

기타 소모품비는 가변비용에 속하며 광(光)파일 스캔작업, 서버
등록, 색인입력 등 디지털화 작업을 하는 데 필요한 종이, 복사비,
소모품비 등에 소요되는 기타 비용이 포함된다.

3.3 편익의 측정

3.3.1 유형편익: 직접편익

유형편익은 직접편익으로 평가되며, 직접편익은 디지털 아카이빙
을 도입함으로써 절감 또는 회피할 수 있는 공간비, 시설비, 복사비
의 합이다. 직접편익은 <그림 3-2>와 같이 기록물 이관, 폐기 및
인쇄 기록물의 디지털 매체변환으로 인하여 발생하는 절감분을 공
공기관의 기록물 관련 법률 시행령에 따라 산출하였다. 공간비 절
감편익은 자료관의 신축 공사비로 추정하며, 시설·장비비 절감편
익은 회피할 수 있는 서가의 추가 구입비용이다.

직접편익 = 공간비 절감편익 + 시설·장비비 절감편익 + 복사비 절감편익
공간비 절감편익 = 99 m^2 : 10,000권 = x : 기록물 이관량
= x (기록물 이관으로 절감된 공간면적) x 신축 공사비
시설·장비비 절감편익 = 99 m^2 : 16개(복식 서가) = x : x1
= x1 (기록물 이관으로 절감된 복식 서가 개수) x 462,000원
복사비 절감편익(공공기관) = 연평균 문서생산량(권) x 200매 x 5%
(보존 기간 20년 이상) x 30원(복사비/1매)

<그림 3-2> 직접편익의 산출식

<표 3-3>에 나타나 있는 공공기관의 기록물 이관량 중 실제치는 2001년과 2002년이며, 2003년부터의 이관량은 추정에 의한 것이다. 2003년과 2004년의 이관량은 담당자의 자문을 토대로 하였으나, 그 이후(2005년~분석 기간)는 기관의 유형별 연평균 문서생산량(2002년 기준)과 국가기록원에서 제공하는 통계치를 근거로 추정하였다. 국가기록원에 의하면 유형별 연평균 문서생산량 중 보존기간 20년 이상(디지털 아카이빙의 대상자료)의 기록물은 평균 5%이며, 이 중 국가기록원으로 이관된 기록물은 일부분(중앙행정기관은 80~90%, 광역지자체는 60%, 그리고 교육행정기관은 30%)에 불과하다.[16)

<표 3-3> 공공기관: 기록물 이관량

(단위: 권)

유형	기관	2001	2002	2003	2004	2005	2006	2007	2008	2009	2010
광역 지자체	A	0	0	0	0	0	0	0	0	0	0
	B	1362	1832	1800	1800	1200[17)	1200	1200	1200	1200	1200
	C	14504	6657	5290	5290	5290	1200	1200	1200	1200	1200
시도 교육청	D	152	468	310	310	310	300	300	300	300	300
	E	704	2016	680	680	300	300	300	300	300	300
	F	0	0	0	0	2317	300	300	300	300	300

한편 일반 기업체에서의 직접편익은 디지털 아카이빙을 도입한 후 이루어진 인쇄문서의 폐기 및 디지털 매체의 생산으로 인해 발생하는 비용의 절감으로 측정하였다. 그러나 이를 정확히 측정하는

---

16) 공공기관에서의 연평균 문서생산량은 광역지자체(16개)는 4만 권(서울특별시는 평균 536,055권, 제 주시 평균 7,120권), 시도교육청은 2만 권임.

17) 기관 B(광역지자체)의 2005년 기록물 예상 이관량 = 40,000권 x 5% x 60% = 1,200권

데 무리가 있으므로, <표 3-4>와 같이 각 기관(일반 기업체)의 담당자가 추정하는 절감된 면적의 절감률을 토대로 공간비 및 시설·장비비 절감편익을 산출하였다.

<표 3-4> 일반 기업체: 자료관 면적의 추정 절감률

(단위: %)

유형	기관	1차년	2차년	3차년	4차년	5차년	6차년	7차년	8차년	9차년	10차년
일반 기업체	G	60	12	12	12	12	12	12	12	12	12
	H	60	12	12	12	12	12	12	12	12	12
	I	34	34	34	34	34	34	34	34	34	34

복사비 절감편익은 디지털 아카이빙을 도입하게 되면서 감소한 복사량으로 인하여 절감된 비용이다. 공공기관의 복사비 절감편익은 보존 기간 20년 이상의 기록물을 한 부씩 복사하는 비용으로 추정하였다. 이는 디지털 아카이빙 도입 전에 적어도 보존 기간 20년 이상의 기록물이 타 부서 회람이나 보존을 위해서 몇 부씩 복사되어 왔기 때문이다.[18) 반면 일반 기업체의 복사비 절감편익은 각 기관에서 디지털 아카이빙 실시 후 추정한 보고 자료의 내역을 근거로 하였다. 복사비는 1매당 30원을 적용하였다.[19)

3.3.2 무형편익: 가치가속 및 가치연결에 의한 편익

본 연구의 무형편익은 가치가속으로 인한 편익과 가치연결로 인한 편익의 두 가지 측정항목으로 나누어진다. 가치가속으로 인한

---

18) 한 부씩 복사하는 비용만을 복사비 절감액에 포함하므로 매우 보수적인 가정치라 할 수 있음
19) 복사비(1장)의 산출내역 = 부품(3원) + 토너(8원) + 드럼(4원) + 종이(10원) + 전기료(5원) = 30원

편익은 접근시간 절감으로, 가치연결로 인한 편익은 의사소통 향상의 정도로 평가된다. 가치가속과 가치연결의 효과는 설문 조사의 결과를 토대로 추정하였다.

(1) 가치가속으로 인한 편익

접근 편익은 기존 인쇄문서보다 신속하게 접근할 수 있어 절감되는 접근시간의 효과로 정의하였다. 디지털 아카이빙의 접근 편익은 디지털 기록물에의 접근이 가능한 곳을 방문하는 데 소요되는 고정시간과 이를 검색할 때마다 발생하는 가변시간으로 구분된다. 고정시간은 컴퓨터가 구비된 장소를 방문하는 데 걸리는 시간이다. 현실적으로 볼 때 기록물의 사용자는 거의 모든 경우 컴퓨터가 구비된 장소에 근무하고 있어서 디지털 아카이빙을 위한 추가 시간이 소요되지 않는 것으로 가정하였다.

디지털 기록물을 검색할 때마다 발생하는 가변비용 역시 킹마의 연구 결과를 토대로 '0'으로 추정하였다. 따라서 디지털 아카이빙의 접근비용은 '0'이므로 인쇄 기록물에 접근하기 위해서 소요되었던 시간이 디지털 아카이빙을 도입함으로 절감되는 것으로 가정하였으며, 절감되는 시간 모두가 기관의 생산적인 활동에 투여된다고 전제하는 일반적인 경제성 이론에 따라 그 경제적 가치를 추정하였다. 본 연구의 접근 편익은 <그림 3-3>과 같이 인쇄 매체에 접근하는 데 소요되는 접근시간에 1인당 평균 기회비용과 잠재 사용자 수를 곱하여 산출하였다.

(단위: 원/1년)

접근 편익= 인쇄 기록물 이용횟수(a) x 인쇄 기록물(1건)에 접근하는 데 드는 시간 (b) x 1인당 평균 기회비용(c) x 잠재 사용자 수(d)

<그림 3-3> 접근 편익의 산출식

(a)와 (b)는 설문지의 응답 결과에 근거한다. (d)는 전자문서관리 시스템 내에 저장된 디지털 기록물을 생산하는 모든 부서 직원 전체의 절반만을 포함하였다. 대부분의 기록물은 생산부서에서만 접근할 수 있도록 제한이 설정되어 있으므로 생산부서에서 가장 많이 활용되는 것은 당연한 현상이라 하겠다.[20] 또한, 기록물 생산부서 직원의 절반만을 잠재 사용자 수에 포함한 것은 소속 부서에서 생산된 기록물이라 하더라도 직위나 담당업무의 특성상 실제로 이를 사용하는 직원은 그 부서 직원의 약 절반 정도로 보는 것이 타당하다는 담당자들의 제언에 따른 것이다.

현실적으로 디지털 아카이빙이 국내에 도입된 것은 최근이므로 현재 자료관에 디지털 아카이빙이 되어 있는 기록물은 일부분에 불과하며 시간의 경과에 따라 더욱 많은 기록물이 자료관 시스템에 탑재되고 잠재 사용자 그룹도 기록물 생산부서뿐만 아니라 외부인이나 시민 등 접근 가능한 사람들에게로 확산할 수 있다. 따라서 현재의 잠재 사용자 수를 연구 기간 내내 동일하게 적용하는 것은 보수적인 추정이라 할 수 있다. 또한, 동일한 부서 내에서도 실제로 활용하는 사용자만을 잠재 사용자 수에 포함함으로써 한 번도 기록물을 이용하지 않는 사용자와 거의 매일 활용하는 사용자를 동일하게 한 명의 사용자로 간주할 수 있는 과대평가의 위험성을 배제하였다.

향후 사용자 수의 추정은 과거의 실제치(실제 사용빈도)를 근거로 로지스틱 함수를 이용하여 추정하였다. 로지스틱 함수를 추정하는 데 있어서 근거가 되는 과거 사용빈도의 추적은 기관 A와 기관 H에서만 입수할 수 있었기 때문에, 이들을 각각 공공기관과 일반 기업체의 대표기관으로 설정하였다.[21] 공공기관의 향후 추정치는

---

20) 인사기록카드 등 전 부서 공통 해당문서는 예외가 될 수 있음.

매년 증가하여 7차년이 되면 거의 상한값에 이르는 것으로 나타났다.[22] 기관 H의 실제치를 근거로 한 일반 기업체의 향후 사용자 추정치는 공공기관보다 초기에는 빠른 속도로 증가하나, 상한값에 가까워질수록 속도가 느려지는 경향을 보인다. 그러나 두 유형의 기관 모두 디지털 아카이빙 도입 후 7~8년이 지나면서 상한값에 매우 근접하게 되는 것으로 나타났다.[23]

(2) 가치연결로 인한 편익

Anselstetter(1986)의 모형을 근거로 본 연구는 디지털 아카이빙의 도입으로 인하여 발생하는 기관 내 의사소통의 향상이 디지털 아카이빙으로 인한 가치연결의 효과를 발생시키는 추진력으로 파악하였다. 따라서 의사소통의 향상 효과로 인해 나타나는 여러 항목 중 측정이 가능한 타 부서 방문 빈도, 전화통화 빈도, 메시지 보내는 빈도, 회의 빈도의 감소를 본 연구의 가치연결의 효과측정을 위한 측정지표로 설정하였다.

4. 사례분석 결과

4.1 기관별 자료관 운영현황

기관의 유형별 설문지 회수현황은 광역지자체(약 66%), 일반 기

---

21) 그 외의 기관들은 디지털 아카이빙의 도입 초기 단계이거나 시스템의 기능이 미흡하여 실제치 추적이 불가능하였음.
22) 공공기관의 로지스틱 함수: 1차년(9.8%), 2차년(38%), 3차년(66%), 4차년(73%), 5차년(93%), 6차년(98.6%), 7차년(99.7%)
23) 일반 기업체의 로지스틱 함수: 1차년(47%), 2차년(70%), 3차년(86.2%), 4차년(94.4%), 5차년(97.9%), 6차년(99.2%)

업체(약 33%), 그리고 시도교육청(약 16%)의 순이며 설문 조사 회수율은 약 38%이다. 이러한 저조한 설문지 회수율은 디지털 아카이빙을 도입한 설문대상 기관들에서 디지털 아카이빙이 아직 활발하게 이용되지 않기 때문으로 분석된다. 시도교육청의 경우에 설문지 회수율이 특히 저조하게 나타난 이유는 3개 기관 모두 디지털 아카이빙의 시범 운영 기관으로, 이를 사용하고 있는 이용자의 수가 매우 제한되어 있기 때문으로 분석된다. 9개 기관의 기관별 자료관 운영현황은 <표 4-1>에 나타나 있다.

<표 4-1> 기관별 사례분석

구분	자료관 설립 년도	디지털 아카이빙 구축연도	면적 (m²)	기록물 보유현황(권)	연평균 문서생산량 (권)	담당 부서	담당 직원	디지털 아카이빙 구축량(권)	잠재 사용자 수(명)
A	1994	2001	2,016	약 42만 (각 실 35만, 문서고 72,000)	536,000	민원과 문서관리팀	정규 직원 10명 임시 직원: 공공근로요원	4,360	2,500
B	2001	2001	887	약 33만 (55개 실과의 문서포함)	40,000	총무과 문서관리팀	정규 직원 11명 임시 직원: 공공근로요원	59,620	2,500
C	2001	2001	560.74	약 13만	40,000	총무과 자료관	정규 직원 10명 임시 직원: 공공근로요원	약 2,646	1,492
D	2001	2001	365	37,389 (문서 26,000 도면 2,000매 카드 9,389매)	20,000	총무과 자료관	정규 직원 6명 임시 직원: 공공근로요원	약 3,000 카드류 9,000매	335

구분	자료관 설립 년도	디지털 아카이빙 구축연도	면적 (m²)	기록물 보유현황(권)	연평균 문서생산량 (권)	담당 부서	담당 직원	디지털 아카이빙 구축량(권)	잠재 사용자 수(명)
E	2000	2000	559.98	50,340 (문서 10,626 카드 28,288매 고교학적부 11,426)	20,000	총무과 자료관	정규 직원 8명 임시 직원: 공공근 로요원	약 3,000	420
F	2001	2001	455.68	26,207	20,000	총무과 자료관	정규 직원 2명 임시 직원: 공공근 로요원	77,236 (문서 22,673건 카드 50,294매, 도면 4,020매, 대장 238, 시청각 자료 11)	300
G	1999	1999	760.33	62,000	파악 불가	인력관리처 문서팀	정규 직원 2명	254만 매	1,068
H	2003	2003	521	8,866	파악 불가	PI 지원실 (Process Innovation)	정규 직원 2명	735,144 (결재문서 170,742 건 포함)	1,675
I	2003	2003	803	-	파악 불가	문서관리실	정규 직원 3명 임시 직원 20명	256 Giga Bytes	1,700

[1] 정부기록보존소에 집계된 통계치에 근거함
[2] 기관 A의 자료관은 1994년에 설립되었지만, 자료관의 기능이 미비하므로 2001년 디지털 아카이빙이 도입된 해에 자료관이 신설된 것으로 가정하고 경제성을 추정함
[3] 현재 전자문서 위주로 생산되므로 문서 이관이 이루어지지 않으므로 파악 불가능함

4.2 편익의 단계적 분석

9개 분석대상 기관 중 8개의 기관에서 경제성이 있는 것으로 나타났다. 직접편익만을 그 가치로 평가하여 디지털 아카이빙의 경제성을 분석하면 1개 기관 외에는 경제성이 나타나지 않았으며, 이는 디지털 아카이빙에 초기 투자비용이 많이 투입되었기 때문으로 분석된다. 직접편익에 가치가속의 효과를 추가하게 되면 경제성이 큰 폭으로 증가하였으나, 2개 기관(D와 E)은 여전히 경제성이 없으며 기관 B와 F에서도 가까스로 경제성이 있는 것으로 나타났다. 기관의 유형별로 보면 일반 기업체에서는 도입 첫해부터, 광역지자체에서는 7차년이 되면서 경제성이 나타나기 시작하였다. 직접편익과 가치가속에 가치연결의 효과를 추가하여 경제성을 분석하면, 일반 기업체는 도입 첫해부터, 광역지자체는 평균 5차년, 시도교육청은 평균 8차년이 되면서 경제성이 있는 것으로 나타났다. 이러한 분석 결과는 디지털 아카이빙의 가치를 유형편익만으로 평가한 기존의 연구들이 디지털 아카이빙의 가치를 얼마나 과소평가했는가를 입증하는 결과라고 할 수 있다(표 4-2 참조).

<표 4-2> 분석 결과

(단위: 천원)

구 분		직접편익		가치가속 포함		가치연결 포함	
		NPV	B/C	NPV	B/C	NPV	B/C
광역 지자체	A	-5853554	0.18	1708447	1.24	17177092	3.42
	B	-6231984	0.03	17829	1.00	9444130	2.45
	C	-3756534	0.08	2819065	1.69	5725838	2.40
	평균	-5280691	0.10	1515114	1.31	10782353	2.61
시도	D	-2535042	0.02	-1013976	0.61	92629	1.04

구 분		직접편익		가치가속 포함		가치연결 포함	
		NPV	B/C	NPV	B/C	NPV	B/C
교육청	E	-3673916	0.02	-2987531	0.21	-1178120	0.69
	F	-1832236	0.04	3402	1.00	1762033	1.99
	평균	-2680398	0.03	-1332702	0.61	161762	1.21
일반 기업체	G	-740639	0.73	16366318	8.18	4074263	18.78
	H	-3143344	0.31	17040920	4.72	55605815	13.15
	I	1815720	1.30	44653953	8.47	51911163	9.76
	평균	-689421	0.78	26020397	7.12	50071724	13.90

4.3 민감도 분석

민감도 분석 결과, 고위수준인 사회적 할인율을 적용하게 되면 편익비용비율이 평균 2.7% 감소한 반면, 저위수준인 물가상승률을 적용하게 되면 평균 6.8% 증가하는 것으로 나타났다. 할인율에 따라 경제성 내역이 가장 크게 변화된 기관은 기관 E와 G로 이들의 변화 내역은 각각 -1.5% -15.2% 그리고 3.6% -17.1%이다. 기관 D 에서 디지털 아카이빙은 경제성이 있는 사업이었으나 고위수준인 사회적 할인율을 적용하게 되면 경제성이 존재하지 않는 것으로 나타났다. 그러나 그 외의 기관에서는 할인율에 따른 경제성 변화 내역이 그리 크지 않은 것으로 나타났다.

반면 공사비 추정 기준의 설정은 디지털 아카이빙의 경제성에 크게 영향을 미치는 것으로 나타났다. 재배치만으로 자료관을 설립할 경우에 모든 기관의 순 현재가치와 편익비용비율은 신축 공사비를 적용하였을 때보다 평균 26.3% 향상되는 것으로 나타났다. 공사비 의 변동에 따라 가장 경제성의 변화 내역이 큰 기관은 기관 A, H, F의 순이다. 즉 재배치 비용을 경제성 분석에 적용하게 되면 신축 공사비를 적용하였을 때보다 편익비용비율이 각각 43.9%, 37.6%,

그리고 **35.2%** 향상되는 것으로 나타났다. 이렇게 경제성 분석에 사용된 공사비(신축 공사비)가 매우 보수적으로 추정되었을 가능성이 큼을 참작하면, 디지털 아카이빙 실제의 경제성은 더욱 높을 것으로 분석된다.

4.4 요인 비교분석

기관의 유형에 따른 경제성을 알아보기 위해 Kruskal Wallis 검증을 실시한 결과 유형 간 통계적으로 유의한 차이(p=0.0273)가 있는 것으로 나타났다. 즉 경제성은 일반 기업체, 광역지자체, 시도교육청 순으로 높게 나타났다. 이러한 경제성의 차이는 디지털 아카이빙 도입에 투입한 비용을 편익으로 전환하는 과정에서 기관의 유형에 따른 경영의 질적·전략적 차이가 존재하기 때문으로 판단된다.

디지털 아카이빙의 도입 목적에 따른 경제성의 차이를 Wilcoxon 검증을 통해 분석한 결과 유의한 차이(p=0.0200)가 있는 것으로 나타났다. 이 결과는 기록물의 활용을 목적으로 도입한 기관들은 기록물의 보존을 목적으로 한 기관들에 비해 디지털 아카이빙 사용을 활성화하기 위한 전략을 통하여 유형의 가치를 크게 발생시킨 것으로 해석된다. 또한, 디지털 아카이빙의 구축 방법에 따른 경제성의 차이를 Wilcoxon 검증을 통해 분석한 결과, 유의한 차이(p=0.0200)가 발견되었다. 외부용역으로 구축한 기관들이 자체 구축한 기관들보다 경제성이 높은 것은 국내에 디지털 아카이빙 전문가가 거의 없으며, 구축 사례가 전무하기 때문에 구축 경험이 있는 외부의 전문기관 용역을 통해 구축하는 것이 효율적임을 입증해 주는 것으로서 도입 초기에 당연한 현상으로 분석된다.

5. 결론 및 시사점

기존의 연구에서는 기록관리의 유형적 편익만이 측정됨으로써 그 유용성이 과소평가 되어왔는데, 이는 무형의 편익을 정량적으로 평가하는 방법이 개발되지 않았기 때문이다. 그러므로 무형의 편익을 정량화할 수 있는 합리적인 모형이 개발되고, 이를 통한 경제성 평가가 이루어지면 국내의 디지털 아카이빙 도입에 따른 시행착오를 줄일 수 있을 것이다.

본 연구는 디지털 아카이빙에 의해 파생되는 부가가치를 파커의 정보경제학 방법론을 토대로 직접편익, 가치가속, 그리고 가치연결의 효과로 분류하여 분석하는 경제성 분석모형을 도출하였다. 이 모형은 포터의 가치사슬 개념을 적용한 경제성 분석의 틀로서 경제성 분석을 위해 현재 디지털 아카이빙을 구축·활용하고 있는 국내 9개 기관에 적용되었다. 사례분석 결과, 자료관에서의 디지털 아카이빙의 도입은 기관의 유형과 관계없이 경제성이 있는 사업이며, 특히 유형의 편익보다 무형의 편익이 큰 사업임이 입증되었다. 따라서 기관의 의사 결정자들은 디지털 아카이빙 도입 여부를 판단하는 데 있어서 가시적인 편익보다는 업무의 효율성, 의사결정 능력의 향상 등 무형의 편익을 고려하여 도입 여부를 결정하여야 할 것이다.

또한, 디지털 아카이빙은 기록물 자체의 보존만을 위한 소극적인 목적이 아닌 자료관에 보유된 기록물의 체계적인 관리와 활용을 위한 적극적인 목적으로 도입될 때 기관의 전략적 목표를 달성하는 데 긍정적인 역할을 하게 되어 더욱 높은 경제성을 기대할 수 있게 된다. 도입 목적 외에 기관의 유형과 구축 방법의 차이에 따른 디지털 아카이빙의 경제성에 미치는 영향을 파악함으로써 디지털 아카이빙의 도입 여부와 경제성을 극대화하기 위한 전략을 제시하는 근거가 될 것이다.

본 연구의 경제성 분석모형에서는 파커가 제시한 다섯 항목 중에서 측정의 임의성이 크기 때문에 연구자의 주관에 의해 과대평가될 수 있는 분석상의 오류가 존재할 수 있음이 지적된 가치재구성과 혁신으로 인한 효과는 배제하였다. 따라서 본 연구가 파커의 방법론에 근거한 디지털 아카이빙의 종합적 편익이라고 주장하기에는 한계가 있다. 또한, 국내에 디지털 아카이빙을 도입하여 활용하고 있는 기관들에 의존하여 실증분석을 수행하기에는 절대적인 표본수가 부족하였으며, 이는 본 연구의 실증 결과에 사용된 통계 분석에 제한적 요소로 작용하였다.

정보화 사회에 부응하여 기록물에의 신속한 접근과 의사소통의 향상을 가져와 효율적인 업무 수행을 가능하게 하는 디지털 아카이빙을 구축하기 위해 선진 각국에서 활발한 움직임이 있으며, 국내에서도 최근에 공공기관을 중심으로 디지털 아카이빙이 도입되기 시작하였다. 앞으로 이러한 추세가 가속화될 예상이며, 디지털 아카이빙의 구축이 더 성공적으로 시행되기 위해서는 국가 및 기관 차원에서 많은 문제점을 극복해야 할 것이다.

현재의 디지털 매체를 미래에도 지속해서 이용할 수 있도록 국가적 차원에서의 연구 및 기술적 지원이 이루어져야 하며 기록물의 중요성에 대한 인식을 확산시키고 정보 공개 서비스 강화를 선도하여야 한다. 또한, 국내에 디지털 아카이빙의 제도적인 정착을 위해선 기록물의 역사적·행정적 가치를 선별할 수 있는 기록관리 전문가(아키비스트)의 양성을 활성화하여야 한다. 이를 위해서는 정부가 자격증이나 인증 등을 제도화하여 공공기관에 우선적으로 시행하고, 단계적으로 민간부문에도 확대될 수 있도록 추진하여야 할 것이다.

　개별 기관이 디지털 아카이빙의 도입을 계획하고 있다면 효율적인 활용을 위한 장기적인 목적을 가지고 디지털 아카이빙을 도입하는 것이 바람직하며 전문 능력을 갖춘 인력을 채용함으로써 체계적인 기록관리 및 자료 선별이 이루어져야 할 것이다. 한편 디지털 아카이빙에 대한 전문기술과 경험을 갖춘 전문 인력이 없거나 기본적인 시설 설비가 미비할 경우 외부 전문 업체에 용역을 주어 디지털 아카이빙을 실시하는 것도 고려해 볼 만하다. 마지막으로 기록물의 이관 작업을 충실히 수행하여야 한다. 기록물의 이관 및 폐기는 기관의 공간, 시설 및 인건비 절감의 근원이 되기 때문이다.

참고문헌

강성홍. 1997. 「의무기록 전산화의 모형개발 및 경제성 분석」. 박사학위 논문. 인제대학교 대학원 보건학과 보건행정학 전공.

고영만. 2003. 정보의 경제성에 관한 담론. 「한국문헌정보학회지」. 37(4): 53-68.

김동건. 1997. 「비용편익분석」 서울: 박영사.

김동석, 조동호, 고영만. 2003. 디지털 도서관의 경제성 평가: 국립디지털도서관 DLP 사례연구. 「한국정보관리학회지」 20(4): 159-193.

김재형, 홍기석, 이승태. 2000. 「2000년도 예비타당성조사 연구보고서: 예비타당성 조사 수행을 위한 일반지침 연구」. 서울: 한국개발연구원.

김효석, 오재인. 1996. 정보기술의 평가모형 개발: K 기업의 사례연구. 「경영과학」 13(1): 29-46.

이국희. 1992. 기업 정보시스템의 평가를 위한 모형. 「경영정보학 연구 2(1): 17-33.

한국감정원. 2002. 「건물신축 단가표」 한국국가기록연구원 편. 2003. 「레코드 관리를 위한 ISO 표준 해설」.

Annand, David. 2002. "Concurrent Development and Cost-Benefit Analysis of Paper-Based and Digitized Instructional Material." *Internet and Higher Education* 5: 47-54.

Anselstetter, R. 1986. "Betriebswirtschaftliche Nutzeffekte der Datenverarbeitung, Anhaltspunkte fuer Nutzen-Kosten-Schaetzungen" ed 2, Springer, Berlin, 44. Quoted in Parker, Marilyn M., Robert J. Benson and H. E. Trainor. *Information Economics: Linking Business Performance to Information Technology*. England Cliffs: Prentice Hall. 1988.

Brumm, Eugenia. 1993. "Cost/Benefit Analysis of the Records Management Program in the State of Texas." *Records Management Quarterly* 27: 2 (April): 30-39.

Cisco, Susan L. and Karen V. Strong. 1999. "Value Added Information Chain." *Information Management Journal* (Jan.): 4-15.

Conway, Paul. 1997. "Yale University Library's Project Open Book." *D-Lib Magazine*. [cited 2004. 6. 5]. <http://www.dilib.org/dlib/february96/yale/02conway.html>

Cummins, Thompson R. 1998. "Cost-Benefit Analysis: More Than Just Dollars and Cents." *Bottom Line* 3(2): 3-7.

Dmytrenko, April. 1997. "Cost Benefit Analysis", *Records Management Quarterly* 31(1) (Jan.): 16-20.

Ericksen, Paul and Robert Shuster. 1995. "Beneficial Shocks: the Place of Processing-Cost Analysis in Archival Administration." *American Archivist* 58 (winter): 32-52.

Kenney, Anne R. "Digital to Microfilm Conversion: a Demonstration Project 1994-1996." [cited 2004. 6. 5]. <http://www.library.cornell.edu/preservation/pub.htm>

Kingma, Bruce R. 2000. "Economics of Digital Access: the Early Canadian Online Project", Michigan in Ann Arbor. PEAK: the Economics and Usage of DL Collection. [cited 2004. 6. 5]. <http://www.si.urnich.edu/PEAK-2000/speakers.htm>

Lincoln, Y. S. and E. G. Guba. 1985. *Naturalistic Inquiry*. Beverly Hills, CA: Sage.

Machlup, F. 1962. *The Production and Distribution of Knowledge in the United States*. Princeton, N.J.: Princeton University Press.

Maher, William J. 1982. "Measurement and Analysis of Processing Costs in Academic Archives." *College and Research Libraries* 43(Jan.): 59-67 Parker, Marilyn M., R. Benson and H. E. Trainor. 1988. *Information Economics: Linking Business Performance to Information Technology*. England

Cliffs: Prentice Hall.

Porat, M. 1977. *Information Economy: Definition and Measurement*. Washington, D.C: U.S. Government Printing Office.

Porter, Michael E. 1985. *Competitive Advantage*. New York: Free Press.

Saffady, William. 1999. *Value of Records Management: a Manager's Briefing: the Business Case for Systematic Control of Recorded Information*. ARMA International.

Sassone, Peer G. 1988. "A Survey of Cost-Benefit Methodologies for Information Systems." *Project Appraisal* (June): 73-84.

Schement, Jorge Reina, Porat, Bell. 1990. "The Information Society Reconsidered: the Growth of Information Work in the Early Twentieth Century." *Information Processing and Management*, 26(4): 453-463.

Silver, Bruce. 1998. "Records Management Rides Again." KM World. February 23. [cited 2004. 6. 5]. http://www.kmworld.com/newestlibrary/1998/februry_23/recmgmtridesagain.cfm>

Skupsky, Donald S. 1991. *Recordkeeping Requirements*. Denver: Information Requirements Clearinghouse.

Wilsted, Thomas, 1989. "Computing the Total Cost of Archival Processing," Technical Leaflet Series 2. Mid-Atlantic Regional Archives Conference: 1-8.

도서관 서비스의 가치평가

목록 아웃소싱의 타당성 분석

1990년대 대학도서관과 국립중앙도서관을 비롯한 공공도서관을 중심으로 도서관의 본질적인 업무로 여겨져 왔던 목록을 아웃소싱하는 사례가 증가하였다. 핵심 업무에의 집중으로 조직의 경쟁력을 강화하겠다는 취지로 시작된 목록 아웃소싱은 도서관 계의 적잖은 논란거리가 되었다. 수년간 몇 군데 대학도서관에서의 실무경험으로 목록이 이용자 서비스에 미치는 긍정적 영향을 실감했던 필자 역시, 이의 타당성에 대한 의구심을 가지게 되었다. 2005년에 게재된 **'목록 아웃소싱의 타당성 분석에 관한 연구'**는 목록 아웃소싱에 관한 경제적 가치를 파악하기 위한 것이다. 타당성 분석을 위해 비용요소에는 아웃소싱 비용을, 그리고 편익에는 목록의 품질을 도입하였다. 사례분석 결과, 목록 아웃소싱의 타당성은 거의 없는 것으로 나타났으며, 이는 목록 납품업체들의 전문성 부족과 위탁 도서관의 특수 상황에 대한 이해 부족 때문으로 파악되었다. 이로 인해 예상치 않게 결과물 납품 후 위탁 도서관 사서들의 목록 품질제어를 위한 시간과 노력에 과다한 비용이 추가로 투입된 것으로 나타났다.

목록 아웃소싱의
타당성 분석에 관한 연구[*]

　　본 연구는 목록 아웃소싱의 타당성 분석을 시도하였으며, 아웃소싱으로 인해 발생하는 부가가치를 정보경제학에 기초한 직접편익, 가치연결의 효과로 분류하여 분석하는 경제성 분석모형을 적용하였다. 직접편익은 비용절감과 비용회피로 가치연결 효과는 목록 품질의 향상 정도로 측정하였다. 분석과 목록 아웃소싱의 종합적인 타당성은 입증되지 않았으며, 이는 납품업체들의 전문성 결여로 품질제어를 하는 데 사서의 시간이 많이 투입되어 실제적인 비용절감에 효과가 거의 없는 것이 가장 큰 요인인 것으로 나타났다. 이렇게 현실적인 타당성이 미흡한 상태에서 목록 아웃소싱을 무리하게 이용할 경우 운영비용의 절감과 봉사 기능의 제고라는 기본 취지를 달성하는 것이 불가능할 것이다.

* 이 논문은 2004년 한국문헌정보학회지 38권 4호(251~270쪽)에 게재되었음.

1. 서 론

최근 기업 환경이 급변하면서 아웃소싱에 관한 관심이 증대되고 있다. 도서관도 예외는 아니어서 1980년대 전산화의 시작과 함께 아웃소싱의 개념이 도입되었다. 특히 제한된 정규인원으로 처리하기 어려운 미정리 자료의 누적 및 정리 직원의 감축 등으로 인해 목록이 아웃소싱 되고 있다. 아웃소싱의 형태로는 업체 직원이 상주해서 목록작업을 하거나, 자료 구입 시 MARC 데이터를 함께 납품받는 경우가 일반적이다. 그러나 목록 아웃소싱을 이용한 경험이 있는 도서관들의 시각은 혼합적이며, 관련 연구에서도 이의 타당성은 입증되지 않은 상태이다.

본 연구에서 '목록'은 목록과 분류를 총체적으로 일컫는 말로 정의된다. '아웃소싱'이란 내부의 기술력 부족이나 핵심 업무 이외의 주변 업무를 외부의 전문 업체가 대행하게 함으로써 기업의 비용을 절감하고 생산성을 제고시키는 전략을 의미한다. 목록 아웃소싱을 긍정적인 측면에서 분석한 Jiang(1998)은 아웃소싱이 도서관 업무의 효율성을 증대시키며, 이는 비용 절감, 미처리분의 감소, 생산성 증대, 자료 접근의 용이성 등의 편익에 의한 것이라고 주장하였다. 이와 유사한 주장을 한 Tsui와 Hinders(1999)는 Dayton 대학(Marian 도서관)에서 수행된 아웃소싱이 검색능력을 향상해 업무의 효율성과 부가적인 혜택을 가져왔음을 증명하였다. 김영규(2000)에 의하면 목록은 무엇보다 노동집약적이며 인적비용이 꾸준히 증가하는 작업이기 때문에 아웃소싱의 주요 대상이 되어왔으며, 이를 이용한 대학도서관은 대체로 그 결과에 만족하고 있다. 그는 아웃소싱 업체의 전문성 부족을 중요한 문제점으로 지적하였으며, 도서관 직원의 참여도가 아웃소싱의 경제성에 직접적인 영향을 미치고 있다고 주장하였다.

한편 Dunkle(1996)은 비용절감을 전제로 하는 아웃소싱의 기본 취지와는 달리, 실제로 제공된 목록 레코드는 품질이 저조하여 오류수정에 추가 인건비 및 업무부담 등의 비경제성이 야기되고 있다고 지적하였다. 또한, 그는 목록 아웃소싱은 목록이 도서관의 핵심 업무가 아니라는 편견과 목록자의 전문성 및 역할에 대한 의사결정자의 인식이 미약하므로 이루어지는 것이며 관리자와 목록자가 효과적인 커뮤니케이션의 부재로 인한 것이라고 주장하였다. 윤정옥(2004)은 대학도서관 목록의 부분적 혹은 전면적 아웃소싱을 수행하였던 국내외 도서관들의 사례를 통하여 목록 아웃소싱의 현황과 이에 관련된 문제점을 지적하였다. 문제점에는 참조할 우수한 공동목록의 부재, 아웃소싱 서비스 제공자의 전문성 결여, 실질적 비용효과 분석, 데이터의 결핍 등이 포함되어 있다.

이와 유사한 연구인 김포옥과 노옥림(2004)은 사서 320명과 업체 직원의 목록기술 내용에 대한 양자 간의 견해를 통해서 아웃소싱을 심층적인 각도에서 조명하였으며, 아웃소싱된 목록을 자관에 반입하는 과정에서 나타나는 문제점을 상세하게 분석하였다. 연구결과, 많은 사서가 아웃소싱에 대한 필요성을 인식하고 있지만 실제로 수행되는 비율은 낮으며 결과에 대한 사서들의 견해에도 찬반이 공존하고 있는 것으로 나타났다. 목록 아웃소싱에 대한 논란의 핵심에는 무엇보다도 실제적인 비용의 절감과 제공된 목록의 품질에 관한 의문이 자리 잡고 있다. 기존의 목록비용이 구체적으로 파악되지 않은 대부분의 도서관에서 아웃소싱의 경제성을 파악하기란 용이하지 않다. 그러나 의사결정에 근거를 마련하기 위해서는 정량

적으로 파악할 수 있는 목록 아웃소싱의 편익을 최대한 고려한 종
합적인 타당성 분석이 요구된다.

이러한 필요성에 따라 본 연구가 수행하고자 하는 연구내용은 다
음과 같다.

첫째, 목록 아웃소싱의 경제성 분석을 위한 기본개념을 찾아낸다.

둘째, 경제성 분석을 위한 목록 아웃소싱의 비용요소와 편익요소를
적합성 평가를 거쳐 관련 연구로부터 추출한다.

셋째, 사례분석을 통하여 목록 아웃소싱의 타당성을 분석한다.

2. 이론적 배경

2.1 아웃소싱의 경제성 분석모형

목록 아웃소싱의 편익에 관한 연구는 정보경제가 체계화되면서 가
능하게 되었다. Porter(1985)가 제시한 가치사슬(value chain) 개념을
토대로 Parker 등(1988)은 정보시스템의 유형편익을 직접편익으로, 무
형편익을 가치가속(value acceleration), 가치연결(value linking), 가치
재구성(value restructuring), 그리고 혁신으로 인한 가치(innovation)로
구분하여 측정하는 경제성 분석모형을 개발하였다.[1] 이로 인하여 직
접편익만 측정하던 종래의 방법에서 탈피하여 더욱 포괄적으로 경제
성을 분석할 수 있는 계기가 되었다.

정혜경(2004)은 디지털 아카이빙의 경제성 분석을 위해서 Parker

---

[1] 가치사슬은 조직의 활동들이 가치사슬 선상에서 연결되어 가치를 부가하는 역할을 함으로써 궁
극적으로 조직의 목표를 달성하는 효과를 가져온다는 개념임.

등이 제시한 무형편익의 항목 중 가치가속과 가치연결을 포함하였다. 가치재구성과 혁신으로 인한 가치는 정량적인 측정이 불가능하고 주관적이라는 Parker 자신과 후속 연구의 주장에 의하여 배제하였다. 직접편익은 디지털 아카이빙의 도입으로 발생하는 인건비, 소모품 등의 비용절감으로, 가치가속으로 인한 편익은 접근 속도의 향상, 그리고 가치연결로 인한 편익은 기관 내 의사소통의 향상으로 측정하였다. Porter가 제시한 정보시스템의 가치사슬 개념을 토대로 목록 아웃소싱의 경제성 분석을 위한 측정요소를 관련 연구로부터 추출해보고자 한다.

2.2 비용의 측정

Hill(1998)은 Alabama 대학도서관을 대상으로 목록 아웃소싱의 경제성 분석을 시도하였다. 목록 아웃소싱의 비용요소에는 목록작업, 준비과정, 품질검토과정에 투입되는 비용요소를, 자체목록에는 카피목록, OCLC 서지 유틸리티 검색, 장비 작업에 필요한 비용요소를 포함하였다. 연구 결과, 아웃소싱의 비용($9.90/종)은 자체목록작업($3.44/종)보다 훨씬 높고, 오류율(30%)도 자체목록(5%)보다 크게 나타나 목록 아웃소싱은 경제성이 없는 것으로 입증되었다.

한편 도서관 목록의 자동화가 비용절감에 미치는 효과에 관한 연구는 Getz와 Phelps(1984), Morris(1992)에 의하여 이루어졌다. 전자는 목록 자동화 이후에도 사서들은 기존의 업무처리 방식을 고수하려는 경향이 있어 그 효과는 제한적이라고 주장하였다. 비용요소에는 <표1>과 같이 목록과 분류, 사전검색, 목록관리, 장비 작업이 포함되어 있다. Morris는 실제 업무량(16주 동안)을 근거로 목록비용을 산출하였으며, 비용요소에 목록, 전거통제, 교육시간을 포함하였다. 목록의 자동화 이후에도 여전히 카피목록에 가장 많은 시간 (36.9%)이 소요되었으며, 오리지널 목록은 현저히 감소한 것으로 나타났다. 한편 재 목록, 전거통제와 교육시간은 많이 증가하였다. 인건비에는 실제 급여 외에 부가급여(연금, 유급휴가, 보험급여)를 포함하였다.

Morris와 Wool(2000)은 Iowa 주립대학을 대상으로 후속 연구를 수행하였다. 목록의 단가는 <표 2>와 같이 직원의 투입 시간에 시간당 급여를 곱하고, 이를 완성된 권수로 나누어 산출하였다. 연구 결과, 레코드 당 편목 비용은 1991년에 비해 감소하였고 완성된 목록의 종수는 30% 증가하지만, 목록작업에 투입된 전체 직원 수 및 시간은 크게 감소한 것으로 나타났다.

2.3 편익의 측정

2.3.1 유형편익: 직접편익

Brumm(1993)은 미국 Texas 주에서 실시된 기록관리 프로그램에 대한 경제성 분석을 시행하였다. 기록관리를 도입함으로써 가시적으로 발생하는 비용 절감과 비용회피의 유형편익을 포함하여 경제성 분석을 하였다. 비용 절감에는 인건비, 공간, 파일 캐비닛과 상업 시설이 아닌 기록관리청의 레코드 센터를 무료로 이용함으로써 절감되는 비용을 포함하여 분석하였다. 연구 결과, 3년 동안 총 $69,973,701의 비용을 절감한 것으로 나타났다.

Dmytrenko(1997) 역시 기록관리의 경제성을 분석하였으며, 편익을 유형편익, 무형편익, 그리고 비용회피로 분류하였다. 비용회피에는 기록관리의 도입으로 더 이상 구입하지 않아도 되는 파일 캐비닛, 공간 등의 비용을 포함하였다. 한편 정혜경(2004)은 디지털 아카이빙의 유형편익을 비용절감과 비용회피로 구분하여 측정하였다.

2.3.2 무형편익: 가치연결로 인한 편익

Parker 등에 의하면 가치연결로 인한 효과는 정보시스템의 도입이 조직의 성과나 기능의 향상으로 파급되어 조직의 효율성 향상을 가져오는 무형의 가치이다. 관련 연구들은 목록이 필요한 가치를 전달하여 이용자의 시간을 절감하고 신속한 의사결정을 할 수 있는 원동력이 되기 위해서는 품질이 우수해야 한다는 데에 동의하고 있다. 미국 의회도서관에서는 '목록의 품질'을 '이용자에게 필요한 상세하고 정확한 서지정보 그리고 시대에 맞는 적절한 접근점 제공'으로 정의하고 있다.

<표 1> Getz and Phelps: 목록 단가 산출식

목록 단가 = (목록 + 분류 + 사전검색 + 목록관리 + 장비 작업) ÷ 권수

<표 2> Morris & Wool(2000): 목록 단가 산출식

목록 단가=(직원의 시간당 급여 x 목록에 투입된 직원의 시간 x 직원 수) ÷ 권수

목록의 품질은 일관성으로 측정되어야 한다고 주장하는 연구들이 있다. Johnston(1990)은 목록의 일관성을 평가하기 위해 18개의 납품업체가 제공하는 전거통제 기능에 대하여 설문 조사하였다. 그 결과 납품업체들이 제공하는 대부분의 전거통제 기능은 평균 이상인

것으로 나타나 목록의 품질이 입증되었다. Tsui와 Hinders(1999)에 의하면, 도서관은 온라인 시스템과 온라인 전거통제 납품업체와의 적절한 협력 체계 안에 있을 때 효과적이고 효율적인 운영이 가능하다. 여기에서 납품업체는 입수된 서지 레코드의 표목을 조사하고 갱신하는 역할을 한다.

Morris와 Wool(1999)은 품질 있는 목록은 규칙을 준수하고 일관성을 유지해야 하며 완전하고 상세하게 작성되어야 한다고 주장하였다. 품질지표로 목록 규칙 준수, 상세성, 완전성, 신뢰성을 제안하였으며, Lam(2001) 역시 일관성 없는 목록은 유용한 자료에의 접근을 보장할 수 없음을 지적하였다.

McCain과 Shorten(2001)은 도서관 목록의 품질지표로 효율성과 효과성을 제안하였으며, 이를 적용하여 26개 대학도서관 목록의 품질을 측정하였다. 효율성은 일정기간 동안에 생산되는 자료의 종수와 권수로 측정되었고, 효과성은 업무분장, 목록대상 후보 자료량, 전거통제, 그리고 데이터베이스 관리 정도로 측정되었다. 이들은 도서관 목록의 품질을 비교하기 위하여 대상 도서관의 운영방식, 아웃소싱 비용과 아웃소싱 대상 순위 등의 유사함이 우선되어야 한다고 주장하였다.

목록의 무결성이나 형식성에 초점을 둔 목록자(또는 목록) 중심의 관점에서 이용자를 중시하는 관점으로 초점을 맞추게 되면서 유용성에 초점을 둔 목록 평가지표가 나오게 되었다. 이제환(2002)은 국내 학술정보시스템인 KERIS가 구축해 놓은 종합목록 DB의 품질을 평가하기 위한 지표로 유용성에 초점을 둔 포괄성, 배타성, 최신성, 중복성, 일관성, 완전성을 제시하였다.

노지현(2003) 역시 유용성을 목록의 품질 측정지표로 설정하였으며, 포괄성, 상세성, 완전성 그리고 정확성을 세부 측정지표로 삼았다. 6개 대학도서관을 사례 분석한 결과, 현 단계의 국내 도서관 목록은 모든 지표에서 품질이 매우 낮으며 특히 정확성이 매우 저조한 것으로 나타났다. 윤정옥(2004)은 아웃소싱 업체에 의하여 제공된 목록이 기술과 접근점에 있어서의 일관성을 유지하지 못하여 정확성, 신뢰성 또한 결여된다면 궁극적인 피해자는 이용자임을 강조하였다.

3. 연구의 방법

3.1 연구의 설계 및 절차

자료수집은 10개 도서관(8개 대학, 2개 공공)의 정리부서를 대상으로 심층 면담과 설문 조사를 병행하여 이루어졌다. 심층 면담은 정리부서의 관리자를 대상으로 하였으며, 설문 조사는 목록의 품질을 평가할 수 있는 관리자와 사서 모두를 대상으로 이루어졌다. 본 연구는 가치사슬 개념에 기반을 둔 Parker 등의 이론을 바탕으로 목록 아웃소싱의 경제성을 유형편익과 무형편익으로 범주화하였다. 유형편익은 직접편익을, 무형편익은 가치연결로 인한 효과로 측정하였다. 각 항목의 측정요소는 관련 분야의 여러 이론과 모형으로부터 보편타당성과 실용성의 적합성 평가를 거쳐 추출되었다.

직접편익은 인건비, 비품, 소모품비 등의 절감분을 측정항목으로 설정하였으며 정량적으로 측정되었다. 한편 가치연결로 인한 편익은 사업의 목적과 직결되는 가장 중요한 효과인 목록의 품질 향상으로 측정되나, 이는 정량적으로 파악하기 어려운 무형편익으로 판단되어 라이커트(Likert)의 5점 척도로 그 효과를 분석하였다. 따라서 본 연구에서 가치연결에 의한 효과는 질적 평가를 통하여 부연설명을 가능하게 함으로써 목록 아웃소싱의 타당성을 종합적으로 이해하게 하는 데 중요한 몫을 하도록 설계되었다.

연구 절차는 크게 세 부분으로 구성된다(그림 1 참조).

첫 번째, 관련 분야의 경제성에 관한 여러 이론과 모형으로부터 목록 아웃소싱의 경제성 분석을 위한 기본개념과 분석요소를 도출한다.

두 번째, 도출된 목록 아웃소싱의 기본개념과 분석요소를 사례분석에 적용하여 목록 아웃소싱의 비용 편익을 분석한다.

세 번째, 목록 아웃소싱의 경제성에 영향을 미칠 수 있는 요인들을 파악하고 목록 아웃소싱의 경제성을 종합적으로 분석한다.

3.2 경제성 분석을 위한 기본개념 및 분석요소 도출

목록 아웃소싱의 경제성 분석을 위해 Porter의 가치사슬 개념을 토대로 Parker 등이 제시한 정보시스템의 편익항목들에 대한 적합성을 평가하였다. 적합성 평가는 보편타당성과 실용성을 기준으로 삼았다. 보편타당성의 기준은 제시된 분석모형이 타 연구에서 적용된 사례가 있는지며, 실용성은 실제 현장에서 사용되고 있는지다.

분석방법으로는 비용과 편익을 함께 측정하고 평가하며, 이와 관련된 여러 원칙과 기준 하에서의 분석이 가능한 비용편익분석을 이용하였다(그림 2 참조).[2]

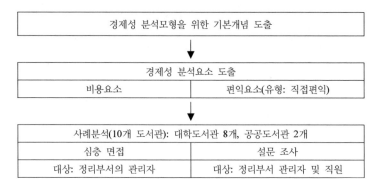

<그림 1> 연구의 절차

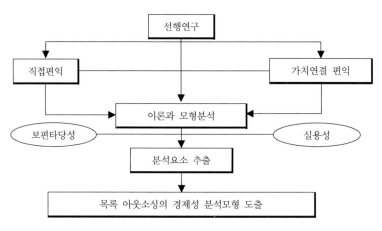

<그림 2> 경제성 분석모형을 위한 기본개념 및 분석요소 도출방법

3.3 사례분석 방법

본 연구는 여러 모형과 이론에서 도출한 경제성 분석요소를 국내

---

2) 비용편익분석은 어떠한 투자사업 대안의 집행에 필요로 하는 비용과 그것에서 얻어지는 편익을 화폐단위로 환산하여 비교 평가하고, 그 대안의 시행이 바람직한가를 검토하는 방법으로, 비용과 편익은 장래 시점에 걸쳐 발생하는 것으로 현재가치로 환산하여 양자의 비율 또는 차이를 가지고 평가 기준으로 삼는 것이 일반적임.

도서관에 적용하는 사례분석을 수행하였다. 목록 아웃소싱에 포함되어야 하는 비용 항목 중 이미 다른 목적으로 투입된 비용은 매몰비용으로 처리하여 제외하였다.

3.3.1 분석대상

목록 아웃소싱을 수행한 경험이 있는 전체 도서관을 파악하기는 쉽지 않다. 국내 도서관으로 비교적 지속해서 아웃소싱을 수행했고 앞으로도 지속할 의사가 있어 타 도서관에 파급 효과를 미칠 수 있을 것으로 파악된 10개의 도서관을 분석대상으로 선정하였다. 분석대상에는 6개의 서울 시내 대학도서관, 2개의 지방대학 도서관 그리고 2개의 공공도서관이 포함되어 있다. 분석대상 도서관의 직원 수와 가장 최근에 수행된 아웃소싱의 현황은 <표 3>과 같다.

3.3.2 자료의 수집

자료의 수집은 2005년 3월 1일부터 4월 30일까지 이루어졌다. 설문지 문항은 크게 두 부분으로 나누어져 있다. 설문지 I은 관리자들과의 심층 면담을 통하여 이루어졌으며, 설문지 II는 아웃소싱으로 제공된 목록의 품질을 관리하는 정리부서 사서들을 대상으로 하였다. 설문지의 문항은 <표 4>와 같이 구성하였다.

<표 3> 분석대상 도서관 현황

도서관		정리부서 직원(인원)	수행 기간	정리 권수(권)
대학	A	과장(1), 사서(6), 시간제(1)	지속적(1년마다 갱신)	65,000
	B	과장(1), 사서(4)	2003.8~2004.9(13개월)	30,000
	C	주임(1), 조교(3)	2004.6~2005.9(방학 중 3회)	10,800

도서관		정리부서 직원(인원)	수행 기간	정리 권수(권)
	D	과장(1), 사무관(1), 주임(2), 사서(14)	2004.11~2005.2(4개월)	6,000~7,200
	E	사서(2), 조교(1)	2004.2~2005.2(1년)	23,530
	F	계장(1), 주임(1), 계원(1), 임시직(2)	2004.3.1~2005.2(1년)	36,400
	G	계장(1), 사서(4), 파견직(1)	2004.5~2005.4(1년)	42,000~48,000
	H	사서(7)	2004.12~2005.2(방학 중 1회)	8,500
공공	I	사서(1)	2004.1~2004.12(1년)	8,300
	J	사서(4)	2005.2~2006.2(1년)	10,000

<표 4> 설문지의 구성내용

설문구성		측정내용	문항	총
	정리부서 현황	자료정리 담당 직원의 수와 직위	1	
		연간 정리자료 권수(유형별)	1	3
		소요되는 소모품비 및 기타 비용	1	
I	아웃소싱	계약 기간	1	
		아웃소싱 때문에 이루어진 자료의 정리작업	1	
		아웃소싱 형태	1	
		MARC 레코드 비용이 책 비용에서 차지하는 비율	1	
		업체선정 방법	1	
		의뢰한 자료의 유형	1	10
		준비하는 과정에 투입된 비용	1	
		목록 아웃소싱에 대한 종합적인 관리자의 인식	1	
		목록 아웃소싱으로 개선된 부분	1	
		목록 아웃소싱을 지속할 의사	1	
II (MARC 레코드의 품질)	일관성	기존 레코드와 접근점 사용에 있어서 일관성이 있다.	2	
		레코드의 구조와 데이터의 표기가 목록규칙을 준수하여 일관된 방식을 따르고 있다.		
	정확성	띄어쓰기 오류, 철자 오류 등의 오류가 거의 없다.	2	7
		자료의 내용을 파악하는 데 직접적인 단서가 될 수 있는 '주제명'을 정확하게 기술하고 있다.		
	완전성	내용을 식별하는 데 도움이 되는 다양한 정보(판차 사항, 발행사항, 형태 사항 등)를 완벽하게 수록하고 있다.	2	
		데이터 필드 자체가 누락되거나 중복된 필드가 많다.		
	분류	분류번호는 주제에 맞게 정확하게 부여되어 있다.	1	
총합			20	

3.3.3 분석 도구

비용편익분석에서 발생하는 모든 비용과 편익은 단기적이 아닌 장기적 시각에서 종합적으로 평가하는 것이 일반적이다. 도서관도 시간이라는 변수는 중요하나, 목록 아웃소싱은 비용과 편익이 동시에 발생하는 것으로 가정하였다. 아웃소싱으로 인한 편익의 발생 여부는 대부분 아웃소싱의 계약 기간 내에 발생한다. 즉 제공된 목록은 자관의 데이터로 반입되기 전에 품질제어가 이루어지기 때문에, 품질이 미흡한 경우에는 이를 교열하기 위하여 투입되는 사서의 시간이 늘어나고, 이로 인해 추가비용이 발생하기 때문이다.

물론 품질제어를 거쳐 이용자에게 제공되는 목록은 지속해서 편익을 발생할 것으로 기대될 수 있다. 그러나 대부분 경우에 아웃소싱으로 제공된 목록은 도서관 사서에 의하여 품질제어 되기 때문에, 이후에 지속해서 발생하는 편익은 자체목록에서 발생하는 편익과 동일하다고 간주할 수 있다. 따라서 본 연구는 시간이라는 변수를 배제한 순 편익(net benefit)과 편익비용의 비율(the ratio of benefit to cost)을 경제성 분석의 도구로 사용하였다.[3](표 5 참조) 한편 정량적인 측정이 불가능하다고 판단된 목록의 품질은 라이커트(5점 척도)에 의하여 만족도를 분석하였다.

순 편익은 목록 아웃소싱으로 인한 편익에서 아웃소싱에 소요된 비용을 차감한 금액을 말한다. 편익은 유형편익인 직접편익으로 측정된다. 순 편익을 기준으로 경제성을 판단한다면, 순 편익이 '0'보다 크면 경제성이 있는 것으로 평가한다. 편익비용비율이 높은 사

---

3) 순 편익: 일반적으로 사업 기간이 1년을 초과하는 경우 돈의 시간가치가 중요한 요소가 되나, 본 연구의 대상인 목록 아웃소싱의 경우 통상적으로 1년 계약으로 이루어지므로 할인율(금리)을 적용하여 현재가치로 전환할 필요가 없음.

업일수록 경제적 타당성이 높은 것으로 평가한다. 편익비용비율이 '1'보다 크면 경제성이 있는 것으로 평가하고 '1'보다 작으면 경제성이 없는 것으로 평가한다. 목록의 품질제어를 담당하는 정리부서의 사서들이 아웃소싱 업체에서 제공된 목록의 품질에 대한 만족도를 라이커트 5점 척도로 측정하였다. 긍정(4점)과 매우 긍정(5점)에 응답한 응답자가 전체에서 차지하는 비율을 목록의 품질에 대한 만족도의 척도로 삼았다.

<표 5> 목록 아웃소싱의 경제성 분석 도구

---

* 순 편익(net benefit) = 편익(benefit) - 비용(cost) > 0 → 경제성 존재
* 편익-비용 비율(ratio of benefit to cost)
  = 편익(benefit) ÷ 비용(cost) > 1 → 경제성 존재

---

4. 목록 아웃소싱의 경제성 분석모형

4.1 경제성 분석 기본모형

목록 아웃소싱의 경제성 분석을 위해 비용편익분석을 사용하였다. 이는 목록 아웃소싱이 가시적인 편익뿐만 아니라 업무의 효율성을 향상하는 무형편익을 크게 발생시키는 특징을 지니고 있음을 고려한 것이다. 목록 아웃소싱 때문에 파생되는 부가가치는 Parker의 정보경제학 방법론을 토대로 직접편익과 가치연결의 효과로 구분하였다. 단, 가치연결의 효과는 목록의 품질에 대한 이용자의 만족도로 파악하였다. 한편 가치가속, 가치재구성과 혁신으로 인한 가치는 적합성 부족 또는 측정의 임의성이 크기 때문에 연구자의

주관에 의해 과대평가될 수 있는 분석상의 오류가 존재할 수 있음이 지적된 바 있으므로 본 연구에서 배제하였다.

4.2 비용의 측정

관련 연구의 이론과 모형에서 보편타당성과 실용성 여부의 적합성 평가를 통해 추출된 목록 아웃소싱의 비용요소에는 목록비용, 교육훈련비용, 품질제어비용, 그리고 행정비용이 포함되어 있다. 동일한 의미이나 여러 연구에서 다르게 표현된 요소들은 한 가지 용어로 통일하여 사용하였다. 다시 말해서 교육시간은 교육훈련비용에, 목록관리 및 전거통제는 품질제어비용에 포함하였다. 사전검색은 행정비용에 포함하였다(표 6 참조).

1) 목록비용

목록비용에는 목록, 분류, 장비 작업을 하는 데 투입되는 비용이 포함된다. 목록의 유형은 오리지널 목록, 카피목록, 그리고 재목록으로 나누어진다. 자료 구입 시 MARC 레코드를 함께 납품받는 경우에는 납품가에 레코드의 비용이 포함되는 것이 일반적이다. 비용은 대상의 유형, 작업의 범위 등에 따라 결정된다.

2) 교육훈련비용

교육훈련비용에는 업체의 직원을 교육하는 데 투입되는 도서관 사서의 인건비가 포함되었다. 아웃소싱 업체의 직원을 대상으로 하는 교육은 초기에 단기적으로 실시되거나 사업 기간에 필요에 따라서 실시되기도 한다.

3) 품질제어비용

품질제어비용에는 아웃소싱으로 제공된 레코드의 교열에 투입되는 사서의 인건비를 포함하였다. 품질제어의 대상에는 제공된 레코드의 띄어쓰기, 철자 오류, 기존 목록과의 일관성 여부, 데이터 필드의 누락 및 중복 여부, 주제명과 분류번호의 적합성 여부 등이 포함되어 있다.

4) 행정비용

행정비용에는 목록 아웃소싱을 위한 사전검색작업, 업체선정, 목록규칙제정, 서류작성, 운송, 포장 및 원부작성 등의 여러 가지 행정에 투입되는 비용을 포함하였다. 정리대상 자료를 업체에 보내어 데이터를 납품받는 경우가 업체의 직원이 도서관에 상주하여 아웃소싱이 이루어지는 경우보다 행정비용이 많이 투입된다.

<표 6> 비용요소 분석표

연 구	비용요소	보편타당성	실용성	적합성 평가결과
Getz and Phelps (1984)	목록(오리지널, 카피)	O	O	목록비용 교육훈련비용 품질제어비용 행정비용
	사전검색	O	O	
	목록관리	O	O	
	물리적 장비 작업	X	△	
Morris(1992)	목록(카피, 오리지널, 재목록)	O	O	
	전거통제(품질관리)	O	O	
	교육시간	O	O	
Morris & Wool (1999)	목록(카피, 오리지널, 재목록)	O	O	
	전거통제	O	O	
	컨설팅/문제해결	X	X	
	교육 훈련/지침개정/문서화	O	O	

4.3 편익의 측정

목록 아웃소싱의 경제성 분석 기본모형은 편익을 유형편익과 무형편익으로 범주화하였다. 유형편익에는 직접편익, 무형편익에는 가치연결의 효과가 포함되었다. 단, 무형편익인 가치연결의 효과는 품질에서 나오는 가치를 정성적 방법으로 측정하여 정량적으로 파악된 직접편익과 함께 목록 아웃소싱의 타당성을 분석하는 데 사용되었다.

4.3.1 유형편익: 직접편익

유형편익은 <표 7>과 같이 직접편익으로 평가되며, 직접편익은 비용절감과 비용회피로 구분되었다. 비용절감은 목록 아웃소싱을 도입함으로써 기존 업무프로세스가 개선되어 절감되는 비용이며, 비용회피는 목록 아웃소싱을 도입함으로써 추가로 발생하지 않아도 되는 비용이 포함되었다. 목록 아웃소싱의 유형은 크게 두 가지로 나누어진다. 자료 구입과 함께 **MARC** 데이터를 납품받는 경우와 업체의 직원이 상주하거나 임시직을 채용하여 미정리자료, 신착자료의 목록작업을 수행하는 경우이다. 전자는 기존 업무의 프로세스가 개선되어 인건비가 절감되므로 여기에서 발생하는 절감분은 비용절감의 측정지표로 설정하였다. 한편 후자는 목록작업을 위한 정규직을 채용하는 비용을 회피할 수 있으므로, 이를 비용회피의 측정지표로 설정하였다. 직접편익의 산출식은 <표 8>과 같다.

<표 7> 유형편익의 항목

편익의 종류	평가항목	세부평가 항목	평가지표
유형편익	직접편익	비용절감	자료 구입과 함께 MARC를 납품받음으로써 업무프로세스가 개선되어 나타나는 인건비, 소모품비 등의 절감
		비용회피	목록을 아웃소싱 함으로써 추가로 발생하지 않아도 되는 인건비, 비품 소모품비 등의 절감

<표 8> 직접편익의 산출식

직접편익 = 비용절감 + 비용회피 = 인건비 절감 + 소모품비 절감 + 비품 절감

비용절감(인건비) = (완성된 권수 ÷ 1인당 평균 정리 권수[4]) x 1인당 평균급여[5]

비용회피(인건비) = 목록업무에 관련된 직원의 수 x 1인당 연평균 급여 x 정리업무 속도향상의 정도(%)

비품 및 소모품비 절감 = 실제로 절감된 비품 및 소모품의 비용

4.3.2 무형편익: 가치연결로 인한 편익

무형편익은 <표 9>와 같이 가치연결로 인한 편익으로 측정된다. 가치연결로 인한 편익은 '목록의 품질'에 대한 만족도를 측정지표로 설정하였으며, 이는 라이커트의 5점 척도로 측정하였다. 본 연구는 목록업무를 수행하고 있는 사서직만을 대상으로 설문 조사가 이루어졌다. 아웃소싱으로 제공된 목록은 자관의 목록에 반입되어 도서관에서 이용되기 전에 목록업무를 수행하고 있는 사서들에 의하여 품질 제어되기 때문에, 이용자는 실제로 최종 목록을 이용할 수 있게 된다. 따라서 아웃소싱으로 제공된 목록이 기존에 도서관

---

4) 각 도서관의 1인당 평균 정리 권수(2004년도 기준)를 적용함.

5) 공공도서관 정규직원의 연평균 급여: 평균직급 7급 10호봉(연평균 급여 총 26,766천 원) 기본급 (11,424천 원)에 각종 수당 및 보조비(정근수당, 가계지원비, 명절 휴가비, 급식비, 직급보조비, 교통보조비 등)를 포함하여 산출함. 사립대학교 교직원의 연평균 급여: 10년 차 교직원(연평균 급여 총 36,569천 원) 기본급에 각종 수당 및 보조비(정근수당, 가계지원비, 명절 휴가비, 급식비, 직급보조비, 교통보조비 등)를 포함하여 산출함.

사서들에 의하여 이루어진 목록과 품질에 있어서 크게 차이가 나지 않는다고 가정하였다.

세부측정지표는 관련 분야의 이론과 모형으로부터 적합성 평가를 거쳐 추출하였다. 적합성 평가를 거쳐 추출된 평가지표는 일관성, 정확성과 완전성이다. 본 연구는 각기 다른 연구에서 유사한 의미로 사용된 상세성과 완전성을 유사한 의미로 간주하여, 더욱 함축적인 의미인 완전성으로 표현하였다. 그리고 관리자와의 심층면담 결과 목록 품질의 가장 중요한 척도가 될 수 있는 분류번호를 포함하였다.

<표 9> 무형편익의 항목

편익의 종류	평가항목	세부평가 항목	평가지표
무형편익	가치연결로 인한 편익	목록의 품질	만족도(라이커트 척도)

<표 10> 목록 품질측정의 지표

품질측정 지표	관련 항목	보편 타당성	실용성	적합성 평가결과
일관성	레코드 구조의 일관성, 데이터 표현의 일관성, 데이터 기술의 통일성	O	O	일관성 정확성 완전성 (분류번호)
정확성	수록 내용의 정확성, 표기의 정확성	O	O	
포괄성	수록자료의 범위, 수록 레코드의 수	X	X	
배타성	독점성	O	X	
상세성	내용식별에 유용한 정보의 상세한 수록 여부, 필요한 데이터 필드의 완벽한 수록	O	O	
완전성	표기의 오류, 레코드 구조의 적합성, 데이터 기술의 완전성	O	O	
최신성	현행성, 신속성, 갱신주기, 타임 래그	X	X	
중복성	동일 지표에 대한 중복데이터의 포함 여부	O	X	

5. 결과 분석

5.1 설문지의 회수현황

8개의 대학도서관과 2개의 공공도서관을 설문대상으로 설정하였다. 설문지 I은 정리부서의 관리자를 대상으로 심층 면담을 병행하여 이루어졌으며, 10명의 관리자 모두에게서 응답을 받았다. 한편 설문지 II의 배포대상과 회수율은 <표 11>과 같다. 전체 10개 도서관의 설문지 회수율은 약 61%이다. 기재된 직급명은 관리자가 작성한 대로 사용되었다.

5.2 기관별 분석

5.2.1 현황 분석

목록 아웃소싱은 크게 4가지 형태로 나눌 수 있다. MARC 데이터를 자료와 함께 서적상에서 납품받는 경우(5), 업체의 직원이 상주하여 목록작업이 이루어지는 경우(3), 업체에 목록대상 자료를 보내어 MARC 데이터를 납품받는 경우(1), 그리고 MARC 데이터를 납품받으면서 동시에 임시직을 채용하여 목록작업을 수행하는 경우(1)로 구분된다.

자료의 유형으로 분석하면, 2개 도서관만이 일서와 비도서를 아웃소싱 하였으며, 나머지는 모두 국내서를 아웃소싱 하였다. 그리고 2개 도서관이 미정리도서를, 나머지 도서관은 신간 도서를 대상으로 하였다. 처리 범위를 살펴보면, 2개 도서관만이 목록, 분류, 장비 작업까지, 나머지 도서관은 목록과 분류작업만을 아웃소싱 하였다. 도서관별 아웃소싱의 현황은 <표 12>와 같다.

5.2.2 직접편익

도서관별 목록 아웃소싱에 투입된 비용과 편익을 요소별로 정리해 보면 <표 13>과 같다. 비용요소에는 아웃소싱 수행 기간에 목록, 교육 훈련, 품질제어 및 행정에 투입된 비용이 포함되어 있다. 자료구매와 함께 MARC 데이터를 납품받으면 발생하는 인건비 절감은 직접편익의 비용 절감으로 측정되었으며, 도서관 A, E, F, G, I, 그리고 J의 경우가 포함되었다. 반면 미정리자료, 특수언어자료의 처리 및 방학 기간을 이용한 단기 아웃소싱에서 발생하는 정규직의 인건비 및 비품 절감은 직접편익의 비용회피 항목에 포함되었고, 도서관 A, B, C, D 그리고 H의 경우이다.

<표 11> 설문지 II 회수현황

유형	도서관	정리부서 직원의 직급(명)	직원 수(명)	응답자(명)	회수율
대학	A	과장(1), 직원(6)	7	5	61%
	B	과장(1), 사서(4)	5	3	
	C	주임(1)	1	1	
	D	과장(1), 사무관(1), 주임(2), 사서(14)	18	4	
	E	직원(2)	2	2	
	F	계장(1), 주임(1), 계원(1), 파견직(2)	5	3	
	G	계장(1), 직원(4), 파견직(1)	6	6	
	H	사서(7)	7	6	
공공	I	직원(1)	1	1	
	J	직원(4)	4	3	
	설문지 회수 전체 수		56	34	

<표 12> 도서관별 아웃소싱의 현황 분석

	형태	자료유형: 권수	처리 범위
A	계약직, MARC 납품	신간 도서(일부 비도서 제외: 65,000)	목록, 분류
B	업체 직원 상주	미정리도서(국내서, 동양서: 32,549)	목록, 분류
C	업체 직원 상주	신간 도서 (국내서, 서양서, 동양서: 140,000)	목록, 분류
D	업체에 자료 보내어 MARC 납품	미정리도서(국내서: 9,000) 미정리도서(일서: 12,793)	목록, 분류, 장비
E	MARC 납품	신간 도서(국내서, 서양서: 21,647)	목록, 분류
F	MARC 납품	신간 도서(국내서: 30,000)	목록, 분류
G	MARC 납품	신간 도서(국내서, 동양서: 22,500)	목록, 분류
H	업체 직원 상주	신간 도서(국내서: 8,000)	목록, 분류, 장비
I	MARC 납품	신간 도서(국내서, 비도서: 8,300)	목록, 분류
J	MARC 납품	신간 도서(비도서: 700점)	목록, 분류

<표 13> 비용 및 편익요소*

도서관	비용요소				편익요소
	목록	교육 훈련	품질제어	행정	직접편익
A	계약직(3) 인건비, MARC 비용 일부 비도서 제외(65,000권)	없음	계약직(1)	없음	비용절감 (정리속도향상, 30%) 비용회피(인건비 절감)
B	국내서 32,549권 (2,885원/권)	직원(1)의 5%	직원(1)의 50%	직원(1)의 30%	비용회피(인건비 절감)
C	국내서 126,000권 (책값의 3%) 서양서 14,000권 (책값의 6%)	직원(1), 조교(3)의 각 128시간	직원(1)의 100% 조교(3)의 각 30시간	직원(1)의 40시간	비용회피(인건비 절감)
D	국내서 9,000권(1,500원/권)	직원(2)의 2주	직원(2)의 2주	직원(1)의 30%	비용회피 (인건비 및 소모품비 절감)
	일서 12,793권(2,849원/권)	직원(1)의 1일	직원(600)의 1일	직원(1)의 1일	비용회피 (인건비 및 소모품비 절감)
E	국내서 20,826권 (책값의 3%) 서양서 821권(책값의 5%)	없음	직원(2)	없음	비용절감 (정리속도향상, 50%)
F	국내서 30,000권 (책값의 5%)	없음	파견직(2)	없음	비용절감 (정리속도향상, 15%)
G	국내서 22,500권 (책값의 3%)	없음	직원(5), 파견직(1) 의 50%	없음	비용절감 (정리속도향상, 50%)

도 서 관	비용요소				편익요소
	목록	교육 훈련	품질제어	행정	직접편익
H	국내서 8,000권(책값의 3%)	없음	직원(3)의 3일	없음	비용회피 (인건비 절감 및 소모품비 절감)
I	국내서 8,300권(책값의 5%)	없음	직원(1)의 50%	없음	비용절감 (정리속도향상, 50%)
J	비도서 700점(1,000원/1점)	없음	직원(1)의 40%	없음	비용절감 (정리속도향상, 30%)

* = 각 항목에 대한 산출근거는 <부록> 참조

도서관 A의 경우는 두 가지 형태의 아웃소싱이 함께 병용되기 때문에 이로 인해 비용절감과 비용회피가 함께 발생한 것으로 분석된다. 도서관 D와 H의 경우는 정리작업이 아웃소싱에 포함되었기 때문에 소모품비의 절감도 발생하였다. 정리부서 관리자는 MARC 데이터를 납품받기 때문에 향상되었다고 인식되는 업무의 속도를 비율(%)로 응답하였다. 6개의 도서관 중 3개의 도서관은 50%, 2개 도서관은 30%, 1개 도서관은 15%로 응답하였다.

직접편익에 의한 효과를 보면 4개 도서관(4개 사례)만이 경제성이 있는 것으로 나타났으며, 만족의 정도는 저조하였다.[6] 도서관별로 비교해 보면 도서관 D(국내서:1.59), A(1.30), C(1.27), B(1.15)의 순이다. 경제성이 가장 저조한 도서관은 E(0.42)와 F(0.43)이다. 도서관 D의 경우, '국내서'와 달리 일서 사례는 0.93으로 경제성이 없는 것으로 나타났다. 일서의 경우는 업체의 MARC 입력수준이 매우 미흡하여 자관의 특성에 맞게 수정하는 데 사서의 시간이 많이 소요되었기 때문이라는 것이 관리자의 설명이다. 아웃소싱 유형별로 분석해 보면, 업체의 직원이 상주하거나 임시직을 채용한 경우(A, B, C)가 그렇지

---

6) 편익비용비율이 1.70 이상이 될 때 경제성은 안정적이라고 할 수 있음(KDI 공공투자센터)

않은 경우보다 경제성이 크게 나타났다(표 14 참조).

5.2.3 가치연결에 의한 효과

가치연결에 의한 효과는 목록의 품질에 대한 사서들의 만족도(5점 만점)로 분석하였다. 평균 만족도는 3.08로 나타났다. 직접편익만으로 경제성이 있는 것으로 나타난 도서관 중 3개 도서관이 평균만족도 이상인 것으로 나타났다. 도서관별로 분석해 보면 도서관 C(3.88) J(3.6), D(3.38)의 순으로 목록의 품질에 대한 만족도가 크며, 가장 불만을 느끼고 있는 도서관은 F(2.5)와 I(2.5)인 것으로 나타났다. 지표별로 분석해 보면, '일관성'(3.6) '완전성'(3.29) '정확성'(2.75), '분류번호'(2.68)의 순이다. 특히 목록의 '정확성'과 '분류번호'의 미흡에 대한 불만족은 아웃소싱 업체들의 전문성이 결여되어 있음을 보여주는 중요한 단면이다(표 15 참조).

<표 14> 직접편익에 의한 효과

도서관		비용(원)	유형편익 직접편익(원)	경제성(편익비용비율)
A		75,400,000	98,396,000	1.30
B		128,898,368	148,470,140	1.15
C		194,785,431	246,787,560	1.27
D	국내	24,317,264	38,656,200	1.59
	일서	117,205,930	109,490,161	0.93
E		86,614,000	36,569,000	0.42
F		46,500,000	20,055,000	0.43
G		113,547,000	103,422,500	0.91
H		12,750,776	12,732,712	1.00
I		17,533,000	13,383,000	0.76
J		11,406,400	8,029,800	0.70

<표 15> MARC 레코드의 품질에 대한 이용자들의 인식

(단위: 라이커트 척도 5점 만점)

구분	A	B	C	D	E	F	G	H	I	J	평균
일관성	3.70	3.70	4.00	4.13	3.75	3.30	3.83	3.08	2.50	3.70	3.60
정확성	2.30	2.80	3.50	3.00	1.25	2.30	2.83	3.00	3.00	3.50	2.75
완전성	3.60	3.30	4.00	3.40	3.25	3.20	3.00	2.92	2.50	3.70	3.29
분류	2.40	2.70	4.00	3.00	2.50	1.20	2.83	2.83	2.00	3.30	2.68
평균	3.00	3.13	3.88	3.38	2.69	2.50	3.12	2.96	2.50	3.60	3.08

5.2.3 분석 결과 요약

본 연구에서 나타난 분석 결과를 요약하면 다음과 같다. 첫째, 정량적 분석이 가능한 직접편익으로 측정하였을 때, 10개의 분석대상 도서관 중 4개(11개 사례 중 4개)에서만 경제성이 있는 것으로 나타났다. 경제성은 도서관 D(국내서: 1.59), A(1.30), C(1.27), B(1.15)의 순으로 나타났다. 둘째, '기존의 인력으로 처리가 불가능한 미정리자료나 신착 자료를 단기적으로 아웃소싱' 하는 형태는 '자료 납품 시 업체에서 MARC 데이터를 지속해서 납품받는 경우' 보다 경제성이 큰 것으로 나타났다.

전자의 경우는 후자보다 일반적으로 MARC의 단위비용이 높게 책정되어 있었지만, 상대적으로 목록의 품질이 더 우수하여 품질제어를 위한 사서의 추가 인건비가 덜 투입되었고 정규직의 채용을 회피할 수 있었기 때문이다. 목록의 품질이 더 우수할 수 있었던 것은 업체 직원에 대한 체크 작업과 교육이 상식적으로 이루어졌기 때문으로 분석된다. 또한, 전자의 경우에는 대부분 업체의 직원이 상주하여 목록업무를 수행하였기 때문에 준비작업이 별도로 이루어지지 않았기 때문이다. 셋째, 아웃소싱으로 제공된 품질에 대해서는 어느 도서관도 만족하지 않는 것으로 나타났다. 따라서 정량적 평가에서 경제성이 있는 것으로 나온 4개 도서관에서 아웃소싱의 종합적인 타당성은 입증되지 않았다.

6. 결 론

목록은 반복적이고 많은 시간이 필요한 업무의 성격상 아웃소싱의 주요 대상이 되어왔다. 그러나 이에 대한 도서관의 시각은 혼합적이며 타당성에 대한 견해도 상반되어 있다. 본 연구 결과, 목록 아웃소싱의 타당성은 입증되지 않았으며, 이는 아웃소싱을 수행하는 업체들의 전문성 부족 때문으로 분석되었다. 본 연구는 목록 아웃소싱 때문에 파생되는 부가가치를 Parker의 정보 경제학적 접근을 토대로 직접편익, 가치연결의 효과로 구분하여 분석하는 모형을 도출하여 10개의 도서관을 대상으로 사례분석 하였다. 직접편익은 비용절감과 비용회피로, 가치연결 효과는 목록의 품질로 측정하였다. 직접편익은 정량적으로 측정하였으나, 목록의 품질은 일관성, 정확성, 완전성 그리고 분류번호를 측정지표로 라이커트(5점) 척도를 이용하여 그 가치를 분석하였다.

직접편익만으로 측정했을 때 경제성이 있는 것으로 나타난 4개 중 3개 도서관은 업체 직원이 상주하여 목록작업을 수행한 경우로서, 문제해결이 즉각적으로 가능하였으며 사전준비와 품질제어에 소요되는 비용을 회피할 수 있었기 때문으로 분석된다. 한편 가치연결의 효과만을 그 가치로 평가할 때 목록 아웃소싱은 어느 도서관에서도 타당성이 없는 것으로 나타났다. 따라서 직접편익만으로 경제성이 있는 것으로 나타난 4개 도서관도 목록의 품질까지 고려한다면 종합적인 타당성이 입증되지 않았다. 이는 아웃소싱 업체의 전문성 결여에 따른 저조한 품질의 목록에 투입되는 불필요한 인건비 때문으로 분석된다.

이러한 현실에서 목록 아웃소싱을 무리하게 적용할 경우 목록업무에 대한 정체성의 훼손 내지 와해로 귀착될 수 있으며, 기본 취지인 운영비용의 절감과 봉사 기능의 제고에 어긋나게 된다. 사서들은 관리자와의 대화를 통하여 목록자의 역할 및 전문성에 대한 확실한 인식을 전달해야 할 필요성이 요구되는 시점이다. 물론 향후 아웃소싱 업체의 전문성 부분이 보완된다 하더라도 장서개발의 문제, 사후관리 및 목록의 일관성은 여전히 해결되지 않은 문제로 남아있게 된다는 사실도 기억해야 할 것이다.

한편 사례분석 대상은 일부에 불과하므로, 여기에서 나온 결과를 보편적이라고 단정하기에는 한계점이 있다. 그러나 비교적 지속해서 아웃소싱을 수행하고 있어 다른 도서관에 파급 효과를 미칠 수 있는 도서관을 대상으로 선정함으로써 한계점을 보완하고자 하였다. 또한, 본 연구에서의 경제성 분석은 Parker가 제시한 다섯 항목 중에서 정량적 추정이 가능한 유형편익만을 가지고 경제성을 분석하였기 때문에 Parker의 방법론에 근거한 목록 아웃소싱의 종합적인 분석이라고 주장하기에는 한계가 있다.

참고문헌

김영귀. 2000. 정리업무와 대학도서관의 아웃소싱에 관한 연구: 부산, 경남지역을 중심으로. 『한국문헌정보학회지』, 32(4): 361-394.

김포옥, 노옥림. 2004. 목록업무의 아웃소싱에 대한 인식도 연구. 『정보관리학회지』, 145- 171.

노지현. 2003. 유용성의 관점에서 본 도서관 목록의 품질. 『한국문헌정보학회지』, 37(2): 107- 134.

이제환. 2002. 공동목록 DB의 품질평가와 품질관리: KERIS의 종합목록 DB를 중심으로. 『한국문헌정보학회지』, 36(1): 61-89.

윤정옥. 2004. 대학도서관 편목 업무 외주의 동향과 논쟁. 『한국문헌정보학회지』, 38(2): 119- 136.

정혜경. 2004. 디지털 아카이빙의 경제성 분석연구. 『한국문헌정보학회지』, 38(4): 251- 270.

Brumm, Eugenia. 1993. "Cost/Benefit Analysis of the Records Management Program in the State of Texas." *Records Management Quarterly,* 27(2): 30-39.

Dunkle, Clare B. 1996 "Outsourcing the Catalog Department: A Meditation Inspired by the Business and Library Literature." *Journal of Academic Librarianship,* Jan: 33-43.

Dmytrenko, April. 1997. "Cost Benefit Analysis", *Records Management Quarterly,* 31(1): 16-20.

Getz, Malcolm and Doug Phelps. 1984. "Labor Costs in the Technical Operation of Three Research Libraries." *Journal of Academic Librarianship,* 10(4): 209-219.

Hill, Debra W. 1998. "To Outsource or Not: University of Alabama Libraries Engage in Pilot Project with OCLC's TechPro." *Cataloging & Classification Quarterly,* 26(1): 63-73.

Jiang, Diana. 1998. "A Feasibility Study of the Outsourcing of Cataloging in Academic Libraries." *Journal of Educational Media & Library Sciences,* 35(4): 283-293.

Lam, Vinh-The. 2001. "Outsourcing Authority Control: Experience of the University of Saskatchewan Libraries." *Cataloging & Classification Quarterly,* 32(4): 53-69.

Johnston, Sarah Hagen. 1990. "Desperately Seeking Authority Control: Automated Systems Are Not Providing It." *Library Journal,* Oct.(1): 43-46.

McCain, Cheryl and Jay Shorten. 2001. "Cataloging Efficiency and Effectiveness." *LRTS,* 46(1):23-31

Morris, Dilys E. 1992. "Staff Time and Costs for Cataloging." *LRTS,* 36(1): 79-95.

Morris, Dilys E., Collin B. Hobert, Lorl Osmus, and Gregory Wool. 1999. "Cataloging Staff Costs Revisited." *LRTS,* 44(2): 70-83.

Morris, Dilys E., Gregory Wool. 2000. "Cataloging: Librarianship's Best Bargain." *Library Journal,* 124(11): 44-50.

Parker, Marilyn M., Robert J. Benson and H.E. Trainor. 1988. *Information Economics: Linking Business Performance to Information Technology.* England Cliffs: Prentice Hall.

Porter, Michael E. 1985. *Competitive Advantage.* New York: Free Press.

Tsui, Susan L., Carole F. Hinders. 1999. "Cost-Effectiveness and Benefits of Outsourcing Authority Control." *Cataloging & Classification Quarterly,* 26(4): 43-61.

While, Herbert S. 1998. "Library Outsourcing and contracting Cost-Effectiveness or Shell Game?" *Library Journal,* Jun 15: 56-57.

학술지 평가모형

급변하는 정보통신기술의 발달은 도서관의 역할에도 적잖은 변화를 몰고 왔다. 출판사들이 유수의 국내·외 학술지를 디지털화하기 시작하면서 기존 인쇄 매체는 전자학술지의 보급에 밀려 점차 감소하는 추세였다. 발 빠르게 움직이는 출판사들은 전자학술지의 연착륙을 위해 전자저널 컨소시엄, 웹 DB 그리고 다양한 가격모델을 앞다투어 선보이면서 학술지 시장은 일대의 전환기를 맞이하게 되었다. 2005년 당시, 필자가 근무하는 KDI대학원 도서관에서는 매해 발생하는 인쇄학술지의 과다한 구독비용(약 200여 종)과 이로 인한 도서관 공간의 부족이 주요 과제로 대두되었다. 특히 인쇄학술지 구독료의 지속적 인상(연평균 약 10%)과 IMF 외환위기 사태로 인한 달러화 강세는 해외 학술지 구독 비중이 높은 대학원 도서관에 큰 걸림돌로 작용하였다(약 64%). 체계적이고 합리적인 학술지 선정을 위해 그리고 도서관 예산의 효과적인 배분을 위해 구독 학술지의 유용성을 평가해야 할 필요성이 제기되었다. 이를 계기로 필자는 도서관 학술지의 가치를 정량적으로 평가할 수 있는 다양한 대안 마련을 모색하였고 도서관의 학술지의 장기 운영계획을 수립하게 되었다.

"전문도서관에서의 학술지 평가를 위한 경제성 분석에 관한 연구(2006)"는 유용성(usefulness)에 기반을 둔 학술지 평가모형을 제시하였다. 이 논문이 제시하는 모형은 편익에 무형편익인 유용도를 적용하였으며, 비용에 학술지의 제본, 주문, 그리고 클레임에 드는 전체 비용을 포함하였다. 유용성은 학술지가 기관의 성격에 맞게 유용하게 활용된 정도에 따라 등급으로 평가되도록 고안되었다. 이용자의 연구 성과물에 직접 인용된 구독 학술지에는 3점, 그리고 전문 다운로드나 검색에 이용된 학술지에는 각각 2점, 1점을 부여하였다. 편익은 개별 구독 학술지의 평균 유용도에 이용 빈도를 곱하여 산출되며, 이용 빈도는 웹 기반의 전자학술지를 대상으로 하였다. 연구대상 학술지는 사례연구 도서관에서 구독하고 있는 4개 전자 DB를 통하여 접근이 가능한 학술지 146종이다. 사례분석 결과, 상위 20% 안에 있는 학술지의 편익이 전체의 75%를 차지하는 것으로 나타났다. 향후 전문도서관은 본 모형을 통해서 측정된 경제적 가치평가를 토대로 학술지의 구매 전략(웹 DB, 전자학술지 only, 인쇄학술지 추가 구매 등)을 위한 기본 틀을 구상할 수 있다. 한편, 평가가 저조한 학술지는 잠정적인 구독중지 대상에 포함하고 요청 시 DDS(Document Delivery Service, 원문복사서비스)를 통하여 제공하는 대안 등을 고려할 수 있다. 이러한 학술지 평가는 일회성이 아닌 다년간 지속해서 축적된 데이터 분석을 기반으로 하는 것이 바람직하다.

　"Evaluating Academic Journals Using Impact Factor and Local Citation Score (2007)"는 학술지의 로컬 도서관 이용 데이터에 객관적인 가치를 함께 고려한 학술지 평가모형을 제시하였다. 이 모형은

CPU(Cost-per-use; 활용/비용)를 토대로 측정한다. 학술지의 로컬 유용성과 객관적인 지표인 Journal Citation Review(JCR)의 피인용지수(Impact Factor; IF)를 1:1의 동일한 비율로 합산한 수치를 활용(편익요소)으로, 학술지의 구독비용과 운영비용을 비용요소에 포함하였다. CPU가 높을수록 경제성이 높은 학술지로 정의된다.

"An Analysis Model of Creating a Core Journal Collection for Academic Libraries (2009)"는 2006년, 2007년 연구와 비교했을 때 학술지 평가를 위한 다양한 측면의 데이터를 최대한 고려한 심층적이고 종합적인 분석모형이라 할 수 있다. 본 연구에서 비용은 구독비용을, 편익에는 JCR의 Impact Factor, 도서관 이용자의 학술지 이용 및 구독 요청 등의 빈도를 환산하여 합한 값을 적용하였다. 본 연구의 분석모형을 사례 대학도서관의 학술지 평가 분석에 적용함으로써 구체적인 실행방법을 제시하였다. 특히, 전문도서관은 위에 제시한 다양한 평가모형 중 도서관의 이용자와 학술지 구독 목적에 적합한 평가모형을 선별하여 학술지의 품질관리와 효율적인 관리체계를 구축하기 위한 기초 자료를 축적할 수 있기를 기대한다.

전문도서관에서의 학술지 평가를 위한 경제성 분석에 관한 연구[7]

본 연구는 학술지 평가를 위한 경제성 분석모형을 도출하였으며, 이를 이용한 사례분석을 수행하였다. 이 모형은 비용요소에 구독비용뿐만 아니라 제본, 주문, 그리고 클레임 등의 관리에 소요되는 총비용을 포함하였으며, 편익요소에는 이용 빈도만을 다루었던 기존의 평가모형과는 달리 유용성을 포함하여 종합적인 분석모형을 제시하였다. 유용성은 학술지가 기관의 성격에 맞게 유용하게 활용되었는지에 따라 등급으로 평가되도록 고안되었다. 이 모형은 최근 연구에 가장 중요한 자원으로 활용되고 있는 웹 기반 전자학술지의 통계를 토대로 측정할 수 있도록 고안되었다. KDI 국제정책대학원 도서관을 대상으로 한 사례분석에서 이용자의 연구 성과물에 활용된 학술지는 가장 높은 등급인 3점을 부여하였으며, 전문 다운로드나 검색에 활용된 학술지는 각각 2점과 1점을 부여하였다. 사례분석은 분석 결과 상위 20위에 포함된 학술지의 편익이 전체의 75%를 차지하며, 이용자의 유형별 학술지 이용행태에 차이가 있음이 나타났다. 이 모형은 특히 전문도서관의 사서들이 학술지의 가치를 평가할 수 있는 기본 틀을 제공할 수 있는 계기가 될 수 있을 것으로 사료된다.

---

7) 이 논문은 2006년 정보관리학회지 23권 1호(121~138쪽)에 게재되었음 [공저: 정은주].

1. 서 론

전문도서관이나 대학도서관의 경우에 학술지 이용에 소요되는 총예산은 도서관 장서 구입 예산의 70에서 80%에 이른다. 여기에는 연평균 약 10%의 높은 인상률을 보이는 인쇄학술지뿐만 아니라 온라인 학술지, 그리고 온라인 데이터베이스의 비용까지 포함되어야 하기 때문이다. 이렇게 높은 비용이 투입되는 정보원임에도 불구하고, 대부분 도서관에서 20%의 구독 학술지가 이용률 80%를 차지하고 있다는 사실이 입증되었다. 따라서 더 많은 학술지가 활용되게 하려면 도서관은 지속적이고 체계적인 학술지 평가를 토대로 더욱 합리적인 의사결정을 해야 할 필요성이 제기되었다. 이는 특히 도서관이 재정 위기 또는 경영 문제 등에 직면했을 때 위기를 극복하는 중요한 계기가 될 수 있다.

이러한 필요성을 토대로 학술지의 선정을 위한 평가 기준이 여러 연구에서 수행되었다. 학술지의 평가 기준으로는 주제의 적합성 여부, 품질, 구독비용, 그리고 이용 빈도 등이 사용되었다. 이 중 인쇄 학술지의 이용 빈도 추정은 학술지의 정량적인 평가를 위하여 유일하게 사용되어 온 연구 방법이다. 그러나 자료수집에 있어서 정확성이 결여되기 쉬우며, 절차가 번거로워 실제 도서관에 적용하기 어렵다는 문제점이 지적되었다. 또한, 이용 빈도에 의한 학술지의 평가는 학술지의 질적 가치를 배제하고 있어서 학술지의 선정을 위한 종합적인 평가방법이라고 볼 수 없다.

한편 학술지의 질적 평가는 JCR(Journal of Citation Reports) 등을 토대로 이루어져 왔다. 그러나 JCR은 ISI사(Institute for Scientific Information)가 구축한 인용 분석의 기준으로서 모든 도서관에 적용할 일반적인 기준치로 보기에는 한계가 있다. 학술지의 유용성은 도서관의 유형 및 특성에 따라 크게 달라질 수 있기 때문이다. '쓸모가 있음', '이용할 데가 있음'의 사전적 의미를 토대로, 본 연구는 학술지의 유용성(utility)을 '구매 목적에 맞게 유익하게 이용됨'으로 정의하였다. 즉 학술지가 도서관의 구매 목적에 부합되게 이용되었다면 유용성 있는 학술지로 구분될 수 있으며, 더 나아가 어떻게 활용되었는지에 따라 유용성의 크고 작음에 차이가 있을 수 있다.

실제로 한 도서관에서 구독하는 학술지는 연구 성과물에 직접 인용되기도 하고, 연구 성과물을 생산하기 위한 지식 축적 또는 기초 자료에 간접적인 용도로 활용되어 그 유용성에서 차이를 보인다. 따라서 본 연구는 이러한 유용성을 토대로 가중치를 부여하는 질적 평가와 이용 빈도를 통한 양적 평가를 모두 고려하여 학술지 평가의 기본 분석모형을 개발하는 것을 연구의 목적으로 삼았다. 후자는 전자학술지의 통계를 토대로 측정하였으므로 연구대상은 구독 중인 인쇄학술지 중 전자적으로 접근이 가능한 학술지를 대상으로 하였다.

이를 위해 본 연구에서 수행하고자 하는 연구내용은 다음과 같다.

첫째, 학술지의 유용도와 이용 빈도를 함께 고려한 종합적인 학술지 평가의 분석모형을 제시한다.

둘째, 제시된 연구모형을 KDI 국제정책대학원 도서관에 적용하는 사례연구를 수행한다. 이를 위해서 KDI 대학원에서 구독한 학술지의 유용성을 평가할 수 있는 항목을 설정하고 설문 조사를 통하여 이용자들의 매체별 학술지 이용행태를 조사한다.

셋째, 본 연구에서 제시된 분석모형이 실제 도서관에서 어떻게 적용될 수 있는지에 대한 기본 가이드를 제공한다.

2. 학술지 평가방법에 관련한 선행연구

2.1 인쇄학술지 평가방법

인쇄학술지의 평가를 위해 이용분석, 인용 분석, 설문 조사, 그리고 비용편익분석 등의 평가방법이 사용되었다. 이용 빈도 분석은 학술지의 이용 빈도를 분석하는 것으로서 대출, 열람, 복사, 상호대차 등에 이용된 빈도를 분석하며, 인용 분석은 학술지가 다른 학술지에 인용된 빈도를 조사하는 것이다. 설문 조사법은 이용자에게 학술지의 내용을 질적으로 평가하도록 하거나 학술지의 등급을 매기도록 하는 방법이다.

Broadus(1985)는 학술지의 평가를 위해서 이용되는 이용분석, 설문 조사, 인용 분석에 대하여 평가하였다. 그는 North Carolina 대학도서관의 학술지를 평가하기 위하여 sweep method 방식을 통한 이용분석을 하였다. 이 연구에서 sweep method는 저렴한 비용이 소요되나 이용 빈도를 정확히 파악하기가 쉽지 않은 단점이 있음이 지적되었다. 또한, 그는 이용자 설문 조사 역시 간단하기는 하나 이용자 기억의 한계로 인한 단점이 있다고 지적하였다. 그리고 미국 ISI(Institute for Scientific Information)가 구축하고 있는 JCR(Journal Citation Reports)을 활용하는 인용 분석방법도 도서관에서 자체적으로 수행하는 정보수집과정을 피할 수 있어 비용 절감을 가져오나 모든 도서관에 적용할 일반적인 기준치로 보기에는 한계가 있다고 주장하였다. 즉 어떠한 평가방법도 단독으로는 완벽한 평가방법이 될 수 없음을 알 수 있다.

Deurenberg(1993) 역시 JCR을 이용한 인용빈도를 주축으로 이와 함께 이용할 몇 가지 기준점을 제시하였다. 먼저 주제별로 범주화한 후, 영향계수(impact factor)를 기준으로 25% 내 학술지를 선정하였으며, 마지막 단계로 즉각 지수(immediacy index)를 평가 기준으로 사용하였다. 이 과정에서 선정되지 않은 40%의 학술지는 Index Medicus에 색인 여부, 이용 빈도, ILL 이용 빈도 포함, 영어 작성 여부, 그리고 출판사의 인지도 등을 고려하여 재평가함으로써 5점(또는 6점)이 되는 학술지만을 구독대상의 학술지로 선정하였다. Deurenberg 역시 JCR은 일반적인 기준치로 볼 수 없다는 데에서 Broadus와 의견을 같이하였다.

한편 학술지의 비용편익분석은 투입된 비용에 대한 편익을 분석하는 방법으로, 비용과 편익에 어떤 요소를 대입하느냐에 따라 결과가 매우 다양하게 나타날 수 있다. 비용에는 구독비용, 그리고 편익에는 이용 빈도를 대입하는 방안이 널리 사용되었다. 본 연구에서는 학술지의 평가방법에 관련한 선행연구 중에서 비용 대 편익에 관련되어 발표된 선행연구를 중심으로 고찰하고자 한다.

Chrzastowski(1991), Milne and Tiffany(1991), Sridhar(1988), 그리고 김석영과 황혜경(2001) 등은 CPU('이용'당 비용, Cost Per Use)를 측정함으로써 학술지의 비용편익분석을 수행하였다. 또한, 비용요소에 학술지의 구독비용, 그리고 편익요소에 이용 빈도가 동일하게 대입되었다.

Chrzastowski와 Milne and Tiffany는 각각 University of Illinois at Urbana-Champaign(미국) 화학도서관 및 Memorial University of Newfoundland 도서관(캐나다)의 학술지를 대상으로 비용편익분석을 수행하였다. 이를 위해 CPU가 사용되었으며, 이용요소에는 학술지의 대출, 도서관 내 열람, 상호대차에 이용된 빈도가 적용되었고, 비용에는 학술지의 구독비용이 대입되었다.

이와 유사한 연구로 Sridhar(1988)는 ISRO Satellite Center Library (인도)에서 구독하는 학술지 최신호(도착 후 3개월)의 CPU를 추정함으로써 비용편익분석을 수행하였다. 한편 비용편익분석은 학술지의 선별을 위한 완전한 해결책은 될 수 없지만, 의사결정을 할 수 있는 단서를 제공해 주고 있어서 다른 요소들, 학술지의 생산지(인도의 학술지가 많이 이용되므로 선호), 출판사의 인지도 등을 함께 고려하는 것이 바람직하다고 주장하였다. 그리고 비용과 편익을 함께 고려하여 低비용/低편익, 高비용/低편익, 低비용/高편익, 高비용/高편익의 4개 그룹으로 나누어 학술지를 평가하는 방법을 제시하였다.

김석영과 황혜경(2001)은 한국과학기술정보연구원이 구독하고 있는 과학기술 분야 해외 학술지의 비용 대 효과를 파악하기 위하여 CPU를 분석하였다. 타 연구와 같이 비용요소에는 복사이용 빈도, 편익요소에는 구독비용을 대입하였다. 여기에서 CPU는 학술지의 2000년도 구독 금액을 연간 평균 복사이용 건수로 나눈 수치이다. 분석결과, 비용 대 효과가 높은 학술지는 이용자의 접근이 쉽고 편리하도록 배가하는 한편, 그렇지 않은 학술지에 대하여는 그 원인을 규명하여 효율적인 장서 관리를 계획해야 한다고 제안하였다.

한편 학술지의 CPU를 추정하는 데 있어서 편익에 단순한 학술지의 이용 빈도가 아니라 상호대차 비용을 적용한 연구를 볼 수 있다. Himt(1990)는 편익에 상호대차 비용을 이용하여 CPU뿐만 아니라 ICR(Institutional Cost Ratio)의 산출식을 제안하였고, 이를 Lawrence Livermore National Laboratory(LLNL)의 구독 학술지(537건)를 평가하는데 적용하였다(표 1 참조). ICR을 산출하기 위한 비용요소에는 학술지 구독에 소요되는 연간 구독비용; 구독 유지비, 그리고 서가 비용이, 편익의 요소에는 학술지의 연간 이용횟수를 토대로 한 상호대차 비용이 대입되었다. 측정 방법으로는 spine-marking method를 이용하였다. ICR이 1.0 이상인 경우만 비용대비 효과가 있는 것으로 간주하였다. CPU의 산출식에는 기록되지 않은 횟수와 자료의 연도 수에 대한 조정 수치가 고려되었다. 연구 결과 CPU가 $28 이하인 학술지는 경제성이 있다고 판단되었다.

<표 1> Hunt의 ICR과 CPU 산출법

ICR = (U * I) / [P + M + (L*S)] U = 연 사용량, I = 상호대차 비용, P = 연간 구독비용, M = 구독 유지비, L = Size of bound collection, S = 서가 및 저장비용($6 / foot) CPU = Cost / Use Cost = 상호대차 비용 / Use = A * B * C A = 1년간 이용횟수, B = 기록되지 않은 횟수를 고려한 조정 수치 1.5 C = 연구에 포함된 자료의 연도 수에 대한 조정 수치

Hasslow와 Svermng(1995)은 Hunt가 제안한 산출식을 Chalmers University of Technology Library(스웨덴)의 ICR을 추정하는 데 적용하였다. 연구 결과 전체 학술지의 74.4%가 '1'보다 작아 경제성이 없는 것으로 판정되었다. 그러나 이들은 Hunt의 산출식에는 환율의 변동, 제본과 미제본 권호, ILL의 실제 비용, 그리고 학술지의 질에 대한 고려가 배제되었음을 지적하였다.

Scigliano(2000) 역시 비용요소에 학술지의 이용횟수에 해당하는 상호대차 비용을 적용하였다. Sciglioano는 Trent 대학 도서관(캐나다)의 학술지를 평가하기 위하여 2년간(1997-1998) 부서당 학술지 사용비율(Rate of Serial Use)과 CPU를 분석하였다. 건당 상호대차 비용은 Deurenberg(1993)에 의하여 제시된 $28/1건을 사용하였다. 연구 결과

CPU는 $2.75~1,002.96이고, RSU는 0.04~6.43(평균 1.59)으로, CPU 와 RSU 사이에는 반비례 현상이 나타났다.

학술지의 평가를 위한 지금까지의 비용 편익 연구가 일반적으로 이용 빈도와 상호대차 비용을 토대로 한 양적인 분석으로 질적인 부분에 대한 평가가 배제되어 있었다. 한편 학술지의 질적 분석인 인용도 분석도 JCR을 활용하는 경우가 대부분이어서 이를 각 기관 의 인용 분석에 그대로 적용하는 것에는 문제가 있는 것으로 분석 되었다.

최귀숙과 황남구(2002)는 SCI와 CMCI에 게재된 포항공대 연구 자의 발표논문에 대한 참고문헌을 분석함으로써 2002년에 구독하 고 있는 해외 학술지(1997년~2001년도)의 비용 편익 분석을 수행 하였다. 이 연구는 포항공대 이용자의 인용도를 분석함으로써 JCR 과 같이 일반적으로 발표된 학술지의 인용 분석을 적용하는 데서 벗어났으나, SCI와 CBCI 외 다른 곳에 게재된 연구 결과의 참고자 료는 인용도 분석 결과에서 누락되었다는 제한점이 있다.

2.2 전자학술지

대출, 열람, 복사, 상호대차 횟수를 토대로 학술지의 이용 빈도를 추적하는 인쇄 형태는 정확한 이용횟수를 파악하기 어려우며 추적 이 불가능한 어려움이 존재한다. 그러나 전자학술지의 경우는 대부 분 이용통계가 제시되므로 이용통계 및 이용 빈도를 집계하기가 비 교적 쉽고 정확하다. 특히 전자학술지의 이용률이 증가함으로 인해 전자정보의 이용행태 및 이용통계를 사용하는 방법에 관한 연구가 활발하게 진행되고 있다.

Monopoli, *et al.* (2002)는 Patrase 대학을 대상으로 이용자들의 전자학술지에 대한 이용행태를 파악하기 위한 설문 조사를 수행하였다. 전자저널을 사용하는 연령대, 사용빈도, 지위별 사용빈도, 사용하는 이유, 사용하는 곳, 검색방법, 인쇄물과의 비교 및 사용하지 못하는 이유에 대한 설문 조사가 이루어졌다. 연구 결과 전자학술지는 모든 연령층에서 사용이 되었으며, 특히 35세 이하의 이용자가 61.8%로 가장 이용 빈도가 높은 것으로 나타났다. 또한, 인터넷 이용자들이 전자학술지를 이용하는 데 가장 큰 문제점으로 너무 많은 정보, 그리고 시간의 부족이 포함되었다.

이와 유사한 연구인 Ke, *et al.* (2002)는 타이완에서 가장 크고 많이 사용되는 원문데이터베이스인 Science Direct On Site E-journal system(SDOS)의 로그 분석을 실행함으로써 이용자의 전자정보에 대한 이용행태를 조사하였다. 연구 결과 또한 이 기관에서 구독하지 않는 인쇄 저널의 64%가 SDOS를 통해서 다운로드 되고 있으며, 대상 이용자 34명 대부분이 구독하지 않는 인쇄학술지를 다운로드하고 있다는 사실을 파악할 수 있었다.

Mercer(2000)는 전자학술지의 이용통계는 해외 학술지의 평가를 위한 의사결정에 기반이 된다고 주장하면서 몇 가지 지표를 제안하였다. 총사용량(히트된 수), 목차, 초록 및 전문의 사용, 사용된 전문의 포맷(HTML 또는 PDF), 검색 수, IP 주소의 수 등이 제안되었다. 심원식(2005) 역시 전자정보 이용통계는 개별 도서관에서 활용하는 자료가 될 뿐 아니라 문헌정보학의 여러 분야에서 활용될 수 있는 연구 자료가 된다는 것에 동의하였다. 그러나 그는 이용통계는 양적인 부분만이 아니라, 이용자가 추구한 목적에 부합되었는가, 이용자에게 어떤 가치를 주었는지 등의 질적인 측면에서 이용통계를 분석하고 해석해야 한다고 주장하였다. 그는 전자정보의 이용통계에는 특정 데이터베이스 안에서의 세션 수, 실행된 검색 수, 전문 다운로드 수, 그리고 세션당 평균 사용시간을 포함하였다.

3. 학술지 평가를 위한 경제성 분석모형의 개발

본 연구는 문헌 조사를 통해 학술지의 양적 평가와 질적 평가를 병행하여 분석할 수 있는 종합적 분석모형을 개발하였다. 분석모형의 기본적인 틀은 비용편익분석이다. 비용편익분석은 학술지의 비용과 편익을 측정하고 비교 평가하여 최선의 대안을 도출하는 방법으로, 이를 파악하기 위하여 대상 학술지의 '이용'당 비용(CPU)을 분석하였다. CPU가 높은 학술지는 낮은 학술지에 비하여 경제성이 높은 것으로 분석된다. 분석대상은 구독 학술지 중 인쇄 매체와 전자매체가 동시에 접근 가능한 학술지이다. 비용요소로는 기존 연구에서 사용된 학술지의 구독가격뿐만 아니라 주문, 분류, 목록, 체크인, 클레임, 배가 등에 드는 모든 관리비를 포함하였다. 한편 학술지의 편익은 '유용성'의 정도에 따라 차등 되어 평가된다. 이 논문의 이론적 근거는 학술지의 구독 목적과 부합되게 이용이 된 학술지일수록 품질이 높다는 것이다.

본 연구는 대부분 대학 또는 기관에서 학술지를 구독하는 목적을 중요도에 따라 다음과 같이 나열하였다.

첫째, 연구 성과물 및 강의에 직접 인용된다. 둘째, 복사, 열람 또는 전문 다운로드를 통해서 필요한 지식을 축적한다. 셋째, 검색 또는 초록을 통해서 연구 주제 및 강의에 관련된 논문들에 대한 정보를 다양하게 입수한다. 예를 들어, 이용 빈도가 높다 하더라도 검색에만 이용이 되었다면 연구 성과물과 강의에 직접 인용이 된 학술지에 비하여 질적으로 낮게 등급이 된다.

본 연구는 경제경영 분야 해외 학술지의 비용 대 편익을 파악하기 위하여 학술지의 CPU를 분석하였다. 이는 이용자의 요구에 대하여 구체적으로 파악하게 해 줄 뿐만 아니라 장서개발 전략에 대한 종합적인 틀을 마련해 줄 수 있다.

학술지의 비용과 편익의 측정을 위해서 포함된 요소는 다음과 같다.

3.1 비용요소

비용요소에는 구독가격뿐만 아니라 학술지의 구매에서부터 보존까지의 관리비용이 포함된다. 학술지의 구독비용은 크게 구독가격과 관리비로 구분된다.

1) 구독가격
분석 대상인 학술지의 실제 연간 구독가격을 대입하며, 여기에 수수료(우송 수수료, 서비스 요금)는 제외된다.

2) 관리비
학술지 1종을 구독하는 데 소요되는 연간 관리비를 산출한다. 관리비의 비용요소에는 인건비, 제본비, 소모품비, 서가비, 그리고 공간비가 포함되며 산출 내역은 <표 2>와 같다.
　① 인건비: 주문, 계약, 정리, 배가, 클레임 등 학술지 관리를 위해서 투입된 모든 인건비를 포함한다. 학술지 관리에 관여하

는 사서들의 인건비는 전체 업무 중 학술지 관리에 투입되는 비중을 토대로 산출한다.

② 제본비: 제본 대상 학술지의 1년간 제본 비용을 토대로 산출한다.

③ 소모품비: 구독대상 학술지의 등록(1년)에 이용된 소모품, 바코드, 청구기호, 감응 테이프(tattle tape), 키퍼(keeper) 등에 드는 총비용이다.

④ 서가비: 대상 학술지(1년)를 배가할 서가를 구입하는 데 투입되는 비용이다.

⑤ 공간비: 제본된 학술지를 배가하는 데 필요한 서가의 공간 비용이다.

<표 2> 관리비 산출 내역

관리비용 = 인건비 + 제본비 + 소모품비 + 서가비 + 공간비 / 학술지 구독 건수

3.2 편익요소

편익은 이용 빈도와 유용도(utility)로 측정된다. 학술지는 도서관의 설립목적에 부합되는 용도로 활용되었는지의 유용도에 따라 차등하여 부여된다. 즉 구독 기관의 설립목적에 부합되는 용도로 활용된 학술지일수록 질적으로 우수하다는 이론을 바탕으로 높은 등급을 부여받게 된다. 또한, 어떻게 학술지가 이용되었는지에 따라서 매번 등급에 해당하는 점수가 <그림 1>과 같이 적용된다.

한 예로, 대학교 도서관의 경우, 이용자(교수와 학생)의 논문 또는 강의에 직접 인용된 학술지는 최고의 가중치인 3점, 전문 다운로드 등에 이용된 학술지는 2점, 그리고 검색 초록을 위해 이용된 학술지는 1점을 부여할 수 있다. 선행연구에서 일반적으로 사용되어 온 인쇄학술지의 이용통계 추적방식은 시간이 오래 소요되며 방법상의 문제를 내포하고 있는 것으로 분석되었다. 따라서 본 연구는 전자학술지의 이용통계를 토대로 인쇄학술지의 이용통계를 추정하였다. 인쇄학술지의 이용통계 추정은 설문 조사에서 파악된 전자학술지와 인쇄학술지의 이용률을 적용함으로써 가능하다.

따라서 본 연구는 인쇄학술지의 이용 빈도를 전자학술지와의 이용비율로 추정하는 방법을 제안하였다. 이는 설문지 또는 인터뷰의 방법을 통해서 추적이 가능하며, 질의내용은 <표 3>과 같다. 설문지의 결과를 토대로 이용자들의 매체별 학술지(전자학술지 vs. 인쇄학술지)에 대한 이용률을 파악한다. 매체별 학술지의 이용률이 분석되면, 전자학술지의 이용통계를 토대로 인쇄학술지의 이용 빈도를 추정할 수 있게 된다. 학술지의 CPU 산출식은 <표 4>와 같다.

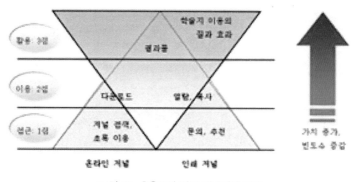

<그림 1> 유용도에 따른 학술지의 등급

<표 3> 전화 인터뷰의 구성내용

1. Please check your position.
   □ Faculty □ Staff □ Outsider □ Student
2. Which resource do you use to find journal articles? (What percent do you use the following for research?)
   □ Online databases: Within KDI School Library (%)
   □ Print formats(association membership): Within KDI School Library (%)
   □ Google, Yahoo! etc.: Not Within KDI School Library (%)

<표 4> CPU 산출식

$$CPU = B / C$$
B = 편익 = (S1 2 3 * 3) + (S2 * 2) + (S1 * 1)
S = 활용도가 기관의 목적에 부합되는 정도에 따른 등급 차등화
C = 비용 = 구독비용 + (관리비 * 구독연수)

4. 사례분석: KDI 국제정책대학원

4.1 분석대상

본 연구는 제시된 분석모형을 KDI 국제정책대학원(이하 'KDI 대학원'이라 명함)에서 구독하고 있는 해외 학술지에 적용하는 사례분석을 시행하였다. 사례분석을 위해 설문 조사와 데이터 분석방법을 병행하였다. 1998년에 개관한 KDI 대학원 정보자료실이 지난 8년 동안 구독한 해외 학술지의 총수는 약 600여 종이며 그 주제는 경제, 경영 및 국제 관련 분야이다. 97년 이전의 학술지는 타 기관을 통하여 기증받은 바 있다. 이들은 모두 영구적으로 보존하기 위하여 제본(약 5,000권)되어 있으며, 5개의 이동 서가(mobile rack)에 배가되어 있다. 이들에 대한 웹상에서의 접근은 EJS[8]를 통해 무료로 또

는 추가비용을 지불함으로써 가능하며 일부는 전자 DB를 통하여 접근하고 있다. KDI 대학원이 구독하고 있는 9개의 전자 DB 중에서 경제·경영 전문 DB인 4개 (EJS, BSP[9]), JSTOR, SD[10])) 만을 분석대상에 포함하였다. <그림 2>에서 보는 바와 같이 2004년과 2005년에 구독한 해외 학술지 205종 중 4개의 전자 DB를 통하여 접근까지 가능한 학술지 146종을 연구대상으로 삼았다.

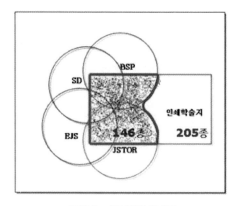

<그림 2> 연구대상 학술지

4.2. 결과

KDI 대학원에서 구독하고 있는 해외 학술지의 비용 편익을 분석하기 위하여 각 학술지 각각의 CPU를 산출하여 비교하였으며, 이의 내용은 다음과 같다. 이는 전문도서관에서 본 연구가 제시한 모형으로 학술지 평가를 하는데 기본적인 틀이 될 수 있다고 믿는다.

---

8) EBSCOHost Electronic Journal Service

9) Business Source Premier

10) ScienceDirect

4.2.1 비용

비용에는 학술지 1종에 해당하는 인쇄학술지 구독비용, 전자 DB 구독비용, 그리고 관리비가 포함되었다.

1) 구독비용

학술지의 구독비용에는 KDI 대학원이 EBSCO를 통해서 구독한 실제 비용을 적용하였으며, 그 외 기증받은 학술지는 0원으로 처리하였다. 한편 전자 DB의 구독비용은 해당 DB의 1년 구독비용을 적용하였다. <표 5>에서 보는 바와 같이 한 종의 학술지에 해당하는 구독비용은 DB의 비용을 제공하는 총 학술지의 종 수로 나누어 산출하였다가 1년 구독료에 해당 DB가 제공하는 저널 종 수로 나누어 1종당 구독비용을 산출하였다. 그 결과는 <표 5>와 같다.

<표 5> DB 제공 저널 수 및 종당 비용

전자 DB 명	평균 구독 비용(원)	종 수	종당 비용(원)
EJS[11]	0	391	0
BSP	22,058,660	9,876	2,234
JSTOR[12]	0	65	0
SD	10,536,091	2,114	4,985

2) 관리비용

학술지 1종을 관리하는 데 드는 비용은 연간 103,315원으로 이는 <표 6>의 산출식을 토대로 한 것이다. 학술지와 연구대상 DB

---

11) 전자학술지에 접근하기 위해 추가비용이 필요한 학술지의 비용이 인쇄학술지 구독비용에 포함.
12) KDI 대학원 도서관 예산으로 충당함.

를 관리하는 데 소요된 인건비, 제본비, 소모품비, 및 서가비가 포함되었다. 따라서 관리비용에 각 학술지의 구독연수를 곱하여 해당 학술지의 총 관리비용을 산출하였다.[13] 인건비에는 학술지와 전자 DB의 관리를 담당하고 있는 사서(1명)와 실장의 급여가 포함되었다. 학술지 관리가 업무에 차지하는 비중과 2005년 급여를 고려하여 산출하였다. 학술지 담당 사서는 50%, 실장은 20%의 시간을 인쇄학술지 및 전자 DB 관리에 할애하고 있는 것으로 나타났다. 제본비에는 2005년에 2차례 걸쳐 실시되었던 총 338권에 대한 제본비(5,500원/권)가 포함되었으며. 소모품비에는 이에 드는 제본 학술지 338권에 대한 감응 테이프(154원/권), 바코드 라벨(21원/권), 청구기호 라벨(8.3원/권), 그리고 키퍼(44원/권)의 비용을 고려하였다. 서가비에는 2005년도 제본 학술지를 배가하는 데 필요한 이동 서가의 비용을 대입하였다. 1개의 이동 서가에는 약 1,000권의 제본 학술지를 배가할 수 있으므로 약 400권에 해당하는 40%의 비용을 고려하였다.[14]

<표 6> 연간 관리비/종

구분	인건비	제본비	소모품비	서가비
계산	(평균급여 * 0.5) (평균급여 * 0.2)	상반기 229권 하반기 109권 (5,500원/권)	감응 테이프(1개) 바코드 라벨(1개) 청구기호 라벨(1개) 키퍼(2개)	한 해에 추가되는 제본저널 서가비
결과	10,315원			

---

13) 실제 학술지 한 종의 비용 산출식은 각 전자 매사 담당자 제언을 토대로 하였음.
14) 서가 배열 시 충분한 공간이 필요하므로 338권의 제본 학술지를 배가하는 데는 충분한 공간이 필요하다는 것을 전제로 하였음.

3) 총 발생비용

앞서 산출된 구독비용과 관리비용을 합산하여 연구 학술지의 총 발생비용을 산출한다. 이해를 돕기 위하여 <표 7>에서 보는 바와 같이 Harvard Business Review의 예를 제시하였다. 이 학술지는 인쇄본으로는 8년간, 그리고 전자로는 2년간(2004년~2005년)만 구독했으며, 이에 투입된 실제 비용을 포함하였다.

<표 7> 학술지 비용 산출 예시

(단위: 원)

학술지명	인쇄본 구독비용	전자 DB 구독비용	연 관리비	총 발생비용
Harvard Business Review	1,462,096	4,468	826,520	2,293,384

4.2.2 편익

유용도(utility)를 분석하기 위하여 전자정보에 대한 이용통계가 사용되었으며, KDI 대학원이 개관된 해인 1998년부터의 통계자료가 토대가 되었다. 인쇄학술지의 이용 빈도를 추적하기 위한 설문조사가 2006년 1월 한 달간 실시되었다. 또한, KDI 대학원의 개교 이래 2005년까지의 전자학술지 이용 빈도와 함께 교수의 연구 성과물, 학생 논문, 그리고 지정도서로 사용된 학술지의 인용빈도가 조사되었다. 이용자들의 매체별 이용 형태를 파악하기 위한 설문조사가 전화 인터뷰를 통하여 실시되었다.

1) 유용성을 반영한 이용 빈도

경제성 분석모형에서 제시한 바와 같이 학술지의 유용성을 반영한 이용 빈도를 적용하였다. KDI 대학원의 학술지 이용자들의 연구와 교과과정을 지원하기 위한 것이므로 본 사례분석에서는 다음과 같이 학술지의 유용도를 설정하였다.

이용자의 연구 성과물에 인용: 3점 / 교과과정에 활용: 3점 / 전문 다운로드: 2점
검색 및 초록에 이용된 학술지: 1점

① 전자 DB 이용통계 편익

학술지 편익의 1, 2점에 해당하는 다운로드, 검색 및 초록에 대해 전자 DB에서 사용되는 용어가 각기 다르므로 <표 8>과 같이 기능별로 범주화하였다. 전자 DB의 이용통계를 토대로 인쇄학술지의 이용 빈도를 추정하기 위하여 전화 인터뷰를 시행하였다. 설문 응답자 106명 중 84명이 도서관 소장 학술지 이용 경험이 있었으며 이들의 매체별 이용률은 전자학술지 47.6%, 인쇄학술지 24.2%. Google, Yahoo, 출판사 웹 사이트 등의 다른 루트를 통하여 이용하는 비율이 28.2%로 나타났다. 인쇄학술지의 이용 빈도를 추정하기 위하여 본 연구가 제시한 산출식은 <표 9>와 같다. 산출식의 이해를 돕기 위하여 Harvard Business Review의 예를 제시하였다.

〈표 8〉 전자통계 용어의 기능별 범주화

	용어	1점	2점	비고
EJS	Abstract Views, Issue Views Journal Views	Abstract Views	Journal Views	Issue Views는 정보제공이 미흡하여 배제
BSP	Total Full Text, PDF Full Text, HTML Full Text, Abstract	Abstract	Total Full Text	N/A

	용어	1점	2점	비고
JSTOR	Browsing, Viewing, Printing	Browsing	Viewing (articles)	Viewing과 Printing 수치는 중복되어 배제함
SD	Full text download, Abstract	Abstract	Full text download	N/A

<표 9> 인쇄학술지 이용 빈도 산출식

전자학술지 이용 빈도 : 인쇄학술지 이용 빈도 = 47.6 : 24.2
인쇄학술지 이용 빈도 = 전자학술지 이용 빈도 * 24.2 + 47.6

ex) Harvard Business Review
인쇄학술지 이용 빈도 = 11,076 * 24.2 + 47.6 = 5,631.08
DB 이용통계 편익 = 전자학술지의 이용 빈도 + 인쇄학술지의 이용 빈도 = 16,707.08

② 연구 성과물을 통한 편익

편익의 3점에 해당하는 성과물을 분석하기 위하여 KDI 대학원 이용자의 지난 8년간의 성과물인 교수 논문 83종, 학생 논문 140종 그리고 3학기씩 8년간(매년 3학기) 교과과정의 강의계획서에 인용된 학술지가 조사되었다. 이때 조사된 146종에 포함되지 않는 학술지 중 인용도가 높은 것은 다음 학술지 선정에서 우선순위를 가지게 된다.

③ 총 발생 편익

전자 DB 이용통계 연구 성과물을 통해 나온 편익을 합하면 한 종에 대한 실제 편익이 산출된다. 계산의 이해를 돕기 위하여 <표 10>을 통하여 Harvard Business Review의 예를 제시하였다.

<표 10> 총 발생 편익 예시

학술지명	DB 이용통계 편익(1점+2점)	성과물 편익 (3점)	총 편익 발생비용 (단위: 원)
Harvard Business Review	16,707.08	984(328회 * 3점)	17,691.08

4.3 결과

4.3.1 학술지의 경제성 순위

학술지의 경제성은 CPU를 통해 산출되었다. CPU를 위해 각 학술지에서 발생한 편익을 투입된 비용으로 나누어 주었으며, 점수가 높은 학술지일수록 경제성이 큰 것으로 분석된다. 연구 대상인 학술지의 CPU 순위는 <표 11>에 나타난 바와 같다. 상위 20위에 포함되는 학술지에서의 편익이 전체의 75%를 차지하는 것으로 나타났다. 이는 타 도서관에서 나타난 결과인 상위 학술지에 대한 이용률 집중 현상을 입증하고 있다. 그러나 위와 같은 전체 순위가 학술지의 재구독을 위한 의사결정을 하는 데는 충분한 자료가 되지 못한다. <그림 3>은 학술지를 A (低비용/低편익), B (高비용/低편익), C (低비용/高편익), D (高비용/高편익)의 4개 그룹으로 나누어 경제성 순위를 비교하였다. 이때 Harvard Business Review, American Economic Review 등이 포함된 그룹 C는 적은 비용으로 가장 많이 활용된 학술지 그룹으로 가장 바람직한 그룹으로 평가되며, Corporate Governance, Risk Analysis 등이 포함된 그룹 B는 높은 비용이 투입되었으나 활용빈도가 저조하여 가장 바람직하지 못한 그룹으로 평가되었다. 따라서 다음 학술지 선정 작업 그룹 B에서 경제성이 가장 낮은 순으로 학술지를 선정한다.

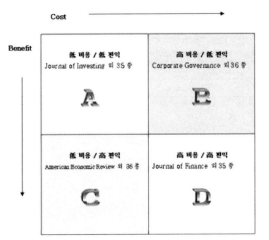

<그림 3> 비용과 편익을 고려한 그룹 설정

<표 11>학술지의 경제성 순위 리스트

순위	학술지명	CPU
1	American Economic Review	8.46
2	Harvard Business Review	7.71
3	Foreign Affairs	5.85
4	Journal of Finance	2.94
5	Journal of Political Economy	2.73
6	Management Science	2.34
7	Econometrica	1.97
8	Quarterly Journal of Economics	1.33
9	California Management Review	1.08
10	Journal of Money Credit and Banking	1.01
11	Review of Economic Studies	0.90
12	Journal of Marketing	0.62
13	Review of Economics & Statistics	0.58
14	Review of Financial Studies	0.57
15	Kyklos	0.49
16	Academy of Management Review	0.48

순위	학술지명	CPU
17	Journal of Industrial Economics	0.45
18	MIT Sloan Management Review	0.42
19	Economic Journal	0.38
20	Rand Journal of Economics	0.36

* CPU는 소수점 셋째 자리에서 반올림하였다. 그리고 용이한 수치 비교를 위하여 모든 학술지의
CPU에 동일하게 1,000을 곱하였으며 이는 순위에 영향을 주지 않는다.

4.3.2 이용자그룹별 학술지 이용행태

논문 및 교과목에 인용된 학술지를 분석해 본 결과 이용자의 유형
별로 학술지 선호도가 다른 것으로 나타났다. <표 12>에서 보는 바와
같이 교수의 경우에는 몇몇 학술지에 이용 빈도가 집중되어 있으며,
학생의 경우는 전체 학술지에 비교적 고르게 분포된 것으로 나타났다.
그러나 가장 선호하는 학술지는 Harvard Business Review이며, 이외
에 10위 안에 5종의 동일한 학술지가 포함되어 있다. 단, 전문 다운로
드, 열람 및 초록에 집계된 통계수치는 여기에서 배제되었다. 이는 이
용자별 로그 추적을 하는 것이 현실적으로 불가능하였기 때문이다.

<표 12> 이용자별 선호 학술지

순위	교수 선호 학술지	이용 빈도(회)	학생 선호 학술지	이용 빈도(회)
1	Harvard Business Review	303	Harvard Business Review	25
2	American Economic Review (Journal of Economic Literature, Journal of Economic Perspective 포함15)	260	American Economic Review	23
3	Journal of Political Economy	133	Journal of World Trade	21
4	Journal of Law and Economics	98	Quarterly Journal of Economics	19
5	Econometrica	69	Administrative Science Quarterly	11

15) Journal of Economic Literature와 Journal of Economic Perspectives는 American Economic Review
를 구독함으로써 같이 오는 학술지이므로 American Economic Review의 편익에 포함됨.

순위	교수 선호 학술지	이용 빈도(회)	학생 선호 학술지	이용 빈도(회)
6	Journal of International Economic Law	57	Journal of Monetary Economics	6
7	Quarterly Journal of Economics	54	Journal of Political Economy	6
8	Journal of Finance	42	World Development	6
9	Foreign Affairs	41	Economic Development and Cultural Change	5
10	Journal of World Trade	38	Journal of International Economics	5

4.3.3 학술지 비용과 편익의 상관관계

학술지 비용과 편익의 상관관계를 알아보기 위하여 Pearson Correlation 의 Two-tailed test를 이용하였다. <표 13>에서 보는 바와 같이 두 가지 요소는 상관관계가 전혀 없는 것으로 나타났다.

<표 13>학술지 비용과 편익의 상관관계

		학술지 비용	학술지 편익
학술지 비용	Pearson Correlation	1	-.043
	Sig. (2-tailed)	.	.606
	N	148	148

* Correlation is significant at the 0.05 level (2-tailed)
** Correlation is significant at the 0.01 level (2-tailed)

5. 결 론

본 연구는 학술지를 평가하는 데 기본 틀이 될 수 있는 경제성 분석모형을 제안하였으며, 이를 이용한 사례분석을 수행하였다. 제시된 모형은 구독비용뿐만 아니라 학술지의 제본, 주문, 그리고 클레임 등의 관리에 소요되는 총비용을 포함하였으며, 편익은 유용성을 반영한 이용 빈도로 측정되었다. 이는 비용과 편익에 각각 구독비용과 이용 빈도만을 고려한 기존의 평가모형과는 달리 간접적이고 무형적인 요소까지 포함한 종합적인 분석모형이라고 할 수 있다.

편익의 측정요소인 유용성은 학술지가 모 기관의 성격에 부합되게 이용되었는지에 따라 등급(1-3)이 부여되었다. 전문도서관과 대학도서관의 성격을 동시에 지닌 KDI 국제정책대학원을 사례분석의 대상으로 하였다. 유용도는 이용자의 연구 성과물에 직접 인용된 경우에 가장 높은 등급인 3점, 그리고 전문 다운로드나 검색에 이용된 학술지는 각각 2점과 1점을 부여하였다.

이 모형에서의 이용 빈도는 학술지 부문에서 점차 중요성이 커지고 있는 웹 기반의 전자학술지를 대상으로 추정하도록 고안되었다. 따라서 이용자의 인쇄학술지 이용 빈도는 설문 조사 결과 파악된 이용자의 매체별 평균 이용률을 대입하여 추정하였다. 이는 인쇄학술지를 대상으로 제안된 모형을 실제 도서관에 적용하는 데 나타날 수 있는 번거로움과 부정확성을 배제한 실용성 있는 모형이라는 점에서 그 의의가 있다고 하겠다.

KDI 대학원의 구독 학술지 중 인쇄와 전자매체가 동시에 가능한 146종을 대상으로 하였다. 이는 본 연구가 제시한 모형이 두 매체 모두에 접근 가능한 학술지에만 적용할 수 있기 때문이다. 사례분석 결과, 상위 20위까지의 편익이 전체 구독 학술지로부터 나오는 편익의 약 75%를 차지하고 있는 것으로 나타났다. 이용률이 저조한 학술지는 DDS(Document Delivery Service, 원문복사서비스)를 통하여 제공될 수 있으므로 대학원의 예산 상황을 고려하여, 잠정적인 구독중지 대상에 포함할 수 있을 것으로 분석된다.

그리고 교수와 학생 그룹의 학술지 선호도에 차이가 있는 것으로 나타났으며 학술지에 투입된 비용과 편익은 전혀 상관관계가 없는 것으로 나타났다.

이 모형을 타 도서관에서 적용하기 위해서는 모 기관의 성격에 따른 유용도의 등급을 설정하는 것이 선행되어야 하며, 공공도서관 보다는 대학도서관, 전문도서관과 학교도서관에서 적용하기에 적합할 것으로 분석된다. 각 도서관에서는 이를 학술지의 평가에 적용함으로써 학술지의 예산 투입 및 선정의 적합성 여부를 판단하는 틀이 될 것으로 본다.

참고문헌

김석영, 황혜경. 2001, 과학기술 분야 해외 학술지의 비용 대 효과 분석 「한국문헌정보학회지」, 35(1): 249-264.

심원식. 2005. 전자정보 이용통계 활용 전략 「정보관리학회지」, 22(2): 5-21.

최귀숙, 황남구. 2002. SCI 논문의 참고문헌 분석을 통한 학술지 평가에 관한 연구 「정보관리연구」, 33(2): 33-48.

Broadus, Robert N. 1985. "The Measurement of Periodicals Use", Serials Review (summer) 157-61.

Chrzastowski, Tina E. 1991. "Journal collection Cost-Effectiveness in an Academic Chemistry Library: Results of a Cost/Use Survey at the University of Illinois at Urbana-Champaign." Collection Management, 14(1/2): 85-98.

Deurenberg, Rikie. 1993. "Journal deselection in a Medical University Library by Ranking Periodicals based on Multiple Factor." Bull Med Libr. Asso., 81(3): 316-319.

Hasslow, Rolf and Sverrung, Annika. 1995. "Deselection of Serials: the Chalmers University of Technology Library Method." Collection Management, 19(3/4): 151-170.

Hunt, Richard K. 1990. "Journal deselection in a Biomedical Research Library: a Mediated Mathematical Approach" Bull Med Libr Asso., 78(1): 45-48.

Ke, et al. 2002. Exploring Behavior of E-Journal Users in Science and Technology Transaction log analysis of Elsevier's Science Direct On Site in Taiwan, Mercer, Linda S. 2000. "Measuring the User and Value of Electronic Journals and Books." http://www.library.ucsb. edu/istl/00-winter.

Milne, Dorothy and Tiffany, Bill. 1991. "A Survey of the Cost-Effectiveness of Serials: a Cost-Per-Use Method and Its Results." Serial Librarian 19(3/4): 137-149.

Millson-Martula Christopher. 1988. "Use Studies and Serials Rationalization; a Review." The Serial Librarian 15(1/2): 121-136.

Monopoli, Maria, Nicholas, David, Georgiou, Panagiotis and Korfiati, Marina. 2002. "A User-Oriented Evaluation of Digital Libraries: Case Study the 'Electronic Journals' services of the Library and Information Service of the University of Patras, Greece." Aslib Proceedings, 54(2): 103-117.

Scigliano, Marisa. 2000. "Serial Use in a Small Academic Library: Determining Cost-Effectiveness." Serial Use in a Small Academic Library 26(1): 43-52.

Sridhar, M.S. 1988. "Is Cost Benefit Analysis Applicable to Journal Use in Special Libraries?" Serials Librarian, 15(1/2): 137-153.

Evaluating Academic Journals using Impact Factor and Local Citation Score[16]

This study presents a method for journal collection evaluation using citation analysis in academic libraries. Cost-per-use (CPU) for each title is used to measure cost-effectiveness and higher CPU scores indicate cost-effective titles. Use data is based on the impact factor and locally collected citation score of each title and is compared to the cost of managing and subscribing to journals. The study also conducts a case study to show how academic libraries could apply the method to their local studies.

---

16) 이 논문은 2007년 Journal of Academic Librarianship 33권 3호(393~402쪽)에 게재되었음.

1. Introduction

The importance of journal evaluation as a critical part in academic libraries has grown, as journal subscription comprises $50 \sim 70\%$ of the acquisition budgets in most academic libraries. In response to annual rise in subscription rates while the budget remains relatively the same academic libraries must decide which journal subscriptions to renew and which to cancel. While some academic libraries base their journal selection decisions entirely on faculty opinion, such decisions are better made if they base their decisions on combined information from local use studies as well as faculty opinion.

Moreover, the Law of Scattering, which predicts about 80% of the citations coming from about 20% of the journal cited, identifies a core list for a local journal collection [1]. If this is true, a core list of journals should be identified, on a regular basis, to support research and teaching capacity of institutions where academic libraries are housed.

Collecting a core list to support research and teaching of academic institutions, while staying within the budgetary limits, often requires citation analysis. It is based on the assumption that journals that are frequently cited have higher qualities. Citation analysis is made using nationally collected citation statistics, and such analysis is often used for library collection development and evaluation.

However, previous studies showed that exclusive reliance on the impact factor or local citation data when making citation analysis raised questions on the validity of journal collection evaluation. The impact factor produced by the Journal Citation Report has been suggested by publishers and some researchers as a tool for making selection decisions [2].

However, a number of studies also raise the question of whether nationally collected citation statistics can substitute for results produced by local use studies, since every library has a different clientele and the clients have different information requirements. Altmann and Gorman (1999) provided a number of reasons to explain why the impact factor is poor predictors for local use [3].

At the same time, some studies argue that the most reliable data for deciding whether to continue to subscribe to or cancel journals are not the number of citations but their use as opposed to the total cost, and select the cost-effective analysis (CEA) as the most important method to decide on journal subscription. The cost per use (CPU) has been often used as an indicator for these measures.

National citation data used in the study are Journal Citation Reports' impact factor developed by the Institute for Scientific Information (ISI). Journal Citation Reports contains four ISI measures for evaluating journals: impact factor; immediacy index;

cited half-life; and citing half-life. The most widely used is the impact factor and it is defined as the number of times the average article in a particular journal over a given time period.

Lancaster (1977) defines cost-effectiveness as the relationship between level of performance(effectiveness) and the cost involved in achieving this level."[4]. The least expensive way to meet the objective is the most cost-effective means. In this study, cost-effectiveness is defined as a core list for a local journal collection satisfying 80% of total user demand [1].

This study aims to present a journal evaluation method to identify most valuable journals for research at academic libraries, based on the concept that national data should be used in combination with local data analysis. The method identified in this study will determine how effectively the library budget can be used in journal subscription. To this end, this study takes the following steps :

1. Identify two essential data sets of cost-effectiveness analysis: cost and use;

2. Develop a method for journal collection evaluation using citation analysis in academic libraries; and

3. Conduct a case study at the KDI School of Public Policy and Management to demonstrate how academic libraries could apply the proposed method to their local studies.

2. Literature Review

2.1 Local Citation Analysis vs. National Citation Analysis

Citation analysis is a method academic library often used to evaluate their collections, as well as a tool for building an effective journal collection. As is well known, citation analysis is based primarily on the Journal Citation Reports' impact factor produced by the Institute of Scientific Information (ISI).

Najman & Hewitt (2003) noted that the impact factor has become a prominent tool for faculty publications for tenure and promotion, since it is often used synonymously with research quality [5]. Some studies have also proposed the use of the impact factor as it provides a systematic, objective way to determine the relative importance of journals within their subject categories [6, 7].

However, several studies have raised questions on the validity of the impact factors. Nisonger (2000) concluded that when calculating the impact factor, self-citations can not be included. In his study, Nisonger argues that the 1994 rankings by the impact factor and total citations received were recalculated with journal self-citations removed and then the recalculated rankings were compared to the original rankings [8].

Coelho (2003) also insisted that, without making adjustments, JCR's impact factor could not be used to compare different journals in different discipline areas. This study adjusted the median journal value of one (1.000)[9]. In a similar study, Archivald and Finifter (1987) pointed out that the impact factor was flawed because it did not account for variations in article lengths [10].

On the other hand, several researchers conducted studies to determine whether the impact factor could be used to predict the local use a title might receive, indicating that every library has a different clientele who have different information requirements. Stankus & Rice (1982) found that the impact factor and national citation study showed a correlation only when the selected journals were similar in subject, scope, purpose, and language and when there was heavy journal use [11].

Altmann and Gorman (1999) used regression coefficients to determine the relationship between actual total usages versus the impact factor for an Australian University Library. The study found that there was low correlation between total local use and the impact factor, and concluded that the impact factor was a poor predictor of local use. It presented two possible reasons for the low correlations-the total uses of a journal depend on the size of the local holdings and a journal's impact factor does not remain constant from year to year [3].

Kreider's (1999) findings were consistent with the view that the impact factor could not predict local use and logical selection decisions could be made only by using the results of a local use study. She studied the University of British Columbia for twenty subject fields in the sciences and social sciences and found the correlation grew much weaker and therefore much less useful for less cited items, even though a strong correlation existed between JCR data and the local data [12].

Representing current trends of research, several studies modeled local citation studies to identify a list of core journals by analyzing only local citations. As an example, Asundi and Kabin (1996) identified a list of core Indian periodicals in horticulture by analyzing citations from 257 master and doctoral theses in a university. The study concluded that a heavy concentration of large numbers of citations remained only in a few periodicals [13].

Dulle (2004) also conducted a study to list core agricultural journals in Tanzania using citation analysis and user opinions. This study analyzed master and doctoral theses submitted at Sokoine University of Agriculture. According to the result of the study, it devised a list of 368 core journals and found that generally agricultural scientists in the country had limited access to comment journals [14].

Leiding (2005) analyzed a sample of ten years' worth of student thesis bibliographies from 1992 to 2002 to determine the adequacy of the collection for undergraduate research. Results provided a base line to track future trends in the use of internet citations and online journals [15].

In a similar study, Burright, *et al.* (2005) analyzed 170 journal articles produced by faculty and doctoral students of the University of Maryland to determine their type, discipline and recent citations [16]. Hurd, Blecic, and Vishwanatham (1999) examined the information needs of a small population of molecular biologists. The study analyzed journal article citations of faculty members within the previous three years and reported the total number of journals cited and their subject disciplines formats of cited references, most-cited journals, and age distribution of molecular biology citations [17]. However, it is difficult to apply the results presented in the local citation studies to other institutions since every library has a different clientele and these clients have different information requirements.

2.2 Journal price studies

Unlike previous studies focus on citation for journal use studies, some studies insist that journals need to be evaluated by the usage related to cost. Total cost is to include administration fees as well as subscription cost. Scanlan (1988) recommended journal price studies for acquisition of journals, citing that journals need to be evaluated not by citation but by their usage related to price. A journal price study is generally conducted in special libraries with fairly limited collections for the purpose of determining which titles to add or cancel [18].

The most commonly used journal price studies cover cost-benefit and cost-effectiveness analysis. The McGraw-Hill encyclopedia defines cost-benefit analysis (CBA) as the ratio of the benefits of a given project to its cost. A closely related concept of cost-effectiveness analysis (CEA) is defined a way of finding the least expensive means of reaching an objective or a way of obtaining the greatest possible value from a given expenditure. Cost-per-use (CPU) is the most frequently used indicator for these studies. Use data are determined based on frequency of articles being cited in journals and are compared to the average cost of an inter-library loan or journal subscription cost. Cost-benefit analysis has taken into account in several journals price studies. The cost dimension added to the use study may influence decisions of which subscriptions to cut. In particular, high cost and low benefit (use) journals need to be carefully considered for cancellation.

However, Wills and Oldman (1977) criticized that the use of cost-benefit analysis (CBA) was inappropriate in journal use studies and questioned whether the 'use' actually equals to 'benefits' [19]. Along the same line, Sridhar (1988) also indicated that CBA might not provide a completely satisfactory solution to issues of journal selection even though it provides some clues as to how to proceed over and above those provided by the sample use study. A systematic random sample of journals was analyzed and compared for their cost-per-use. The sample study of CBA of journals indicates that such a method [20]. Cost-effectiveness, another journal price study methodology, is often used to maximize the usefulness of materials purchased under the library budget. According to Chrzastowski (1991), effectiveness was defined as a core journal collection satisfying 90 percent of total demand for journals [21].

Kim and Hwang (2001) analyzed cost-effectiveness on the usage of overseas scientific and technical journals in the Korea Institute of Science & Technology Information. The study used CPU of a journal to assess journals subscribed to by the library. The study found that 80 percent of the demand for journals was met by 40 percent of total subscription cost [22].

While the study simply used annual subscription cost as use data it suggested that, for future research, journal cost refers to total costs including administration fee as well as subscription. Estimating effects were also suggested to cover indirect benefits such as research output derived from use of journals.

Impact fact data have also been used to investigate cost-effectiveness of journal collection. Barschall (1988) as well as Barschall and Arrington (1988) calculated the ratio of the cost per printed character of 1,000 physics journals in relation to the JCR impact factor. They termed this measure "the cost/impact ratio" and contended that this ratio is the most significant measure of the cost-effectiveness of the journal [23, 24]. Milne and Tiffany (1991) computed an approximate CPU for each title and compared the cost for subscribing to a serial against the cost of providing inter-library loans for evaluating their serials [25].

Hunt (1990) developed a mathematical formula for journal selection decision which serves as a means to compare the cost of owning a journal with the cost of acquiring individual articles through inter-library loans at any given level of use. The cost of owning a journal covers the cost for subscription, maintaining a subscription, shelving and storage. Use was counted by using spine-marking method. This method enabled the library to reduce subscription cost by 46 percent, while reducing only 8 percent of the total use [26].

Institutional cost ratio (ICR) of each subscription title, another indicator for cost-effectiveness analysis, is also used in local studies. Haaslow and Sverrung (1995) used Hunt's formula for selection of journals at Chalmers University. Two methods, ICR and CPU were used and selection was made based on quantile and usage from the result. Cost elements such as subscription, staff, shelving and storage were considered in combination with the level of use to determine the ICR and CPU [27].

3. Methodology

This study proposes a new methodology the combines both the national citation data and local citation data while adjusting these data to be comparable values. Since the measurement units of national citation data (impact factor) and local citation data are quite different, the results can be influenced differently unless these data are adjusted to be the same unit.

Suppose the impact factor of a journal is 3.110 and the sum of the impact factors of all sample journals is 151.323. To get the adjusted score, the journal's impact factor, 3.110, is divided by the sum of the impact factors, 151.323. Then the adjusted score in percentage is 2.055. Similarly, the journal's local citation score is 2.980, is divided by the sum of local citation scores, 31.490. Then the adjusted score in percentage will be 9.463. These two ratios, adjusted impact factor and adjusted local citation score, are benefit ratios of the study.

This study also presents a correlation between local use data and national citation data. Cost-per-use (CPU) is taken to measure cost-effectiveness of each title and two sets of data are required for this purpose: one on cost and one on use. CPU is calculated as the cost divided by use, with higher CPU scores indicating greater cost-effective titles <Figure 1>. Subscription prices and administration fees for each journal title are used as cost elements. Use is determined by the impact factor of JCR and by locally collected citation score.

Journal selection and cancellation may be done on the basis of use and cost-effectiveness to maximize the usefulness of journals. Titles that meet these criteria and are held by the library and fall within the specified JCR subject category are chosen as a sample for the study.

$$\text{CPU of Journal } A = \frac{Use\ A}{Cost\ A}$$

· Cost A = Cost A_S + Cost A_D + Cost A_A
· Use A = Use I_A + Use L_A

$$\text{Use } I_A = \frac{I_A}{Total\ Use\ I} \times 100$$

$$\text{Use } L_A = \frac{L_A}{Total\ Use\ L} \times 100$$

$$\text{Total Use } I = \sum_{k=A}^{n} I_k = I_A + I_B + \cdots + I_{n-1} + I_n \ (A \leq k \leq n)$$

$$\text{Total Use } L = \sum_{k=A}^{n} L_k = L_A + L_B + \cdots + L_{n-1} + L_n \ (A \leq k \leq n)$$

$$L_A = \sum_{k=1}^{n} M_k F_k = M_1 F_1 + \cdots + M_n F_n$$

----

* Use I_A = Impact Factor   * Use L_A = Local Citation Score
* I_A = Use I of Journal A * L_A = Use L of Journal A
* M = Value of Research Output   * F = Frequency of Citation
* Cost A_S = Subscription Price of Journal   * Cost A_D = Price of Aggregator Database
* Cost A_A = Administration fee of Journal A

<Figure 1> Formula for Calculating CPU of Journal *A*

3.1 Cost

Cost is based on journal subscription prices and administration fees for each journal titles.

1) Subscription price

Subscription of a journal is the sum of actual subscription prices for print and online format. For journals in aggregator databases, average subscription price of a title was used; since it was purchased by bundle, there is no individual price for each title. For example, if a title appears in more than one aggregator database, average subscription prices for each database would be summed.

2) Administration fee

The administration fee covers the annual recurring costs of receiving and processing issues, claiming parts not received, replacing missing issues, preparing issues for binding, and so forth. Unlike most of the previous studies, the model covers administration fee since administration fee is too large to ignore.

Total administration fee is determined by computing the total cost of administering all journal's subscriptions, including staffing, supplies and overhead. The average administration fee is the total cost of administering divided by the total number of subscriptions as shown in <Table 1>.

<Table 1> Administration fee per title

Administration fee = Staffing + binding + supplies + overhead / number of subscribed journals

Staffing cost covers expenses for managing journals such as, ordering, organizing, claiming, etc. Personnel were asked to indicate an extent to which they devote their time to manage journals in order to estimate the staffing cost.

The cost of supplies covers expenses such as bar-code, call number label, tattle tape, etc. required for bound journals. The overhead cost covers shelf and space cost and others. Shelf cost refers to the purchase cost of shelves where journal subscriptions are displayed and space cost covers the cost of space that is required to keep the shelves carrying annual journals.

3.2 Use

Use is determined by citation rather than downloads and hits. Both the impact factor and the local citation score of each journal are considered to determine total usage. The scores are adjusted at one-to-one ratio. The data sample is selected from the journals that are held by the library and simultaneously fall within the specified JCR subject category <Figure 1>.

1) Use 1: National Citation Score (Impact factor)

As the national citation data, the impact factor of the Journal Citation Reports (JCR) is used to give the local journal collection an objective value. Adjusted national citation score for a journal (Journal A) is calculated as follows:

① Review the impact factor of Journal A;

② Sum all of the subscribed journal's impact factors; and

③ Divide Journal A's impact factor (①) by the total journal's impact factor (②). Then calculate adjusted impact factor, the first benefit ratio.

2) Use 2: Local Citation Score

Local citation score is based on total citations of Journal A received and how the journal is used in an institution. Citations are checked against the measure guideline, in which researcher's output falls under different categories. As shown in <Figure 2>, this means that a journal cited in one of the publication group with a score of 100 may be used twice as effectively as that with a score of 50.

This study is based on the following assumptions. First, research performance of faculty members is evaluated based on a point system developed by each institute following their research measure guidelines. Second, journals with frequently cited articles have higher value in an organization. Third, the value of the cited journals and citing publications have a close relationship.

Calculation procedures to determine local citation score for Journal A are as follows:

① Based on the institution's measures, group faculty publications by score;

② Count the citation number of journal A by each group;

③ Multiply the group score of journal A by citation use;

④ Add all the citation scores of Journal A from all groups;

⑤ Add all the journal's citation scores; and

⑥ Divide Journal A's citation score by the total journal's citation score. Then identify the Journal A's adjusted local citation score, second benefit ratio. For example, if journal A is cited two times to a research output in a publication group with a score of 100, and is cited three times to a research output with a group with a group with a score of 50, journal A receives 350.

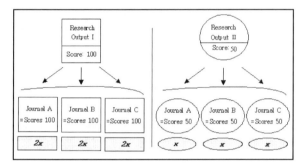

<Figure 2> Relation between research output and the reference

4. Case study analysis

A local citation study of the journal collection was undertaken in a small-sized academic library, KDI School of Public Policy and Management Library. The KDI School is an international graduate school that was started with the support of the Korean government and Korea Development Institute (KDI), one of Korea's most respected economic think-tank. The mission of the school is to train and educate public officials and private sector managers from around the world.

The population of this case study consists of all tenure track and non-tenure track faculty (N=24) employed at the KDI School. Graduate students are excluded from the population, as their work does not represent current trends in research, which helps libraries to make more accurate decisions about collecting journals. Also, Master's theses are not required to graduate from the KDI School.

4.1 Cost

The cost of a journal covers the subscription prices and average administration fee for a title. The subscription prices of a journal include the cost for print, on-line format and aggregator databases. Subscription prices for print and on-line journals were taken from the Libraries' Handbook (EBSCO Industries, 2005).

The aggregator databases subscribed by the KDI School library are Business Source Premier (BSP) and Science Direct (SD). Other databases accessible to the user-Electronic Journals Service (EJS) and JSTOR (Journal Storage Project)-are subscribed by the KDI, with which the KDI School is affiliated and therefore allows full access to their library collection, leaving only benefits without producing any costs as shown in <Table 2>. For example,

3> shows the cost calculation process of 'Journal of Financial Economics'. The KDI School library holds three subscriptions to the title: one in print format and two subscriptions through aggregator databases, BSP and EJS. The annual subscription price for print format journal is 1,930,500 won (US$ 1,930).

As can be seen in <Table 2>, the annual average subscription price of the BSP title is 2,234 won and 0 won for EJS, and thus the total cost is 2,234 won a year, which was multiplied by 2 to get the total cost, 4,468 won for two years. Average administration fee for each title was added to determine the total cost of a journal. Administration fee covers staffing, binding, supplies, and shelf costs for journals. Total administration fee (19,939,757 won) was divided by the total number of subscribed journals (193 titles) to get the annual administration fee (103,315 won). And it was multiplied by 2 to get 206,630 won, since this study was conducted under over a two-year period.

The staffing cost covered two librarians who are responsible for managing journals. A periodical librarian was found to devote 70 percent of her time towards managing journals, while the chief librarian only devoted 20 percent. By multiplying each librarian's monthly pay to the portion of time they devoted towards managing journals and adding the two results together, we found the staffing cost to be 17,383,930 won (per year). The binding cost for journals at the KDI School Library was approximately 1,859,000 won, which came from multiplying the number of bound journals (338 volumes) by the cost per bound (5,500 won). The supplies cost was approximately 76,827 won. To identify this number, we added the individual cost of tattle tapes (154 won/volume), bar-code labels (21 won/volume), call number labels (8.3 won/volume) and keeper (44 won/volume) and multiplied it by the total number of bound journals (338 volumes). The shelf cost for bound journals (338 volumes) covered mobile racks, which were required to accommodate bound journals belonging to the year of 2005. This cost turned out to be approximately 620,000 won, which was 40 percent of a mobile rack.[17)

<Table 2> Web-based electronic DB in the KDI School

(unit: korean won)

Title	Annual subscription price	Number of title	Price per title
EJS	0	391	0
BSP	22,058,660	9,876	2,234
JSTOR	0	65	0
SD	10,536,091	2,114	4,985

<Table 3> Journal of Financial Economics: cost analysis calculation data

(unit: korean won)

Title	Printed format	On-line format	Web-based Electronic DB	Administration Fees	Total Cost
Journal of Financial Economics	3,861,000 (1,930,500 / year)	0	4,468 (2,234 / year)	206,630 (103,315 / year)	4,077,600 (2,038,800)

---

17) 1 mobile rack holds about 1,000 volumes and costs 1,550,000 won based on year 2005).

4.2 Use

The use of a journal was measured by the sum of the impact factor (national citation score) and locally collected citation score for each title.

1) National citation score (The Impact Factor)

National citation scores for 139 titles were determined by the JCR's impact factor. <Table 4> shows journals as ranked by the impact factor. The adjusted impact factor, which was calculated by dividing journal's total impact factor (151.323) by a journal's impact factor, was compared to local citation score, one-to-one ratio. For instance, the adjusted impact factor of 'Quarterly Journal of Economics' is 2.916.[18] The highest impact factor was given to 'Quarterly Journal of Economics' (4.412; 2.916), 'Journal of Economic Literature' (4.400; 2.908), and 'Academy Management Review' (3.717; 2,456).

<Table 4> Journals as ranked by impact factor

Ranking	Journal title	Impact factor	Adjusted IF
1	Quarterly journal of economics	4.412	2.916
2	Journal of Economic Literature	4.400	2.908
3	Academy management review	3.717	2.456
4	Administrative science quarterly	3.405	2.250
5	Health affairs	3.369	2.226
6	Journal of finance	3.110	2.055

18) The impact factor of the journal/Journal's total impact factor = 4.412/151.323 = 2.916

Ranking	Journal title	Impact factor	Adjusted IF
7	Journal of marketing	3.100	2.049
8	Journal of economic perspective	2.951	1.950
9	Medical care	2.907	1.921
10	Journal of political economy	2.622	1.733
. . 139	. . Journal of the Japanese and international Economies	. . 0.038	. . 0.025
Total		151.323	100.000

2) Local Citation Score

The sixty-nine articles published by twenty-four faculty members were considered for analysis in this study. Key areas of faculty research are management, economics and public policy. However, ten articles did not have citations, only 987 citations from 59 articles were analyzed. The 139 journal titles were subscribed to by the library that falls within a given JCR subject category.

As the bibliographies from the twenty-four faculty papers were received, the data from the citing journals were recorded and used to check for its library subscription and whether it was covered by the JCR category during the two consecutive years. Availability of full-text articles through aggregator databases was also checked for the study. And then the total number of citation for each journal was counted and scored based on how it was used. The 'Faculty Research Measure Guideline' provided by the KDI School is shown in <Table 5>. It can be largely categorized into four categories, which are divided into twenty-three sub-categories (scores range from 10 to 400). Multiplying its group score and the total citation number of journal and adding all the results of a journal from all groups calculated local citation score of a journal.

As shown in <Table 6>, when 'Journal of Financial Economics' was cited 75 times in various publications: 7 times in the 'internationally accredited journal (B)' (150 points), 46 times in the 'domestically accredited journal (A)' (100 points), 12 times in the 'international working paper' (50 points), 9 times in the 'international conference report (30 points)' and 'domestic working paper' (20 points) and the local citation score was 6,540 <Table 6>. The adjusted local citation score (20.768) was calculated by dividing the journal's total local citation score (31,490) by the journal's local citation score (6,540). The local citation score was adjusted to match national citation score.

According to the result, the highest local citation score was given to 'Journal of Financial Economics (6,540; 20.768)', and then Harvard Business Review (3,550; 11.723), followed by 'Journal of Finance (2,980; 9.463)', 'Journal of Public Economics (2,650; 8.415)'. <Table 7> shows that the most frequently cited journal was 'Journal of Financial Economics (75)' and 'Journal of Finance (32)', 'Journal of Public Economics (27)', 'Harvard Business Review' (23), and 'American Economic Review' (22).

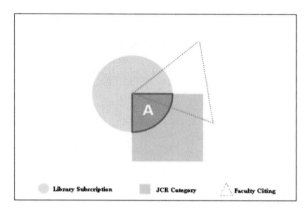

<Figure 3> Sample data

<Table 5> Faculty research measure guideline

Category	Major indicators	Score	Number of citations
Research papers	Internationally accredited journal (A)	400	0
	Internationally accredited journal (B)	150	12
	Domestically accredited journal (A)	100	3
	Domestically accredited journal (B)	75	2
	Domestically accredited journal (C)	50	0
	International authorized criticism, a book review etc.	30	1
	Domestic authorized criticism, a book review etc.	12	4
Research books	International research book (A)	600	1
	International research book (B)	300	0
	Domestic research book (A)	200	1
	Domestic research book (B)	100	2
	International book chapter (A)	120	1
	International book chapter (B)	80	0
	Domestic book chapter	40	5
	International book editing	100	0
	Domestic book editing	40	0
Translated	Translated books	50	1

Category	Major indicators	Score	Number of citations
Conference proceedings	International conference report	30	10
	International proceeding	50	1
Conference proceedings	International working paper	50	19
	Domestic conference report	10	4
	Domestic proceeding	20	1
	Domestic working paper	20	1
Total			69

<Table 6> Journal of Financial Economics: local citation analysis calculation data

Journal of Financial Economics
Local score of 'Journal of Financial Economics'
= (7*150)+ (46*100)+(12*50)+(9*30)+(1*20)]= 6,540
Total local score = 31,490
Adjusted score = 20.768 = 6,540/31,490*100

<Table 7> Local citation score

Ranking	Title	Local citation score (frequency of citation)	Adjusted Score	Cumulative Score
1	Journal of Financial Economics	6,540(75)	20.768	20.768
2	Harvard Business Review	3,550(23)	11.273	32.042
3	Journal of Finance	2,980(32)	9.463	41.505
4	Journal of Public Economics	2,650(27)	8.415	49.921
5	American Economics Review	2,230(22)	7.082	57.002
6	Health Affairs	1,875(14)	5.954	62.956
7	National Tax Journal	1,600(16)	5.081	68.037
8	Econometrica	1,200(16)	3.811	71.848
9	International Security	720(7)	2.382	74.230
10	Quarterly Journal of Economics	650()	2.064	76.294
. 139	. . .	. . .	. . .	. . .
Total		31,490		100

4.3 Results

This case study was designed to show how academic libraries could apply the proposed economic model to a local citation study and how to determine the cost-effectiveness of the journal collection. The bibliographic citations in local publications (articles published by the KDI School faculty members) during 2004 and 2005 were collected.

The 139 journal titles that covered both by the JCR (2004) and subscribed to by the library in 2004 to 2005 were compared and ranked. Cost-per-use (CPU) for each title is used to measure cost-effectiveness and higher CPU scores indicate cost-effective titles. Adding total costs and diving it by total use of a journal measured the CPU. The top three cost-effective titles were 'Harvard Business Review (22.236)', and 'Health Affair (16.293)', 'International Security (10.323)'. The original CPU of each title was converted based on a 100 points scale in order to get a cumulative score. The result shows that a core journal collection satisfying 80 percent of users is found to be forty titles (20.7%) as shown in <Table 8>.

The JCR's impact factor for the journals greatly differed from the local citation score. For example, 'Harvard Business Review' was found to be the most valuable journal at the School, although its impact factor was ranked at 52nd. Pearson Correlation Analysis was also used to test if the impact factor may substitute the results of local use studies. As <Table 9>

shows, two-tail Pearson Correlation test of significance indicated no significant relationship between the impact factor and local citation score. Accordingly, it was proved that the impact factor could not be a substitute for local use study.

According to the result, it was found that 40 out of 193 titles (21 percent) proved to be satisfying 80 percent user demand. The findings are consistent with other previous studies indicating that about 80 percent of the citations come from about 20 percent of the subscribed journal. Additionally, the study examined the frequently cited title lists, based on titles that are not held by the library. The most frequently cited title, as shown in <Table 10> was 'Journal of Business Ethics' (17) and, 'Public Finance (9)' and 'Journal of Accounting and Economics (9)'.

The findings confirmed that the most cost-effective journals were usually held by the library and covered by the JCR. However, there were some titles that were cited by faculty but not held by the library and considered as good candidates for new subscription. On the other hand, the least cost-effective are candidates for cancellation.

<Table 8> Journals ranked by cost per use (Korean won)

Rank	Title	Use 1	Use 2	Total use	Total cost	CPU*	Adjusted score	Cumulative score(%)
1	Harvard Business Review	0.759	11.273	12.032	541,098	22.236	9.180	9.180
2	Health Affair	2.226	5.954	8.818	502,098	16.293	6.726	15.906
3	International Security	1.589	2.382	3.970	384,630	10.323	4.261	20.167

Rank	Title	Use 1	Use 2	Total use	Total cost	CPU*	Adjusted score	Cumulative score(%)
4	National Tax Journal	0.052	5.081	5.583	541,098	10.317	4.259	24.426
5	Journal of Finance	2.055	9.463	11.519	1,151,128	10.006	4.131	28.557
6	American Economic Review	1.094	7.082	8.175	991,098	8.249	3.405	31.962
7	Journal of Economic Literature	2.908	0.699	3.606	471,098	7.655	3.160	35.122
8	Foreign Affairs	1.522	1.048	2.570	369,098	6.963	2.874	37.997
9	Quarterly Journal of Economics	2.916	2.064	4.980	744,098	6.692	2.763	40.759
10	Journal of Economic Perspective	1.950	0.953	2.903	471,098	6.162	2.544	43.303
40	Journal of International	0.850	0.000	0.850	665,310	1.277	0.527	80.027

*For easy viewing, 1,000,000 was already multiplied to CPU

<Table 9> Pearson Correlation between the impact factor and local citation score

		Impact factor	Local citation score
Impact factor	Pearson Correlation	1	0.137
	Sig. (2-tailed)	.	0.145
	N	214	115

** Pearson two tail test significant at the p<.01 level

<Table 10> Use survey

Ranking	Title	Frequency
1	Journal of business ethics	17
2	Public finance	9
3	Journal of accounting and economics	9
4	Journal of financial and quantitative analysis	8
5	Applied financial economics	5
6	Journal of multinational financial management	5
7	New England journal of medicine	4
8	American journal of public health	4

5. Conclusions

Effective access to information is an essential requirement for the success of any academic libraries. Rising journal prices and the increasing number of published journals make it difficult for libraries to provide researchers with all the information they need.

Citation analysis is a useful tool for evaluating the use of libraries' collection, particularly when used in conjunction with cost data. However, previous studies have raised the question whether citation analysis – either through nationally or locally collected citation statistics – is a valid method for journal collection evaluation. This study presented a method for local citation analysis, which combined with the national citation index.

Cost-per-use (CPU) is used to measure cost-effectiveness of each journal with higher CPU scores indicating greater cost-effective titles. Cost is defined as the sum of journal subscription prices and administration fees for each title. Use is defined as the sum of nationally collected citation score, which is based on the impact factor of JCR, and the locally collected citation scores. The local citation score of a journal composed of the number of citations for each journal, and the scores journals received in accordance with the institution's research measure guidelines.

This study proves that the nationally collected citation score is no substitute for conducting a local use study and the locally collected citation score does not reflect the objective value of the academic journal.

This study is more comprehensive than the previous studies in that it enables a more qualitative analysis as it incorporates the cost elements, which cover the overall costs, including administration fee and subscription prices. In order to achieve a more objective result, this study combined the nationally collected citation score and locally collected citation score at one-to-one ratio.

However, the method has limitations and the best results for collection development should be obtained by using convergence of data from all available sources. Further study is warranted in the area of measurement of cost-effectiveness of journals by their material type.

Reference

1. A.S, Tobias, "The Yule Curve Describing Periodical Citations by Freshmen: Essential Tool or Abstract Frill?" *Journal of Academic Librarianship*, 1(1)(1975): 14-16.
2. L.P. Miller, *Publicity Letter* (August 1996).
3. Klaus G. Altmann & G.E. Gorman, "Can Impact Factors Substitute for the Results of Local Use Studies?: Findings from an Australian Case Study." *Collection Building* 18(2) (1999): 90-94.
4. F.W. Lancaster, *The Measurement and Evaluation of Library Services* (Washington, D.C.: Information Resources Press, 1977)
5. J. M. Najman & B. Hewitt, "The Validity of Publication and Citation Counts for Sociology and other Selected Disciplines", *Journal of Sociology* 39(1): 62-80.
6. Robert N. Broadus, "A Proposed Method for Eliminating Titles from periodical subscription lists." *College & Research Libraries* 46 (1985): 30-35.
7. Theresa Dombrowski, "Journal Evaluation Using Journal Citation Reports", *Collection Management* 10(3/4) (1988): 175.
8. Thomas E. Nisonger,"Use of the Journal Citation Reports for Serials Management in Research Libraries: An Investigation of the Effect of Self-Citation on Journal Rankings in Library and Information Science and Genetics", *College & Research Libraries* (May 2000): 263-275.
9. P.M.Z. Coelho, Antunes, C.M.F., Costa, H.M.A. Kroon, F.G., Lima, M.C. Sousa, and Linardi, P.M., "The Use and Misuse of the Impact Factors A Parameter for Evaluation of Scientific Publication Quality: a Proposal to Rationalize its Application", *Braz J. Med Biol Res* 36(12)(2003): 1605-1612.
10. Robert B. Archibald & David H. Finifter, "Biases in Citation-Based Rankings of Journals", *Scholarly Publishing* 18(1987): 131-38.
11. T.Stankus & B. Rice, "Handle With Care: Use and Citation Data for Science Journal Management", *Collection Management* 4(3) (1982):   95-100.
12. Janice Kreider, "The Correlation of Local Citation Data with Citation Reports", *Library Resources & Technical Services* 43 (Apr 1999): 92-96.
13. A.Y. Asundi & S.H. Kabin, "Evolving Criteria for Identification and Selection Core Periodicals in a Subject: A Case of Indian Horticulture." *Library Science with a Slant to Documentation* 33(2) (1996): 73-83.
14. F.W. Dulle, M.J.F. Lwehabura, D.S. Matovelo and & R.T. Mulimila, "Creating a Core Journal Collection for Agricultural Research in Tanzania", *Citation Analysis and User Opinion Techniques* 53(5) (2004): 270-277.
15. Reba Leiding, "Using Citation Checking of Undergraduate Honors Thesis Bibliographies to Evaluate Library Collection", *College & Research Libraries* (Sep 2005): 417-429.
16. Marian A.Burright, Trudi Bellardo Hahn, & Margaret J. Antonisse, "Understanding Information Use in a Multidisciplinary Field: A Local Citation Analysis of Neuroscience Research", *College & Research Libraries* 66(3) (2005): 198-201.
17. Julie M. Hurd, Deborah D. Blecic &, and Rama Vishwanatham, "Information Use by Molecular Biologists: Implications for Library Collections and Services", *College & Research Libraries* 60 (Jan 1999): 31-43.
18. Brian D. Scanlan, "Coverage by Current Contents and the Validity of Impact Factors: ISI from a Journal Publisher's Perspective", Serials Librarian 13 (1988): 57-66.

19. G. Wills, C. Oldman, "An Examination of Cost-Benefit Approaches to the Evaluation of Library and Information Services", in *Evaluation and Scientific Management of Libraries and Information Centers* edited by W.Lancaster (Leiden: Noordhoff Leyden, 1977).

20. M.S. Sridhar, "Is Cost Benefit Analysis Applicable to Journal Use in Special Libraries", *Serials Librarian* 15(1/2) (1988): 137-153.

21. Tina E. Chrastowski, "Journal Collection Cost-Effectiveness in an Academic Chemistry Library: Results of a cost-Use Survey at the University of Illinois at Urbana Champaign", *Collection Management* 14(1/2) (1991): 85-98.

22. Suk-Young Kim & Hye-Kyung Hwang, "A Cost-Effectiveness Analysis on the Usage of Foreign Scientific and Technical Journals", *Journal of the Korean Society For Library and Information Science* 35(1) (2001): 249-264.

23. Henry H. Barschall, "The Cost-Effectiveness of Physics Journals", *Physics Today* 41 (July 1988): 56-59.

24. Hery H. Barschall & J.R. Arrington, "The Cost of Physics: A Survey" *Bulletin of the American Physical Society* 33 (July-Aug 1988): 1437-1447.

25. D. Milne & B. Tiffany, "A Survey of the Cost-Effectiveness of Serials: A Cost-Per-Use Method." *Serials Librarian* 19(3/4) (1991): 137-149.

26. Richard K. Hunt, "Journal Deselection in a Biomedical Research Library: A Mediated Mathematical Approach." Bulletin of Medical Library Association 78(1) (1990): 45-48.

27. Rolf Hasslow & Annika Sverrung, "Deselection of Serials: the Chalmers University of Technology Library Method." *Collection Management* 19(3/4) (1995): 151-170.

28. Hye-Kyung Chung & Eun-Joo Jung, "An Analysis Model for Journal Evaluation in Special Libraries", *Journal of the Korean Society for Information Management* 23 (2006): 121-138.

An Analysis Model of Creating a Core Journal Collection for Academic Libraries[19)]

This study presents an analysis model for setting up a core journal for academic libraries. The model uses multiple factors based on the concept that convergence from all available sources should be used in core journal due to the inherent limitations of each source. The factors considered in the study are the locally collected citations, local use, impact factor, and subscription price. The scores of journals range from '0' to '400' with about 20% of the total collection representing the core list. This study also conducts a case study to demonstrate how academic libraries could apply the model to formulate a list of core journals for their collections.

---

19) 이 논문은 2009년 Library Collections, Acquisitions, & Technical Services 33권(17~24쪽)에 게재되었음.

1. Introduction

In response to steadily rising journal prices while the budget remains relatively the same, academic libraries must determine which journal subscriptions to renew and which to terminate. How are core journals selected in academic libraries? They may base their journal selection decisions purely on faculty opinion, which is very subjective.

Some libraries use the tagging method as this is more likely to record the full spectrum of uses compared to other methods. The method affixes a paper tag on the front cover of every unbound issue or bound volume to collect or analyze circulation and re-shelving statistics. However, the method has been criticized for tracking only about 38% of serial's total use, since it would not be able to capture such brief uses as in-house browsing and quick reference for relevance.

Citation analysis is a useful tool in order to identify a core journal collection. Journals are ranked by citation counts and those with high citation counts are considered to be of high use and thus ranked accordingly. Citation analysis studies may be global or local in scope. Some studies have questioned whether national impact factor and the locally collected citation score could be substituted for conducting a local use study and concluded that they were not substitutable (Altmann & Gorman [1]; Burright et al. [4]; Kreider [13]).

Many studies agreed upon its limitations and proved that there was no single factor that could be used to determine an academic library's core journals. Several studies suggested that such decisions were better made if they based their decisions on the use of convergence of data from all available sources (Segal [19]; Bourne [2]; Dulle et al. [9]; Nisonger [17]; Kim and Lee [12]; Chung [8]). The factors may cover subscription cost, impact factor, user request, journal coverage, language of the publication availability elsewhere, local usage, and local citations.

This study aims to present a journal evaluation method for identifying core journals for research and teaching at academic libraries, recognizing that there is no single indicator that can adequately perform this assessment.

To this end, this study takes the following steps:

1. Identify essential data sets of evaluating core journals;

2. Develop a method for journal evaluation using essential data; and

3. Conduct a case study at the KDI School of Public Policy and Management to demonstrate how academic libraries could apply the proposed method in their local studies.

2. Literature review

It is important to explore how to measure the 'utility' or 'value' of journals in academic libraries. However, journal selections in some academic libraries are still based on faculty opinion, which asks a faculty group what journals they consider to be the most valuable. The method is relatively simple, but it may be too subjective to represent local usage.

Different kinds of utilization studies have been carried out to provide quantitative measures in evaluating journal titles such as every day observations, the tagging method, analysis of re-shelving or circulation statistics. These measures are potentially very useful tools for predicting how frequently each journal is used in a specific library, but they are very time consuming and inaccurate.

Murphy [16] suggested that the impact factor was the most important measure of quality. Smith [20] also argued that the impact factor is quite helpful in comparing two journals in the same subject area, since differences among disciplines in citation practices, research progress, and other factors can undoubtedly affect the outcome of the comparison.

However, Altmann and Gorman [1] found that the JCR's impact factor was no substitute for local citation studies, and it could be only used in conjunction with data from local use studies. Nisonger [17] also concluded that serials collection management decisions should not be made strictly on the basis of impact factor, but in conjunction with other traditional factors such as cost, use or potential usage, indexing, and relevance to the library's collecting priorities. Likewise, although they found that there was a correlation between JCR data and locally collected data for the most-cited items, Burright, et al. [4] and Kreider [13] proved that this correlation grew much weaker and therefore much less useful for less-cited items.

Many studies proved that there was no single factor that may be used to analyze an academic library's core journals. They suggested that the best method for formulating an optimal journal collection was to combine data from all available sources. Dulle et al. [9] suggested that citation analysis combined with user opinions were found to be useful in determining core journals in a library. The study analyzed 295 graduate-level theses reserved at the Sokoine University of Agriculture in Tanzania.

Kim and Lee [12] compared and analyzed the evaluation indicators for core journals and proposed nine evaluation criteria to be considered for collection management from the top 40 academic libraries in Korea. The study employed a web survey method to investigate various selection criteria (27 for printed journals and 37 for electronic journals). The top candidates in determining core journals were user request, followed by subscription price, degree of journal use, impact factor, and local citations.

Hunt [11] developed a mathematical formula for comparing the cost of owning a journal with the cost of procuring articles through an inter-library loan (ILL), at a specific level of use. While ILL costs were computed by totaling the annual cost of staffing, supplies, and ILL-related lending library charges, the cost of owning a journal was determined by the total cost of maintaining each title. Hasslow and Sverrung [10] applied the formula to their study and found that 64.2% of their journals were cost-effective and about 300 journals were canceled representing a cost saving of approximately $100,000.

There are studies that suggest that journals need to be evaluated by usage related to cost, and core journals are required to maximize local usage and minimize cost. They suggested the cost-benefit analysis (CBA) in assessing journal values, considering several benefit factors including coverage, impact factor, use, location, and inter-library loan requests, as well as subscription cost. However the studies agreed upon the limitation that the results could not be truly effective without the help of intuitive value judgment (Byrd & Koenig [5]; Sridher [21]).

Sylvia (1998) conducted a cost-effective study to examine the bibliographies of undergraduate and graduate students of St. Mary's University. Use data was based on citation analysis and cost was determined through the journal's subscription price. In the study, the most cost-effective and commonly-assessed titles constituted good candidates for new subscriptions and least used titles were candidates for subscription cancellation.

Similarly, Chrzastowski [6] conducted a six-month journal-use survey at the University of Illinois Urbana-Champaign Chemistry Library to determine the cost-effectiveness of the collection. Use was defined as circulation of journals within the library in the form of re-shelving and both inter-library borrowing and lending. Cost was based on 1988 subscription prices. Effectiveness was measured by identifying a core journal collection satisfying 90% of total demand.

Milne and Tiffany [15] developed a method for evaluating the cost-effectiveness of journals in order to estimate the cost-per-use (CPU) of a journal at its current subscription price. The study estimated whether the subscription cost of a journal was more than the total cost of inter-library loans a library has to provide for it. Scigliano [18] requested the library users of the Memorial University (Canada) to tick the tag every time they used a journal to estimate usage.

Chung [8] presented a method for journal collection evaluation using CPU. Use data was consisted of the impact factor and locally collected citations score of each journal title. Cost data was based on the subscription prices and average administrative costs associated with a title. However, this study suggested that the best way to develop a journal collection was to use convergence of data from all available sources in addition to citation data.

Some studies questioned whether the use of cost-benefit and cost-effective analysis was appropriate in evaluating journals, since 'use' actually does not equal 'benefits'. And from the user's viewpoint, a 50% proportion of the cost is likely to be viewed as too large, even though it seems to be acceptable from a library's point of view. Accordingly, cost-benefit and cost-effective analyses are limited in that the results are difficult to apply at user oriented academic libraries since the findings are heavily affected by the cost invested (Wills & Oldman [24]; Sridhar [21]).

McDonald [14] examines the relationship between print and online journal use and local citations. The regression results demonstrated that print journal use and locally recorded online journal use were significant predictors of local citations. Online availability of a journal was also found to significantly increase local citations.

3. Methodology

The total value of each journal is determined by a combination of several criteria: impact factor, locally collected citation, local use, and journal subscription price. Based on the concept that the best results for collection development are obtained by converging data from all available sources, the model both international data and locally collected data which is not completely substitutable for international data.

International data is important, since it provides generally accepted objective viewpoints. Locally collected data also plays a significant role in determining core journals, as each library has different users with different information needs. The impact factor and journal subscription price are used to give international data, whereas locally collected citations and local use scores are used to cover local data.

The score of each criterion is adjusted to a one-to-one ratio to generate the total score. The adjusted score of each criterion for a journal is then totaled. Since the unit of each criterion is different, the scores must be adjusted to comparable numbers. Accordingly, the total score of each journal ranges between '0' and '400', with the core list constituting about 20% of the total collection, a proportion used in many empirical studies (Trueswell [23]; Burrell [3]' Chrzastowski & Olesko [7]).

As shown in Fig. 1, the process for calculating the total score of each journal is as follows:

1. Identify the raw score for each criterion;

2. Transform the raw score into a comparable score between '0' and '100';

3. Add up all of the score from the four criteria;

4. Compare the score to other journals; and,

5. Determine if the journal falls among the top 20% of the total collection to qualify for the core list.

$$Local\ Usage\ =\ \frac{Number\ of\ citation\ for\ journal\ A}{Total\ Number\ of\ citation\ for\ journal\ A}\ \times\ (Total\ Number\ of\ online\ usage)$$

<Figure 1> Formula for calculating local usage of *Journal A*

3.1. Local citation score

The local citation score of a journal is local in scope. This criterion is determined by the total number of times a journal is cited in a given period by library users, with higher scores indicating core journals inside a library. The local citation score of a journal may be counted against the Research Measure Guidelines, in which publications fall under different categories according to their score, as shown in Chung [8]. For example, if one journal is cited in a category of publication with a score of 200 and another journal falls into another category of publication with a score of 100, the difference in scores represents the concept that the journal cited in the former category may be used twice as effectively as that with the score of the latter category.

The steps for calculating the locally collected citation score for a journal (*Journal A*) are as follows:

1. Count the number of times *Journal A* is cited by each category in a measure guideline;
2. Multiply the category score of *Journal A* by citation frequency;
3. Add the entire categories to get the raw citation score of *Journal A*;
4. Convert the score to a comparable figure between '0' and '100'.

3.2. Local use score

In the previous literature, different kinds of methods have been used to conduct local use studies in academic library settings, including an analysis of circulation, re-shelving statistics, a tagging method or a tag-ticking approach. However they are very labor intensive, time-consuming and inaccurate, and thus would not be a realistic endeavor for institutions with large journal collections.

This study used online use statistics to avoid the drawbacks of referring to print journal use statistics for journal collection development. Most online databases automatically provide use statistics and the number of times the site was accessed. Moreover, this study was limited to measuring downloads of each journal's full text, as this measurement is a more effective indicator of a journal's future use than data related to other parts of the journal such as the table of contents or abstracts (McDonald [14]).

For journals for which online use statistics are not available, local use scores are predicted by a calculating the ratio of the citation number to the number of full text downloads for all subscribed journals. Calculation procedures to determine the local usage score for a journal *(Journal A)* that does not use an online format are as follows.

1. Add the number of citations *Journal A* receives;
2. Calculate average citation number of the entire journal collection;
3. Calculate the ration of (1) and (2);
4. Multiply the figure by the total number of full text downloads to predict the local use exclusively available by print format; and
5. Adjust the figure to a comparable value between '0' and '100'.

The formula for calculating the use of e-journals is as shown in Fig. 2.

$$TS_A = N_A + [\sum_{n=1}^{12}(L1_n)_A] + [\sum_{n=1}^{5}L2_n]_A + [\sum_{n=1}^{3}L3_n]_A + P_A$$

TS_A=Total score for journal A

N_A=Citation frequency for national data(impact factor) of journal A

$L1_A$=Citation frequency for local data of journal A

$L2_A$=User opinion for local data of journal A

$L3_A$=Usage for local data of journal A

P_A=Price score for national data of journal A

<Figure 2> Evaluation model to select core journals

3.3. International impact factor

In this study, the use of a journal was measured by the sum of the international citation score and locally collected citation score. The international citation score is determined by the impact factor of the Journal Citation Reports (JCR), which is the most widely used assessment tool for deciding which journals should be added or canceled, Journal impact factors provide quantitative tools for evaluating journals. The impact factor is the ratio of the number of times a journal is cited in a given period to the number of articles produced by that journal in the same period. The impact factor for each journal is recorded and then converted into an adjusted score between '0' and '100' is assigned to those journals with the highest impact factor in the total collection.

The steps for calculating the international impact factor for a journal (*Journal A*) are as follows:

1. Check the impact factor of *Journal A* in Journal Citation Report;

2. Compare the impact factor score of *Journal A* with other journals in this criterion; and

3. Convert the score to a comparable number between '0' and '100'.

3.4. Subscription price

Subscription price is national in scope. The subscription price of a journal is the sum of the actual subscription prices of the print and online formats. The subscription price is only one of the four criteria and constitutes 25%, unlike cost-benefit or cost-effective analysis in which it constitutes 50% of the total factors affecting core journal determination. From the user's perspective, this criterion may not be significant enough to compromise 50% of all criteria in selecting core journals. The total cost score of a journal is recorded and then adjusted to a comparable number between '0' and '100'. That is, a journal with the highest subscription price receives an adjusted of '0', while a journal with the lowest subscription price scores a '100'.

4. Case study

A case study was conducted at the KDI School of Public Policy and Management (KDI School) to demonstrate how academic libraries could apply the proposed model in determining their own core journals. The KDI School is an international graduate school that was founded with the support of the Korean government and Korea Development Institute (KDI), one of Korea's most respected economic think tanks. The mission of the School is to train and educate public officials and private sector managers from around the world.

The library reserves 47,000 volumes and subscribes 202 current journals with emphasis on the field of public policy, business administration, asset management, and foreign direct investment, etc. The subscribed journal titles in print or online format are listed as sample journals (n=209 titles). The KDI School Library acquisition's budget is allocated annually for books and periodicals. A high proportion of the allocated budget (45%) is spent on journal subscriptions.

During the consecutive year of 2006 and 2007, a total of 122 publications were analyzed for the 33 faculty members and 46 graduate students included in this case study. The publications included 27 journal articles, 14 books, 34 working papers, one conference proceedings, and 46 master theses.

Journals and working papers constituted about 50% of the items cited, followed by theses (37%), books (11%), and proceedings

(1%). These results support the need for the library to allocate a significant percentage of its budget to journal subscriptions if they are to adequately support research and teaching activities.

Local citation scores are counted against the Faculty Research Measure Guideline (see Table 1) provided by the KDI School, in which researcher's output falls under different categories. The Guideline is largely categorized into 4 categories and then divided into sub-categories (scores range from 10 to 400).

The most frequently cited journal in the Library was '*Journal of Finance*' (8100), followed by '*American Economic Review*' (5875), '*Journal of Financial Economies*' (5750), and '*Journal of Political Economy*' (5350). Both '*Journal of Finance*' (8100) and '*American Economic Review*' (5875) were adjusted to 100 – a perfect score.

<Table 1> Faculty Research Measure Guideline

Category	Major indicators	Score	Number
Research papers	Internationally Accredited Journal (A)	400	7
	Internationally Accredited Journal (B)	150	13
	Domestically Accredited Journal (A)	100	4
	Domestically Accredited Journal (B)	75	3
	Working Paper (KDI)	50	34
	Working Paper (Non-KDI)	50	-
	Books	50	14
Conference Proceedings	International Proceeding	50	1
	Domestic Conference Report	50	-
Theses	Master & Ph. D. Thesis	100	46
Total			122

For example, '*Journal of Finance*' was cited 78 times in various publications; 7 times in publications from the category 'Internationally Accredited Journal (A)' (400 points), 14 times in publications from the category 'Internationally Accredited Journal (B) (150 points), 7 times in publications from the category'Domestically Accredited Journal (A)' (100 points), 5 times in publications from the category 'Translated Books' (50 points), 9 times in publications from the category 'International Proceeding' (50 points), and 36 times in publications from the category 'International Working Paper' (50 points). The local citation score of the journal came out to be 8100 (see Table 2).

<Table 2> *Journal of Finance*: Local citation analysis calculation data

Local citation score of '*Journal of Finance*'
= (7*400) + (14*150) + (36*50) + (5*50) + (9*50) + (7*100) = 8,100
Total raw score = 8,100
Adjusted score = 100

The local use score for each journal was determined by the number of full text downloads, when the online version was available. However when an online version is not available, local use scores for print only journals are designed to be predicted by calculating the average ratio of local citations to the number of full text downloads for all subscribed journals. For example, '*Journal of Health Politics, Policy, and Law*' was cited 450 times and the number of online full text downloads was predicted at

904.1, based on the average ratio of full text downloading (892) to local citations (444), which was about 2:1 (see Table 3).

<Table 3> Predictable usage of print format journals

Title	citation counts	Online use
Average	444	892
Journal of Health Politics, Policy, and Law	450	*x*

X=Potential usage of 'Bulletin of the Institution of Ethnology Academy'
444:892 = 450: *X*, *X* = 450*892/444=904.1

The most frequently used journal at the KDI School was '*Journal of Finance*' (18,336), followed by '*Journal of Economic Literature*' (12,979), '*Journal of International Economic Law*' (12,029) and '*Quarterly Journal of Economics*' (11,903). Since 18,336 is an ultra-high score, 12,979 was converted into score '100'. As a result, 18,336 also got 100 points. The 24th ranking journal, *American Journal of International Law*, was never full text downloaded or locally cited, so the local use score of the journals was '0'.

In an attempt to apply an international point of view for journals, the impact factor for each journal was taken from ISI's Journal Citation Reports. As shown in Table 4, among the core journals at the KDI School, the journal with the highest impact was '*Journal of Marketing*' with 4.831 points. On the other hand, those journals not covered by the JCR received no score or a '0' as shown with '*European Journal of International Law*'.

<Table 4> Top 10 core titles of the journal collection of the KDI School

Rank	Title	Indicators					
		Citing	Request	Usage	IF	Price	Total
1	J. of Finance	100	0	100	27.8	96.2	324.0
2	J. of Accounting & Economics	28.7	80.0	14.4	28.7	93.5	245.3
3	Quarterly J. of Economics	46.4	0	64.9	33.6	97.8	242.8
4	J. of Political Economy	93.0	0	16.1	27.3	98.2	234.7
5	J. of Economic Literature	16.5	0	70.8	39.9	100.0	227.2
6	American Economic Review	100.0	0	10.7	16.0	98.0	224.7
7	Econometrica	78.3	0	27.5	20.5	97.2	223.5
8	Psychological Bulletin	3.5	20.0	1.7	100.0	96.9	222.1
9	J. of World Trade	0	100.0	18.0	0	93.4	211.5
10	Applied Economics	7.0	0	100.0	4.5	100.0	211.4

The sample journals were also analyzed by subscription price. The highest subscription price among core journals was for 'Journal of Financial Economics' at US$ 19,111.58, receiving an adjusted score of '0'. Those journals that cost nothing to access received adjusted scores of '100'. 'Journal of Finance', priced at US$ 729.39, received an adjusted score of 77.3.

Once the original score for each criterion was identified, they were converted to an adjusted score between '0' and '100'. The adjusted scores of each criterion for a journal were then totaled. Accordingly, the total score of each journal ranges between '0' and '400', with the core list constituting about 20% of the total collection. Table 4 provides ranked lists of the top 41 core journals at the KDI School. The top three titles are 'Journal of Finance' (344.7), 'Journal of Economic Literature' (313.1) and

'*Quarterly Journal of Economics*' (306.4). The total range of the journal scores varied widely from 344.7 to 15.7.

5. Conclusion

This study presents a model that combines several factors in determining core journals based on the concept that selection of such journals can not be based on any single factor. The model uses four journal selection tools - impact factor, locally collected citation score, local use, and subscription price. The scores of the four factors are combined at a one-to-one ratio (each compromising 100 points) to determine the quantitative level of each journal.

This model combined international data and data, based on the concept that national data is no substitute for local use studies. International data used in the study are impact factor and subscription price and local data are locally collected citation score and local use. It is assumed that the top 20% of all journal collections constitute good candidates for core journals in an academic library.

This study conducted a case study to demonstrate how academic libraries could apply the model to formulate a list of core journals for their libraries. The results pointed to a list of core journals (41 titles) in the library (see Table 4). At the same time, the lowest scored journals should be considered for cancellation.

One or two year's data alone are inconclusive since the core list in an academic library does not remain constant from year to year. Thus accumulated data going back four to five years may be applied when selecting core journals. User trends need to be analyzed through accumulated data in order to obtain the information necessary for strategic journal selection.

This method is also different from Chung [8] in the following ways:

First of all, it adds local use into the citation and subscription price criteria of the previous study, to enable a more accurate analysis by analyzing the specific information needs of the library. While the data sample covers local use of online format journals, use data of each print format journal is predicted by calculating the ratio of the average number of times a journal is cited to the average online usage of a journal in a given period.

Secondly, the proportion of the cost factor has been reduced to 25% down from 50% in the previous paper. This is because the cost criteria may not be significant enough to compromise 50% in selecting core journals from the user's perspective.

Furthermore, the previous study limited the data sample to journal titles that are held by the library and simultaneously fall within the JCR list. However, this study covers both print and online format journal titles which are subscribed to by the library in the data sample, since there are possibilities that the core journals of a library may include titles that are not covered by the JCR.

Finally, this method is realistic for institutions with large journal collections, since the total number of citation for each journal is counted solely based on how often the journal is cited by users. It is less labor intensive than the previous study, which was designed to check against the measure guideline of each institution, in which researcher's output falls under different categories.

The proposed model is expected to be applicable to any academic library where online journals and their own usage are available. By using convergent data obtained from both subjective and objective viewpoints, this study is greatly expected to improve the validity of journal collection evaluations and minimize the limitations of previous studies that exclusively relied on single sources from citation, local use, or cost elements.

Once the basic framework is established, it can be used for the long term. Libraries may replace old scores for academic journals and produce updated scores for them for the target period. Further research may also broaden the scope of this case study to identify a more representative sample than the journal collection of the KDI School of Seoul, Korea.

Notes

[1] Altmann, K.G. & Gorman, G.E. (1999). Can impact factors substitute for the results of local use studies?: Findings from an Australian case study", *Collection Building*, 18(2), 90-94.

[2] Bourne, C.P. (1975). "Planning serials cancellations and cooperative collection development in the health sciences: Methodology and background information". *Bulletin of the Medical Library Association*, 63(4), 366-377.

[3] Burrell, Q.L. (1985). The 80/20 rule: Library lore or statistical law? Journal of Documentation, 41, 124-139.

[4] Burright, M.A., Hahn, T.B., & Antonisse M.J. (2005). Understanding information use in a multidisciplinary field: A local citation analysis of neuroscience research. College & Research Libraries, 66(3), 198-210.

[5] Byrd, G.D. & Koenig, E.D. (1978). Systematic serials selection analysis in a small academic health sciences library. *Bulletin of Medical Libraries Association*, 66(4), 397-406.

[6] Chrzastowski, T.E. (1991). Journal collection cost-effectiveness in an academic chemistry library: Results of a cost-use survey at the University of Illinois at Urbana-Champaign. *Collection Management*, 14(1-2), 85-98.

[7] Chrzastowski, T.E., & Olesko, B.M. (1997) Chemistry journal use and cost: Results of a longitudinal study. *Library Resources and Technical Services*, 41(2), 101-111.

[8] Chung, H.K. (2007). Evaluating academic journals using impact factor and local citation score. *Journal of Academic Librarianship*, 33(3), 393-402.

[9] Dulle, F.W., Lwehabura, M.F., Matovelo, D.S. & and Mulimila, R.T. (2004). Creating a core journal collection for agricultural research in Tanzania: Citation analysis and user opinion techniques. *Library Review*, 53(5), 270-277.

[10] Haaslow, R. & Sverrung, A. (1995). Deselection of serials: the Chalmers University of technology library method. *Collection Management*, 19(3/4), 151-170.

[11] Hunt, R.K. (1990). Journal deselection in a biomedical research library: A mediated mathematical approach. *Bull. Med. Libr. Assoc.* 78(1), 45-48.

[12] Kim, S.Y. & Lee, C.S. (2004). Analysis of evaluation indicators for the development of evaluation models of foreign academic journals. *Journal of the Korean Society for Information Management*, 21(2), 45-67.

[13] Kreider, J. (1999). The correlation of local citation data with citation data from journal citation reports. *Library Resource & Technical Services*, 43(1), 28-36.

[14] McDonald, John D. (2006). Understanding journal usage: A statistical analysis of citation and use. *Journal of the American Society for Information Science and Technology*, 57(13), 1-13.

[15] Milne D. & Tiffany, B.A. (1991). Cost-per-use method for evaluating the cost-effectiveness of serials: A detailed discussion of methodology. *Serials Review*, 17(2), 7-14.

[16] Murphy, P. (1996). Determining measures of the quality and impact of journals. National Board's Commissioned Report Series. Canberra, Australian Government Publishing Service.

[17] Nisonger, T.E. (2000). "Use of the journal citation reports for serials management in research libraries: An investigation of the effect of self-citation on journal rankings in library and information science and genetics", *College and Research Libraries*, 61(3), 263-275.

[18] Scigliano, M. (2000). Serial use in a small academic library: Determining cost-effectiveness. *Serial Review*, 26(1), 43-52.

[19] Segal J.A. (1986). Journal deselection: A literature review and an application. *Sci Technon Libr.*, 6(3), 25-42.

[20] Smith, T.E. (1985). Journal citation reports as a deselection tool. *Bulletin of the Medical Library Association*, 73(4), 387- 389.

[21] Sridhar, M.S. (1988). Is cost benefit analysis applicable to journal use in special libraries? *Serials Librarian*, 15(1/2), 137-153.

[22] Sylvia, M.J. (1998). Citation analysis as an unobtrusive method for journal collection evaluation using psychology student research bibliographies, *Collection Building*, 17(1), 20-28.

[23] Trueswell, R.L. (1985). Some behavioral patterns of library users: The 80/20 rule. *Wilson Library Bulletin*, 43, 24-39.

[24] Wills, G., & Oldman, C. (1977). An examination of cost-benefit approaches to the evaluation of library and information services. In W. Lancaster (Ed.), *Evaluation and Scientific Management of Librarie and Information Centers*. Noordhoff Leyden: Leiden.

도서관과
가상가치평가법(CVM)

공중(대중)에 의하여 소비되는 공공재는 시장에서 거래되는 민간재와 달리 시장가격이 형성되어 있지 않아, 필요할 때 그 가치를 정량적으로 입증하여야 한다. 도서관이 제공하는 정보서비스도 대표적인 공공재의 하나라고 할 수 있다. 2000년대 초반에 들어오면서, 기관 또는 국가 예산형성의 주요한 결정 과정에서 선 순위를 득하기 위하여, 도서관은 타당성 평가 체제를 구축하기 위한 노력에 주력하기 시작했다.

Aabø, Svanhild 등을 비롯한 해외 학자들의 도서관 가치에 관한 정량적 분석 연구가 이러한 노력에 물꼬를 트기 시작하면서 국내 도서관계에도 변화의 조짐이 나타나기 시작했다. 이들 연구는 생태계나 환경 서비스 등 여러 분야의 비시장 재화의 가치측정에 유용하게 사용되어 온 가상가치평가법(contingent valuation method, CVM)을 도서관 분야에 적용하는 계기가 되었다. 가상가치평가법은 공공재의 가치를 추정하기 위한 거의 유일한 방식으로 인정되었으며, 가상적 상황에 대한 설문 조사에 따라 다양한 공공재에 대한 소비자의 지불의사액(willingness to pay; WTP)을 추정하는 방식이다.

첫째, **"Measuring the economic value of special libraries (2007)"**
는 가상가치평가법을 적용한 전문도서관의 경제적 가치 분석모형을
제시하였다. 본 모형은 도서관의 정량적인 가치평가를 위해 기존에
사용되어 온 '시간 절감'의 편익을 가상가치평가법과 접목하였다는
데에 그 특징이 있다. 비용에는 도서관 운영 예산을 대입하였다. 사
례연구에서 총 경제적 편익은 1.97인 것으로 나타났다. 본 연구는 도
서관의 편익을 시간 절감에만 국한하였다는 한계가 있음에도 불구하
고, 후속 연구들이 나올 수 있는 기반을 마련하였다는 데에 그 의의
가 있다고 하겠다.

둘째, **"공공도서관의 가치평가를 위한 가상가치평가법 분석 (2007)"**
은 가상가치평가법의 인지 부조화 편의를 최소화하기 위한 전략 대안
으로 DM(Dissonance Minimizing) 포맷을 제시하고 있다. 인지 부조
화는 자신의 행위와 신념으로는 이해하지 못하는 상황에서 느끼는 갈
등이다. 설문지에 설정된 가상적 상황이나 환경을 충분히 이해하지 못
하게 될 때 응답자는 인지 부조화 상태를 경험하게 되면서 설문에 무
의식적으로 긍정을 해버리거나 응답 거부를 하는 편의를 유발할 수
있다. 본 연구에서 제시된 DM 포맷은 가상가치평가법 운용에서 발생
할 수 있는 인지 부조화 편의의 영향력과 대처방법을 살펴보고, 이를
해소하기 위한 대안을 제시하였다. 본 연구는 도서관의 실제 가치를
좀 더 정확하게 추정할 수 있는 기반을 마련하였다는 데에 그 의의가
있다고 하겠다.

셋째, **"The contingent valuation method in public libraries (2008)"**

는 선행연구의 핵심 주제인 DM 포맷은 IBM 포맷과 함께 가상가치평가법의 설문 문항에 사용될 경우, 편의를 최소화하는 데 더욱 효과가 있음을 공공도서관의 사례분석을 통해 입증하였다. IBM (information bias minimizing; 정보 편의 감소) 포맷은 설문 문항의 정보 부족이나 불확실성으로 인해 응답자가 공공재에 대한 가치평가를 유보하거나 잘못 응답하는 경향을 줄이기 위해 고안된 포맷이다.

넷째, **"Assessing the warm glow effect in contingent valuations for public libraries (2010)"**는 가상가치평가법의 핵심 편의로 알려진 웜글로우 효과(warm glow effect; 자선심)를 제어할 수 있는 설문모형의 구축에 초점을 두었다. 응답자의 웜글로우 성향이 가상가치평가법의 지불의사액에 영향을 미치게 될 때 가치 추정치가 실제 지불의사액보다 과대평가될 위험이 존재한다고 주장하였고, 이를 공공도서관을 대상으로 한 사례연구에서 입증하였다. 웜글로우 효과를 배제한 설문지와 통제되지 않은 전통적인 지불의사액과 비교·분석한 결과, 통제되지 않은 설문의 경우에 실제 지불의사액보다 약 40.6% 과대평가될 위험이 존재하는 것으로 나타났다.

다섯째, **"Analyzing altruistic motivations in public library valuation using CVM (2012)"**은 가상가치평가법 운용에서 발생할 수 있는 또 하나의 편의인 배타적 동기(altruistic motivations)를 다루고 있다. 본 연구는 타인을 배려하는 응답자의 배타적 동기가 도서관의 가치를 실제보다 과대평가하는 요인이 될 수 있음을 입증하고 있다. 본 연구는 배타적 동기를 두 개의 카테고리로 범주화하여 근본 원인을 보다 심층적으로 도출하기 위한 시도를 하였다: local vs. global; paternalistic vs. non-paternalistic. 배타적 동기를 최대한 통제한 설문지와 그렇지 않은 설문지의 지불의사액을 비교·분석한 결과, 전자가 후자보다 약 22% 높은 것으로 나타났다.

여섯 번째, "도서관의 경제적 가치측정 연구의 탐색적 메타분석 (2009)"[1]은 도서관의 경제적 가치를 실증적으로 측정한 국내·외 선행연구를 총망라하여 상이하게 나타난 경제적 수치에 대한 메타분석을 수행하였다. 메타분석이란 특정 연구 주제에 대하여 독립적으로 수행된 선행연구들의 상이한 수치 결과를 통합하여 통계적으로 결론을 내리는 방법이다. 관련 연구 41건을 취합하여 6개의 변인(연구 시기, 도서관의 유형, 연구 방법, 혜택 범위, 서비스 범위, 1인당 GDP)을 중심으로 지불의사액과 경제성 수치의 비율이 상이하게 나타나는 현상의 이유를 정밀하게 유추하기 위한 것이 목적이다.

---

1) 이 논문은 제한된 지면으로 본문에 포함하지 못함. 2009년 한국문헌정보학회지 43권 4호(117~137 쪽)을 참조하기 바람

Measuring the Economic Value of Special Libraries[2]

This study aims to present a new approach to measuring the economic value of special libraries, concluding certain time saving effects that the contingent valuation method application can not exclusively prove. The benefits of such libraries are based on estimates of how much the user is willing to pay for the service, as well as the cost of time saved as a result of his contact with library services. According to the case study, the economic value of its library services measured in terms of a B/C ratio was 1.97, serving as strong justification for the library's existence. It is hoped that the model will help analyze the strength of each library service as well as the total economic value of the library.

2) 이 논문은 2007년 Bottom Line: Managing Financial Economics 20권 1호(30~44쪽)에 게재되었음.

1. Introduction

Identifying the economic value of special libraries is, without a doubt, critical to their funding, support and, ultimately, their existence. Particularly as institutional resources become increasingly scarce, it is vital for special libraries to prove the value and, in the process, justify their continuation. Library services constitute a significant element for measurement and play a large role in the economic value of special libraries by virtue of their intended purpose of carrying out the mission of special libraries.

Although many studies have shown that special libraries have positive value, the effort to precisely measure and define the value is difficult and ongoing. A key approach to assessing the value of special libraries is measuring the opportunity cost of the time users saved as a result of the services offered by the libraries. In other words, the value users place on library services must be, at a minimum, greater than or equal to the value of their spent time. This study does not make any attempt to estimate benefits other than time saved and thus may correspond to a 'lower bound cost benefit' or 'marginal value of the exercise'.

On the other hand, the contingent valuation method (CVM) has been most widely used for estimating through surveys a user's overall perceived value of all kinds of non-market services. The CVM is used to measure the perceived value of various services offered by the special library by assessing the user's 'willingness to pay' (WTP) and 'willingness to accept' (WTA) alternatives to no library services provided. Because the contingent valuation method is based on asking people questions as opposed to observing their actual behavior, the approach has certain limitations.

One of the major biases that may affect this study is the possibility that the respondent is actually answering a different question than the surveyor intended. In particular, most respondents are accustomed to receiving library services at no cost and therefore are not familiar with placing monetary values on library services. Hence, the CVM needs to be modified so that the respondent has an adequate basis to be able to make an educated, well-founded assessment of values they would apply to the special library setting.

According to the *Encyclopedia of Library and Information Science,* the 'economic value' within the library science field is defined as "1) services that save a user's time in looking for information; and 2) services that put supplies to use with beneficial effects." On the other hand, economic value is defined as "the perception of actual or potential benefit" by those who view the library as part of the economic chain that gets information from "author to reader" (Poll, 2003; Sumsion, *et al.,* 2003). Based on these definitions, we conclude that the 'economic value' of special libraries can be defined as the alternative cost of library services as measured by the value users perceive of various services offered by the libraries.

This study aims to present a new approach to measuring the economic value of special libraries, concluding certain time saving effects that the CVM application can not exclusively prove. The study is based on the concept that the time saving effect is considered the key benefit when measuring the economic value of special libraries. The method identified in this study will help reduce the biases that might emerge from the CVM and determine how a library can effectively budget its resources when providing services.

To this end, this study takes the following steps:

1. Categorize the economic benefits that users receive from their interactions with special library services;

2. Present a modified CVM and provide calculation methods for measuring their benefits; and

3. Conduct a case study at the KDI School of Public Policy and Management to demonstrate how special libraries can apply the proposed method to their local studies.

2. Literature Review

Matthew (2002) discusses the different ways in which libraries add value, and the different evaluation techniques and methodologies used to assess this value. He reviews various measures of input, output and processes, and provides suggestions on how to determine the impact of a special library on the organization, as well as the means by which the resultant value may be represented and communicated.

Time valuation is a method special libraries often use to measure their value, as well as a tool for building effective library services. Special libraries are designed primarily to be of value to the user by saving the user's time. The time valuation method is used to measure and compare the relationships between the time saved and costs avoided against the cost of library services.

While several scholars have researched this topic, the key players are Griffiths and King. Their accumulated research results are all combined in their 1993 work, *Special Libraries: Increasing the Information Edge.* Griffiths and King developed methodologies to value libraries and library services in terms of the cost of the time users expended in acquiring information. Several King Research concluded that the cost to the user amounted to an average of $610 per professional per year when compared to what it would cost the user in time and effort to obtain information elsewhere. In addition, the studies also assumed that the time saved correlated positively with enhanced efficiency (Griffiths and King, 1993; Griffiths and King, 1994).

Koenig (1992) examines and analyzes correlations between

the expenses of library or information services and corporate productivity. Using the cost benefit analysis, he demonstrated that the time saved was positively linked to enhanced efficiency and greater productivity - ultimately leading to an increase in the profitability of the corporation.

Tenopir and King (2000), MacEachern (2001) are consistent with the view that library value could be assessed in terms of the amount of time a user expends for the purpose of visiting a library. Tenopir and King estimated the cost incurred by multiplying the user-time taken by the user's hourly salary rate, arguing that the figure represented the marginal value of the exercise.

In a study by MacEachern, the New Zealand Parliamentary Library compared the time cost to users with the purchase cost of the assets used to provide a library service and found the services had a value of between two and 20 times the annual library budgets. As shown in these studies, the time saving effect is the most important benefit users receive from their contact with special library services. This effect, however, is just one of various benefits. Thus valuation by time saved methods, which is based solely on users' time experience, may represent the "lower bound cost benefit" or "marginal value of the exercise"(Griffiths and King, 1993, p. 71).

There are very few attempts to estimate either the overall benefits of special libraries or specific benefits. Some papers have provided estimates of the economic value of library benefits using the CVM. The CVM is used to estimate economic values for all kinds of non-market services, such as ecosystem and environmental services. It involves directly asking people, in a survey, how much they could be willing to pay for specific services.

Holt *et al.* (1999) asked users of the St. Louis Public Library Services what extra sum of money they would be willing to pay in taxes to ensure that libraries remained open, as well how much taxes would have to be reduced for them to accept the library's closure. The study showed that users were willing to pay an extra $1 for every $1 in current taxes for all libraries to remain open. On the other hand, users requested $9 paid back for every $1 in current taxes in exchange for library closures. He concluded that the monetary value of the 'willingness-to-pay' was lower than that of the 'willingness-to-accept'.

Using the same CVM, Morris, *et al.* (2001) calculated the proxy price for borrowing books in public libraries in Great Britain by asking users when they returned the books if they had benefited from the books. When the user responded positively, he was asked how much he would have been willing to pay to borrow the book. The average price users were willing to pay was compared to the actual cost of the books, indicating that the value of borrowing the books amounted to about 7 to 8 percent of the purchase price of the book.

AabØ (2005) used the WTP amount derived in the contingent valuation method to provide a better understanding of the total value – including economic value – of Norwegian public libraries. Based on empirical data, a cost-benefit ratio of about 1:4 was determined, concluding that the public viewed Norwegian public libraries to be, overall, worth their price. Thus far, this study has provided examples of how the CVM is used to measure the value of public libraries, which are more commonly accepted as non market goods. Although the CVM has been widely used for the past two decades, there is considerable controversy over whether it adequately measures people's willingness to pay for services. Since most people are unfamiliar with the concept of thinking about library services in terms of monetary value.

Assessing the value of special libraries, however, requires a modified CVM since more than a single principle yardstick is needed to take into consideration the unique properties inherent to special libraries. For a more accurate assessment, therefore, the CVM that respondents understand – in particular the service in question – is needed to solicit users' true preferences in the contingent market just as they would in an actual market.

3. Methodology

3.1 Pre-survey

A pre-survey was conducted to show that because of the nature of the study, a significant level of uncertainty would surface in the way respondents answered the CV questions. The pre-survey would also help determine the reason for this uncertainty. The sample (N=100) of participants for the pre-survey was randomly selected from students, faculties, staff and visitors who visited the library and used any of its services in July 2005. As shown in <Appendix II>, the pre-survey consisted of 5 questionnaires aimed at determining the following items: frequency of use, reasons as to why the library was not used, what visitors considered the library's most valuable service, the user's perceived value of the library, and the level of certainty in their response.

Among the sample selected for the survey, 92%(92 persons) completed the pre-survey in its entirety. The remaining 8% failed to fill out the pre-survey completely. The pre-survey concluded the following order of items as the most to least valuable library service: reference service, use of library materials, use of physical facilities, online database workshop, document delivery service (DDS), and tutoring service.

The fourth question was not intended to identify the respondents' perceived value of library services, rather, to measure their reaction towards the question. The fifth question was added for those who answered the fourth question to permit respondents to describe their certainty with the fourth question. In addition, the fifth question entailed a follow-up interview question for those who did not answer the fourth question (84%, 77 respondents out of 92) - "Why did you skip the previous question?"

Among the reasons why respondents skipped CV question four <Table 1>, more than half the respondents (68%) indicated that they were not accustomed to thinking about library services in monetary terms because they had always considered the services to be free of charge. Twenty six percent responded that they could designate a specific price that would properly reflect the value of the library, while 5% said they could not understand the question itself.

3.2 A new approach to the economic value of special libraries

It has been suggested that the CVM needs to be modified so that the respondent has an adequate basis to be able to make an educated, well-founded assessment of values they would apply to the special library setting. This study presents a new approach to the economic value of special libraries, concluding certain time saving effects that the CVM application can not exclusively prove. The survey for this study uses a modified format that combines the contingent valuation method and time valuation effects.

This study uses cost-benefit analysis, which has been widely recognized as an appropriate tool for measuring the benefits of the services a library delivers while carrying out its objectives. A cost-benefit score is performed by calculating the cost divided by the benefit. The higher score indicates greater economic value and enables library managers to solicit and justify adequate funds for their services [12]. For this purpose, two sets of data are required: one on cost and one on use. Cost is defined as the sum of the prices for providing library services. Benefit is determined by estimating the willingness to pay by users for library services.

To derive the benefit elements, the study breaks down the services provided by the library into two categories based on the value that intermediaries offer the users. One category of benefits is achieved through a physical intermediary (collection, facility), while the other category of benefits is achieved using a personal intermediary (trained librarians).

The CVM involves directly asking people, in a survey, how much they would be willing to pay for specific services. This is called "contingent" valuation because people are asked to state their willingness to pay, contingent on a specific hypothetical scenario and description of the service. The study determines the value that the two categories of benefits bring to the user, as well as the method for measuring the value.

3.2.1 Benefits achieved through physical resources

Services that use a physical intermediary elicit two types of benefits to the user: a time-saving effect and the value of the physical resources. Library services may include loan service, in-library use (on-line databases, library collection), and use of facilities. Users of the loan service, for example, benefit immediately through the time saved with the existence of the library, and also benefit in the long-term as the contents of the borrowed resources add value to the user.

<Table 1> Why respondents skipped question four

Reason	Number of response	Response rate
I do not understand the question.	4 persons	5%
I think the service has always been offered free of charge, so I am not accustomed to thinking about library services in monetary terms.	53 persons	68%
I am unable to designate a specific price that would properly reflect the value of the library.	20 persons	26%

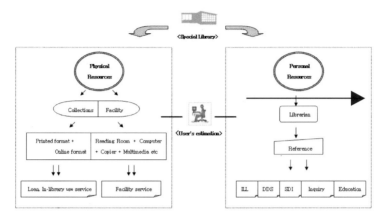

<Figure 1> Categorization of library services

The benefit of the time saving effect is the result of the user not having to expend his time visiting other libraries or institutions to borrow resources. The study points out that the effect is required to be added to the traditional CVM and to measure the value of special library services. Respondents are requested to respond to the following question: "Suppose this library no longer existed. How much in fees would you be willing to pay to access the library services as they exist today, taking into consideration the benefits of time, effort, and travel saved, as well as other factors?" Users were asked to select from among eight price ranges.

The other benefit is the value of the physical resources that the user realizes in various ways. For example, the material may assist the user in solving various questions and/or problems. This study also reflects the added value of physical resources that a CVM application exclusively can not prove. Such data is collected in the survey that directly asks respondents how they determined the value of an item that they borrowed.

Respondents are asked to respond to the following question: "Suppose this library no longer existed. How much in fees would you be willing to pay for the item you borrowed considering how your life has benefited from this item?" Users can select from among eight price ranges. One of the assumptions of this study is that the time saving effect has taken place before the user has been in contact with the service, and the value of the resource is realized during and after utilization of the service. In other words, the two benefit elements may be generated in a continuum before and after users contact the service as shown in <Figure 2>.

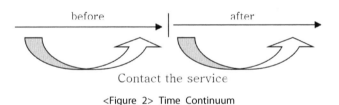

<Figure 2> Time Continuum

Calculation procedures to determine the benefit score deriving from use of physical resources are as follows:

① Add all monetary values for time saved (first benefit element).

② Add all monetary values for resources used (second benefit element).

③ Add ① + ② to obtain the total estimated monetary value for all respondents.

④ Divide the total monetary value by number of respondents.

⑤ Multiply the use frequency to measure the actual benefit of the service for the year.

⑥ Compare this figure to the cost of providing the service.

The outcome can be simplified into the following equation. The benefit realized through the use of physical resources:

<Table 2> Formula for the Valuation of Services using Physical Resources

The benefit realized through the use of physical resources $= [(T_1 + T_2 + \cdots + T_N) + (I_1 + I_2 + \cdots + I_N)] \div N \times U - C$
T_i = Value of saved time I_i = Value of resources N = Number of respondents   U = Use frequency C = Purchasing price

3.2.2 Benefits achieved through personal resources

Services that entail the use of a personal intermediary – such as reference services and other related services – may bring about a time-saving effect to the user. Specifically, the vital benefit is the time saved for the user because of librarian assistance available through reference services. For example, although many users are capable of accessing library electronic databases directly, they will often turn to a trained intermediary for assistance in their search to save time.

In this regard, the survey asks the question: "Suppose this library no longer existed. How much in fees would you be willing to pay for the service, taking into consideration the benefit of saved time to you as the user?" The value may vary depending on the needs of the respondents, reflecting the value generated through the exchange of the user's time and effort for the assistance of librarian.

Calculation procedures to determine the benefit score achieved as a result of the use of personal resources are as follows:

① Add all the monetary values of time saved;

② Divide the total figure by the number of respondents;

③ Multiply the use frequency to measure the actual benefit of the service for the year; and

④ Compare this figure it to the cost of providing the service.

The outcome can be simplified in the equation seen in <Table 3>.

<Table 3> Formula for the Valuation of Services using Personal Resources

The benefit realized through the use of personal resources
$= [(T_1 + T_2 + \cdots + T_{N}) \div N \times U] - C$
T_i = Time Saved   N = Number of respondents   U= Use frequency (Annual)
C= Cost of providing the service

4. Case study analysis

A case study was undertaken in a small special library at the Korea Development Institute (KDI) School of Public Policy and Management. The KDI School was founded as an international graduate school with the support of the Korean government and KDI, one of Korea's most respected economic think thanks. The mission of the school is to train and educate future leaders in the domestic, international, corporate and public issues of today's rapidly changing and globalizing economy facing mid-career professionals.

The case study consisted of constructed scenarios that asked respondents to choose from a selection of alternative actions and a willingness to pay (WTP) measure. The benefit was measured based on users' willingness to pay, followed by the survey that took place immediately after their contact with the service. Estimating the value of online database use, however, could not be measured immediately after the user made contact with the service. Hence, this benefit was measured based on general use. Each question was posed under the assumption that the library no longer existed.

Users are asked to place a monetary value on library services ranging from 0 and 200,000 won based on their experience with the library service on that day, as well as other days in general. In the event users wanted to place a value higher than 200,000 won, they were asked to specify the amount.

4.1 Benefits achieved through physical resources

The services using physical resources in the library include loan service, in-library use, online database, and facility use. The cost of providing the services includes the cost of the books in the library's collection, online database, and facility use. The library offers extensive economic, business, policy and government materials for the students and researchers at the KDI School. Housing both online and offline materials, the library is one of the most comprehensive digital libraries in Korea in the economics and management field.

For the online database, the cost to the institution is entailed in the actual price of purchasing the two databases subscribed to by the KDI School library - Business Source Premier (BSP) and Science Direct (SD). Other databases accessible to users such as the Electronic Journals Service (EJS) and Journal Storage (JSTOR) are subscribed to by KDI, with which the KDI School is affiliated and therefore has full access to, which then translates into only benefits to the School at no cost.

The cost of providing for the facility's use includes the cost of actual purchasing a lobby sofa, new chairs, and other items during the year 2005. The benefit of facility use was then measured based on users' willingness to pay for using the facility and the existence of the library for its facility under the assumption that the library no longer existed.

The benefit of the services was measured by the sum of the monetary values that users perceived over the materials used and time saved as a result of the existence of the KDI School library. Respondents are asked to indicate their willingness to pay for the item they used and valuate the saved time as a result of the existence of the library in the event the library no longer existed.

4.2 Benefits achieved through personal resources

Services using personal resources in the library consist of reference services, including DDS/ILL, online database workshops and inquiry service. The cost of the services covers two librarians who manage and provide services such as planning, educating, and responding to reference questions. Two librarians are asked to indicate the extent to which they devote their time to these specific services as a way to estimate the staffing cost.

The benefit of services through personal resources was measured by asking respondents to rate specific services in the survey immediately after users made contact with the service. Respondents were asked to place a monetary value on the time saved as a result of the existence of the library and its services and determine how much they would be willing to pay in the event the library no longer existed.

4.3 Results

The period selected for this study is July 2005 because the month contains the fewest number of holidays or other special events that could cause irregularities for the data collected compared to other times of the year. The cost-benefit analysis is used as a tool to determine if the benefits of the special library services outweigh the costs to provide the services. According to the results of the survey, the economic value of library services through the medium of the library's physical resources was 2.44 in terms of the benefit-to-cost ratio (B/C ratio). This figure indicates that library services in the form of physical resources hold economic value.

For services through the medium of the library's physical resources such as loan service, in-library use, and online databases, their benefits were calculated as the sum of the estimated values of the time and effort saved as a result of the access to the service, as well as the sum of the values of the resources used. When looking in more detail into the results, the service that produced the largest economic value was facility-use (B/C ratio: 5.71), followed by loan and in-library use (B/C ratio: 2.97) and reference (B/C ratio: 0.76), and online database (B/C ratio: 0.63) as shown in <Table 4>.

On the other hand, the economic value of library services through personal resources was 0.76 in terms of the benefit-to-cost ratio (B/C ratio) as shown in <Table 5>. For reference services such as document delivery service, database workshops, and citations, the benefit was estimated based on the user's perceived value of the time and effort saved as a result of having access to the service. According to the survey, services through the medium of the library's personal resources were not found to hold much economic value.

<Table 4> Economic value of library services through physical resources

Type		Benefit (Time saved + Resource value) (unit: Korean won)	Cost (unit: Korean won)	B/C
Collection	Book Loan	372,049,838 (162,042,486 + 210,007,352)	171,964,578[1]	2.97
	In-Library Use	138,250,909 (60,544,091 + 372,049,838)		
	Online Database	43,443,400 (18,460,750 + 24,982,650)	69,482,885	0.63
	Total	568,138,747 (245,661,460 + 322,554,160)	241,447,463	2.33
Facility		37,365,000(16,892,160 + 20,472,840)	6,541,100	5.71
Total		605,503,747	247,988,563	2.44

[1]171,775,378(Collection cost) + 1,892,000(Binding cost) / see also appendix III

<Table 5> Economic value of library services through personal resources

Type	Benefit (Time saving + Resources value) (unit: Korean won)	Cost (unit: Korean won)	B/C
Document Delivery Service	15,996,000 (15,996,000 + 0)	97,602,158	0.76
Online DB Workshop	2,203,877 (2,203,877 + 0)		
Citation	55,736,755 (55,276,755 + 0)		
Total	73,936,632	97,602,158	0.76

The direct economic benefit of KDI School Library expenditures was 679,440,379 won while the library's total expenditure for operational purposes was 345,590,721 won. Thus, it can be said that the existence of the library resulted in a benefit totaling 330 million won for the mother institution, which also translates into an investment return of 197% for every 1,000 won the institution spent on the library as shown in <Table 6>.

<Table 6> Economic Value of Library Services

Type	Benefit	Cost (unit: Korean won)	B/C
Physical Resources + Personal Resources	679,440,379	345,590,721	1.97

According to the case study involving the KDI School Library, the economic value of its library services measured in terms of a B/C ratio was 1.97, serving as strong justification of the library's existence. The service that produced the largest economic value was facility use (B/C ratio of 5.71), followed by loan and in-library use (B/C ratio of 2.97), and reference service (B/C ratio of 0.75). The relatively low ratio recorded for reference service is an indication of the need to attract more users to the library's reference service, which will in turn raise its the economic value.

5. Conclusion

As scrutiny and studies of the value of library services increase, it is important to explore and introduce new approaches to assessing the economic value of special libraries such as the one involving the KDI School. Specifically, this study proposes a new approach to reducing the occurrence of biases from the CVM. It was found that respondents in the CVM study actually interpreted the question differently from what the surveyor intended. As a result, the degrees to which the preferences that they indicated for the contingent market are reflective of the real market are marginal.

This new approach adds the time saving effects that the CVM application can not exclusively prove. Because of its ability to prove the time saving effects, the CVM, despite being the most widely used method in public library studies, may often overlook the major benefit of the opportunity cost of users' time saved as a result of the services offered by the special library.

The cost-benefit analysis served as a tool in this study to determine if the benefits of library services outweighed the costs to provide the services. Cost is defined as the sum of the prices of providing library services. Benefit is determined by the willingness to pay technique derived from the contingent valuation method. To identify the benefit, the study broadly categorized special library services according to the resource the service delivered: physical resources or personal resources.

The benefit achieved through the use of a physical intermediary is categorized into two types: time saved as a result of the existence of the library and the value of the physical resources. On the other hand, the benefit achieved through the use of a personal intermediary is users' saved time as a result of the assistance of a librarian.

A case study was conducted at the KDI School of Public Policy and Management to show how special libraries could apply the proposed model to their library settings to measure the value of library services. This study sought to improve on previous studies that were often conducted long after users actually utilized the library services, leading to inaccurate results. To achieve a higher level of accuracy, the model was designed to measure benefits immediately after respondents utilized the special library's services.

This study is more specific and accurate than previous studies in that it enables an individual analysis for each service special libraries offer and focuses on the types of benefit derived. However, the study has limitations in that it requires more time and effort since respondents need to be administered the survey as soon as a library service is utilized. In addition, further study is warranted in the area of measuring the economic valuation of library services by type of CVM survey.

References

AabØ, Svanhild (2005), *Libraries: a voyage of discovery.*
http://www.ifla.org/IV/ifla71/Programme.htm.

Griffiths, J.M. and King D.W. (1993), "Special libraries: increasing the information edge." Washington, D.C: Special Libraries Association.

Griffiths, J-M and King, Donald W. (1994), "Libraries: the undiscovered national resource." In *The value and impact of information,* London, Bowker-Saur. (British Library Research: Information Policy Issues): pp. 79-116.

Holt, G.E., Elliott, D. and Moore, A. (1999), "Placing a value on public library services." *Public Libraries,* Vol. 38: pp. 98-108.

Koenig, Michael E.D. (1992), "The importance of services for productivity: under-recognized and under-invested." *Special Libraries* 83(4): pp. 199-210.

MacEachern, R. (2001), "Measuring the added value of library and information services." *IFLA Journal.* Vol. 27, pp. 232-6.

Mason, Robert M. and Peter G. Sassone (1978), "A lower bound cost benefit model for information services." *Information Processing & Management,* Vol. 14 No 2, pp. 71-83.

Matthews, Joseph R. (2002), *The bottom line: determining and communicating the value of the special library,* Westport, Connecticut: Libraries Unlimited.

Morris, Anne, Hawkins, Margaret and Sumsion, John (2001), *"The economic value of public libraries"* London: The Council for Museums, Archives and Libraries.

Poll, Roswitha (2003), "Measuring impact and outcome of libraries." *Performance Measurement and Metrics,* Vol. 4 No. 1, pp. 5-12.

Sumsion, John, Hawkins, Margaret, Morris, Anne (2003), "Estimating the Economic Value of Library Benefits." *Performance Measurement and Metrics,* Vol 4 No. 1, pp. 13-27.

공공도서관의 가치평가를 위한
가상가치평가법 분석3)

본 연구는 공공도서관의 가치평가를 위한 새로운 접근방법을 모색하였다. 기존에 사용되던 가상가치평가법의 한계점을 지적하였으며, 아울러 이를 개선하기 위한 대안으로 Dissonance Minimizing (DM) 포맷을 적용한 가상가치평가법을 제시하였다. 가치평가의 도구로는 비용편익분석이 사용되었고 비용에는 서비스에 투입된 총비용을, 편익에는 서비스에 대한 이용자의 지불의사금액 (willingness to pay)을 적용하였다. 그리고 사례분석을 통해 'J 공공도서관'의 가치를 추정하여 DM 포맷이 공공도서관의 가치를 평가하는데 어떻게 사용되는지 보여주었다.

---

3) 이 논문은 2007년 정보관리학회지 24권 1호(187~208쪽)에 게재되었음 [공저: 정은주].

1. 서 론

공공도서관은 적극적으로 재정을 지원받기 위하여 자관의 가치를 정확하고 효과적으로 의사 결정자에게 전달해야 할 필요성이 있다. 이를 수행하기 위하여 국내외적으로 공공도서관의 가치를 평가하는 기초 데이터로 이용통계 및 성과측정 등의 방법이 오랫동안 사용되었다. 그러나 이들이 공공도서관의 가치를 측정하는 완벽한 지표라 하기는 어렵다. 이용통계의 경우 도서관을 이용할 때마다 이용자 편익이 발생하는 것이 아니므로 질적 평가가 불가능하며, 성과측정법 역시 공공도서관의 가치에 대한 질적 평가는 이루어지지만, 정량적 평가는 가능하지 않기 때문이다.

최근에 공공도서관의 가치를 정량적으로 평가하는 방법으로 가상가치평가법(contingent valuation method; CVM)이 소개되었다. 가상가치평가법은 생태계나 환경 서비스 등 여러 분야에 광범위하게 적용되어온 방법으로 비시장 재화의 가치에 대한 가상적인 상황이나 시장을 설정하여 이용자의 지불의사를 조사하는 방법이다. 가치평가를 위한 기법은 크게 직접적 방법과 간접적 방법으로 구분되며, 가상가치평가법은 직접적 방법에 속하여 간접적 방법에는 여행비용접근법, 만족가격접근법 등이 있다.

가상가치평가법은 비시장 재화에 대하여 정량적으로 평가할 수 있는 거의 유일한 방법임에도 불구하고, 여러 가지 원인으로 인하여 응답자의 정확한 지불의사금액을 왜곡시킬 수 있다는 지적을 받고 있다. 이는 설문지에 사용될 가상적인 상황이나 질문이 공공재의 가치를 정량적으로 측정하는 데 익숙하지 못한 이용자들에게는 매우 난해한 질문이 될 수 있기 때문이다.

Cummings, *et al.* (1995)는 가상가치평가법의 전형적인 질문형태인 이선 선택형 (dichotomous-choice, DC)[4]이 무의식 긍정 바이어스를 유발하여 지나치게 가치가 높게 추정된다고 주장하였다. 실제로 유사한 몇몇 연구에서 지불의사금액은 실제 가치보다 2~3배 높게 나타난 것으로 파악되었다(Champ, *et al.* 1996; Seip and Strand, 1992). 그러나 국내에서는 가상가치평가법을 이용하여 경제적 가치를 추정한 사례는 볼 수 있으나, 이로 인하여 왜곡될 수 있는 문제점을 지적하거나 이를 개선하기 위한 노력은 거의 찾아볼 수 없다.

본 연구는 가상가치평가법을 이용하여 공공도서관 서비스의 가치를 평가한 지금까지의 연구가 지닌 한계점을 지적하고 이를 개선하기 위한 대안을 제시하고자 한다. 이를 위한 구체적인 연구내용은 다음과 같다.

첫째, 가상가치평가법 관련 선행연구를 통하여 기존에 공공도서관에서 사용되어온 가상가치평가법의 문제점과 새로운 대안을 제시한다.

둘째, 기존의 가상가치평가법과 새로운 대안을 'J 공공도서관'에 적용하여 지불의사금액을 비교·분석함으로써 어떤 바이어스가 감소하였는지 살펴보고자 한다.

이 연구에서 사용되는 '가치(value)'는 실제적이거나 잠재적인 편익이 있는, 중요하거나 귀중한 어떤 것으로 정의되고 있다. 서비스의 가치를 측정하는 것에는 서비스로 인한 결과에 대한 측정을 포

---

4) 이선 선택형은 제시한 일정한 가격에 대하여 "예" 또는 "아니오"를 선택하는 두 가지 선택으로 구성되어 있음.

함한다. 다시 말해 결과는 서비스로 인한 단기적인 편익이며, 가치는 이용자가 서비스로 인해 받은 장기적인 결과 또는 효과(effect)라고 할 수 있다(Poll, 2003). 따라서 본 연구는 서비스의 가치를 "이용자가 서비스를 이용한 결과로 나타나는 장기적 효과"라고 정의한다. 한편 Dissonance Minimizing (DM) 포맷은 응답자들이 설문 문항을 완벽하게 이해하지 못하거나, 원하는 답변이 설문 문항의 예시와 정확하게 일치하지 않기 때문에 느끼는 모호함을 줄이기 위하여 고안된 설문형식으로 정의될 수 있다.

2. 선행연구

Holt와 Moore (1999)는 Saint Louis 공공도서관의 가치추정을 위하여 가상가치평가법을 이용하였으며, 비용-편익 분석방법을 도구로 경제성을 분석하였다. 연구 결과, 투입되는 $1에 대하여 수용할 의사가 있는 비용(WTA)과 지불할 의사가 있는 비용(WTP)은 각각 $7과 $1로 나타났다. 또한, 이용자의 그룹에 따라 서비스로부터 받는 편익의 정도가 다르게 나타나는 것을 볼 수 있었다.

Griffiths and King (2004)은 Florida 공공도서관의 회귀분석 (ROI) 비율을 알기 위해 가상가치평가법을 이용하였다. 이 연구는 응답자의 지불의사금액에 대하여 대안(代案)에 대한 문항을 추가하였다는 점이 다른 연구와 차별화된다. 즉, "만약 공공도서관이 없어서 당신의 필요를 충족할 수 없다면, 어떤 대안을 찾을 것인지"라고 질문하였다. 연구 결과, Florida 공공도서관으로 인하여 이용자들이 받는 편익은 납세한 $1에 대해 $6.54 (ROI: 6.54%)인 것으로 나타났다. 이 연구는 공공도서관의 가치를 정량화하였을 뿐만 아니라 이용자들이 도서관을 가장 빈번히 이용하는 시기와 이용자에 따른 가치추정액의 변화 추이를 관찰하였다.

Barron *et al.* (2005)은 South Carolina 공공도서관의 경제적 가치를 평가하고, 이들이 사회 전체에 미치는 경제적인 파장의 정도를 측정하였다. 이 연구는 가상가치평가법과 이용자 통계 분석방법을 병행하였으며 대상으로는 직접 이용자뿐만 아니라 간접 이용자를 포함하였다. 그 결과 South Carolina 공공도서관의 총 경제적 가치는 $1의 예산 대비 $4.48인 것으로 나타났으며, 이는 회기 분석(ROI)으로 환산했을 때 350%이다.

그 외 Noonan (2003)은 박물관이나 도서관과 같은 문화공간의 가치평가를 위해 가상가치평가법을 적용하여야 한다고 주장하였다. 이어 AabØ (2005)는 노르웨이 공공도서관의 가치평가를 위해 가상가치평가법을 적용하여 지불의사 추정액을 조사하였다. 그 결과 한 가구당 지급하는 세금의 4배에 달하는 편익이 공공도서관에서 발생한다는 결론을 내렸다.

이렇게 공공도서관의 가치를 측정하는 데 있어서 가장 보편적인 방법으로 알려진 가상가치평가법은 주로 해외에서 수행되어왔으며, 국내에서는 그 사례가 많지 않다. 한 예로 국립디지털도서관에서 건립사업에 앞서 경제성을 분석한 사례가 있다. 이 연구는 가상가치평가법을 이용하여 미래에 건립될 국립중앙도서관의 가치를 추정하였다. 판매가격이 만 원인 디지타이징 된 자료에 대한 사용자의 지불의사비용(willingness to pay)을 추정하였다. 여기에서 나온 지불의사비용에 디지타이즈 된 도서자료의 평균 판매가격을 곱하여 추정하였으며, 그 결과 편익-비용-비율이 1.7로 나타나 경제성이 있는 것으로 추정되었다.

헌법재판소 역시 도서관 신축의 경제적 타당성 분석을 위하여 가상가치평가법을 사용하였다. 이 연구에서 제시된 설문 문항은 "헌법재판소 도서실에서 이용해보신 경험이 있는 정보자료의 가치를 금전적으로 평가한다면 1회 이용 시 평균적으로 어느 정도의 금액이 됩니까?"이다. 평균 지불의사금액에 평균 개별 이용자의 연간도서관 이용횟수를 추정하여 헌법재판소 도서관의 경제적 가치를 추정하였다.

이 외에 정혜경(2005)은 "전문도서관을 위한 경제성 평가"에서 도서관의 가치는 도서관에서 제공하는 서비스의 합과 같거나 그 이상이라고 하였다. 그리고 제공서비스를 물적 서비스와 인적서비스로 구분하여 서비스별 이용통계와 지불의사금액을 각각의 서비스별로 구하는 방법을 제시하였다. 그 결과인 경제적 가치가 작게 나온 서비스에 대하여 문제점을 파악하고 분석하도록 제안하였다.

이와 같은 광범위한 이용에도 불구하고, 가상가치평가법은 여러 가지 원인으로 인하여 응답자의 정확한 지불의사금액을 왜곡시키고 있음을 지적하는 연구들이 수행되었다. Champ *et al.* (1997), Seip and Strand (1992), Navrud (1992)는 모두 가상가치평가로 인한 결과가 실제 가치보다 높게 책정되는 경향이 있어 신뢰하기 어렵다는 결론에 도달하였다.

가상가치평가법에서 나타나는 과대평가의 주요 요인은 제안된 금액에 대하여 '예'와 '아니오'만 대답할 수 있는 이선 선택형 질의로 인한 무의식 긍정(yea-saying)인 것으로 지적되었다. Ready, *et al.* (1995) 역시 응답자의 무의식 긍정이 가치를 과대평가하는 근원이라고 주장하였으며, Kanninen (1995)은 무의식 긍정자의 비율은 전체 응답자의 20%에 달한다는 통계적 수치를 발표하였다.

가상가치평가법의 결과를 왜곡시키는 또 하나의 원인으로 응답 거부(Protest answer bias)가 지적되었다. 이는 응답자들이 설문에 대하여 확실하게 이해하지 못하기 때문에 설문 응답을 거부하려고 하는 경향이다. 다시 말해서 응답자들은 설문지의 질문에 대하여 분명하게 이해하고 있지 못하거나, 도서관의 가치를 비용으로 환산하는 것에 대하여 익숙하지 못하기 때문에 본인의 지불의사금액에 대하여 확신하기 어렵다.

Champ et al. (1997)은 이를 파악하기 위해 응답자들에게 그들이 한 응답에 대하여 얼마나 확신하고 있는지에 대하여 '매우 확신하고 있다 (10)'부터 '확신이 전혀 없다(1)'까지 10개의 척도로 측정하였다. 이 연구에서 '10' 이하에 답한 응답자들의 지불의사금액을 '응답을 안 함'과 동일하게 처리하면, 실제 지불의사금액에 근접할 수 있다고 주장하였다.

한편 Ready et al. (1995)는 Opaluch and Segersen (1989)의 이론을 토대로 설문 응답자들이 지불의사금액을 추정하기 전에 보이는 모호한 (ambivalence) 느낌을 줄일 수 있다면, 훨씬 정확한 가치평가가 가능할 것이라고 주장하였다. Ready et al.에 따르면 '모호함'은 여러 가지 태도나 인지가 상반되어 있을 때 나타나는 감정으로 정의된다. 이러한 바이어스를 줄이기 위해서는 기존의 이선 선택형 질문보다는 선택할 수 있는 다양한 응답 문항을 제공하여 가장 비슷한 내용을 선택하도록 하는 것이 바람직하다고 주장하고 있다.

Ready et al.은 '응답자가 느끼는 모호함'을 줄이기 위하여 설문 문항을 추가하였으며 이를 Dissonance Minimizing(DM) 포맷이라고 명명하였다. 이는 다양한 응답 문항을 제공함으로써 응답자들이 지불의사금액과 관계없이 프로그램이나 서비스 자체를 지지하는지를 표현할 수 있도록 고안되어 있다. 이를 통하여 이용자들은 무의식 긍정과 응답 거부 바이어스를 줄일 수 있다는 것이 이 연구의 주장이다. Blamey *et al.* (1999) 역시 Ready가 주장한 DM 포맷은 가상가치평가법이 가지고 있는 주요한 문제점인 무의식 긍정과 응답 거부의 문제점을 해결해주는 데 중요한 역할을 한다는 부분에 동의하였다. DM 포맷에서 사용되는 문항은 다음과 같다.

다음의 문항에서 귀하의 의견에 가장 가까운 문항에 'O' 표를 하시오.

(1) 프로그램 A를 지지하며 이를 위하여 인상된 세금을 납부할 의사가 있다.

(2) 프로그램 A를 지지하며 여기에 세금의 사용은 허용하나, 이 프로그램을 위하여 $10 이상을 낼 수는 없다.

(3) 소득세를 올리지 않는다면, 프로그램 A를 지지하겠다.

(4) 얼마를 지불해야 하는지에 상관없이 프로그램 A를 지지할 수 없다.

여기에서 (1) 번을 선택한 사람은 비용을 지불하는 것에 대하여 '예'로 취급되는 반면, (2), (4)를 선택한 사람은 '아니오'로 취급될 것이다. 또한 (3)을 선택한 사람은 다시 구체적인 지급방법에 대하여 응답하는 단계를 거치게 될 것이다. 위에서 검토한 바와 같이 가상가치평가법을 적용할 때 응답자들의 진실한 지불의사금액을 왜곡시키도록 하는 바이어스에 관한 연구가 매우 중요한 부분을 차지함에도 이에 관한 연구는 공공도서관 분야에서 국내외적으로 수행된 사례가 거의 없다. 이에 대한 심도 있는 연구를 통하여 비시장재인 공공도서관의 가치가 제대로 추정될 수 있다면 가상가치평가법은 공공도서관의 가치를 평가하는 중요한 도구로 자리매김할 수 있을 것으로 기대한다.

3. 서비스의 경제적 가치평가를 위한 가상가치평가법

본 연구는 공공도서관의 대표 서비스를 이용하여 공공도서관의 경제성을 평가하며, 이를 평가하기 위한 기본적인 틀로 비용 편익분석방법을 사용한다. 이때 비용에는 서비스를 제공하기 위한 인적·물적 자원 투입비용을, 편익에는 서비스의 가치에 대한 지불의사금액을 적용한다. 선행연구에 따르면 기존 가상가치평가법을 적용하였을 경우, 공공도서관의 가치는 실제보다 과다하게 추정됐음이 입증되었다. 본 연구는 가상가치평가법에서 기본적으로 나타나는 바이어스로 인해 왜곡되는 결과를 통제하기 위해 DM 포맷을 적용할 것을 제안하였다.

DM 포맷은 기존의 전통적인 가상가치평가법을 적용하였을 때 나타날 수 있는 과다한 추정금액을 조정할 수 있는 대안으로써 사용되어왔으나 이를 사용하여 도서관의 가치를 평가하는데 이를 적용한 사례는 거의 찾아볼 수 없다. 본 연구는 국내 공공도서관의 가치를 추정하는 데 있어 DM 포맷을 적용하였을 때 기존의 가상가치평가법과 비교하여 지불의사금액이 어떻게 변화하는지, 그리고 그 원인은 무엇인지 분석하고자 한다. 공공도서관의 경제적 가치평가에 요구되는 비용과 편익은 다음과 같이 추정된다.

3.1 비용의 추정

공공도서관에서 제공하는 대표 서비스에 투입되는 비용은 크게 물적 자원비용 및 인적자원비용으로 구성된다. 여기서 물적 자원비용이란 도서관 서비스를 운영·유지하기 위하여 도서, 시설, 집기 등 물리적인 자원에 소요된 비용을 의미하며, 인적자원비용이란 이를 관리하는 인력을 고용하기 위해 소요된 비용을 의미한다. 비용을 추정하기 위한 산출식은 <표 1>과 같다.

<표 1> 서비스 비용 산출식

서비스 비용 = 물적 자원비용 + 인적자원비용

3.2 편익의 추정

편익[5])은 공공도서관의 서비스가 가지는 실제 특성 또는 상황을 가상적으로 설정하고, 이를 응답자에게 인식시킨 후 서비스 1회 이용에 대한 응답자의 지불의사금액을 통해 추정한다. <표 2> 참조.

<표 2> 서비스 편익 산출식

서비스 편익 = 응답자의 평균 지불의사금액 × 실제 이용횟수

기존의 가상가치평가법에서 사용된 문항들은 다음과 같다.

가) 서비스의 가치를 금전적 가치로 평가한다면, 어느 정도의 비용

---

5) 엄밀한 의미에서의 편익은 사용자가 서비스를 매번 이용할 때마다 발생하는 서비스에 대한 지불의사금액을 추정해야 하나 이는 실질적으로 거의 불가능한 작업임.

이라고 생각하십 니까?" _____원

나) 서비스의 추가 제공을 위해 <u>10,000원</u>의 비용(또는 세금으로)
을 지불해야 한다면 이에 응하시겠습니까?" 예 □ 아니오 □

설문 문항 가)는 가장 보편적으로 사용되는 사례이다. 설문 문항 나)의
경우는 설문자가 몇 가지 비용을 제안하고 응답자는 이에 '예'와 '아니
오'로만 응답하게 되어 있다. 한편, 본 연구에서는 가장 보편적으로 사용
되고 있는 설문 문항 가)를 이용하였으며, 응답법은 개방형으로 고안되
었다. 이는 설문자가 폐쇄형(closed-ended)을 통하여 의도적으로 지불의
사금액을 왜곡시키는 바이어스를 완화하고자 하는 것이다. 또한, 해당 서
비스를 이용해 본 경험이 있는 이용자만이 지불의사금액을 추정할 수 있
도록 제한하였다. 이는 본 연구가 공공도서관을 실제 이용함으로써
경험한 가치에 근거를 두고 경제성을 평가하기 때문이다.

3.2.1 기존 가상가치평가법

<그림 1>에서 보는 바와 같이 기존의 가상가치평가법은 해당 서
비스를 이용해 본 경험이 있는 응답자가 가상적으로 설정된 질문에
대하여 지불의사금액으로 응답하도록 구성되어 있다. 이러한 질문
유형은 응답자가 가상의 상황을 정확하게 파악할 수 있도록 정보제
공을 하거나, 분명하게 응답할 수 있는 충분한 문항이 없는 것이
일반적이다. 이러한 이유로 인하여 응답자는 응답을 회피하거나 정
확한 지불의사금액을 제시할 수 없게 된다. 따라서 지나치게 높게
가치가 평가되어 왜곡된 결괏값을 가지고 온 것으로 나타났다.

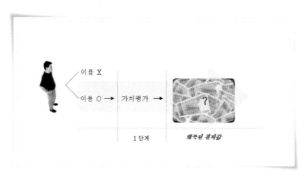

<그림 1> 기존의 가상가치평가법

3.2.2 Dissonance Minimizing (DM)

Blamey *et al.* (1999)와 Ready *et al.* (1995)에 의하여 제안된 DM 포맷을 공공도서관 서비스의 가치평가에 적용하였다. DM 포맷은 지불액수 또는 지불하는 방법 때문에 서비스를 지지하지 못하는 응답자들과 서비스 자체에 대하여 가치가 없다고 생각하여 서비스를 지지하지 않는 응답자들을 분리하도록 고안된 유형이다. 기존의 가상가치평가법에서 응답자들이 서비스 자체는 가치가 있다고 생각하고 있으나 지불방법 또는 액수 때문에 진실한 지불의사금액을 제시하지 못하거나 응답을 거부함으로써 나타나는 바이어스를 최소화하기 위한 것이다. 기존의 가상가치평가법에 2개의 문항을 추가하였으며, 그 문항들은 다음과 같다.

"이 서비스에 대한 귀하의 생각과 가장 근접한 문항에 체크하여 주십시오.

1) 가치가 있다고 생각한다. 따라서 비용을 지불할 의사가 있다.

2) 가치가 있다고 생각하나, 비용을 지불할 의사는 없다.

3) 가치가 있다고 생각하나, 상황에 따라 지불 여부를 결정할 것이다.

4) 가치가 없다고 생각하기 때문에 어떤 비용도 지불할 의사가 없다."

비용 지급 여부와 관련하여 (1) 번에 응답하는 사람은 '예'로, (2) 번과 (4) 번에 응답하는 사람은 '아니오'로, (3) 번에 응답하는 사람은 '조건부 예'로 구분되었다. 위의 문항에서 2) 번과 4) 번에 응답한 이용자는 지불의사금액에 응답하지 않고 다음 서비스로 넘어가게 된다. 그리고 1) 번에 응답한 경우에만 지불의사금액을 추정하는 항목으로 넘어가게 된다. 한편 3) 번에 응답한 자(조건부 '예')는 아래의 설문에 추가로 응답하게 되며, 본 연구가 설계한 문항 내용은 아래와 같다.

"상황에 따른 비용 지급에 대한 설문입니다. 귀하의 생각과 가장 근접한 문항에 체크 하여 주십시오.
  1) 국가의 예산이 부족하여 기존 세금으로 더 이상 지원받을 수 없다는 확신이 있는 경우에만 비용을 지불하겠다.
  2) 추가로 세금을 부과하지 않고 기존 세금으로 지원되는 경우에만 응하겠다.
  3) 적절한 수준의 비용이 제시된다면 지불할 의사가 있다."

위의 문항에서 2) 번에 응답한 응답자는 서비스에 대한 비용을 지불할 의사가 없으므로 지불의사금액을 제시하지 않게 되며, 1) 번과 3) 번에 응답한 이용자만 지불의사금액을 추정하게 되어 있다. <그림 2>에서 보는 바와 같이 기존의 가상가치평가법에서 이용자가 도서관의 가치를 지불의사금액으로 측정하기까지의 과정이 1단계였던 것에 비하여 DM 포맷을 적용한 가상가치평가법에서는 무의식 긍정과 응답 거부 바이어스를 감소시킬 수 있는 2단계를 더 추가하도록 고안되었다.

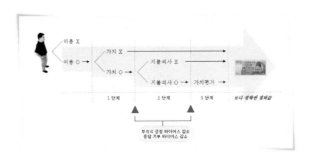

<그림 2> DM 포맷을 적용한 방법론

3.3 경제적 가치평가

공공도서관의 경제성은 한 해 동안 해당 서비스를 운영·유지하면서 발생한 비용과 창출된 편익을 비교함으로써 알 수 있으며 그 결과가 "1"을 초과하였을 때 그 서비스는 비용·효과적으로 운영되었다고 할 수 있다. 공공도서관 전체에 대한 가치평가와 개별 서비스에 대한 가치평가를 분리하여 분석하고자 한다. 공공도서관 서비스의 경제적 가치평가를 위한 산출식은 <표 3>과 같다.

<표 3> 공공도서관 서비스의 경제성 분석 산출식

경제성= 총 발생 편익(Benefit) / 총 발생 비용(Cost)

$$\frac{B}{C} = \sum_{n=0}^{n} \frac{B_n}{(1+r)^n} \div \sum_{n=0}^{n} \frac{C_n}{(1+r)^n}$$

4. 사례분석

'J 공공도서관'의 경제적 가치를 평가하기 위해 DM 포맷을 적용한 가상가치평가법을 사용하였다. 또한, 이를 기존의 가상가치평가법과 비교·분석하였다.

4.1 분석대상

1999년에 개관한 'J 공공도서관'은 40만 명 이상의 인근 주민을 대상으로 문화-교양센터 역할을 하고 있다. 본 연구에서는 'J 공공도서관'에서 제공하는 서비스 중 공공도서관의 대표적 서비스인 자료서비스, 시설서비스, 참고서비스, 그리고 교육 프로그램 서비스를 통하여 경제적 가치를 추정하고자 한다. 'J 공공도서관'은 자료서비스를 운영·유지하기 위하여 119,501종의 장서를 보유하고 있고, 시설서비스에는 개인 독서실, 컴퓨터 관련 각종 시설 등이 포함되어 있다. 또한, 17가지 교육 프로그램을 제공하고 있다. 대표적 서비스를 포함한 도서관 업무를 위하여 2007년 2월 현재 31명의 인력을 고용하고 있다. 여기에는 행정직 3명, 사서직 15명 등이 포함되어 있다.

4.2 자료수집방법

자료수집은 'J 공공도서관' 이용자를 대상으로 2006년 12월 26일부터 2007년 2월 2일까지 배포, 수거되었다. 설문지는 기존의 가상가치평가법을 적용한 "*설문 A*"와 DM 포맷을 적용한 "*설문 B*"의 형식으로 구분되어 무작위로 배포되었다. "*설문 A*"는 166명에게 배포되어 90부가 응답하였고(회수율 약 54%), 이 중 86부(활용률 약 96%)만이 유의미하였다. 한편 "*설문 B*"는 167명에게 배포되어 148부 응답하였고 (회수율 약 89%), 이 중 140부(활용률 약 95%)가 유의미하였다. 이때 영유아는 설문대상에서 제외되었으며, 1~3학년의 초등 아동들의 경우는 학부모가 대리로 작성하였다

4.3 결과

'J 공공도서관'의 대표 서비스에 대한 비용과 편익을 추정하였으며, 그 내용은 아래와 같다.

4.3.1 비용의 추정

비용에는 투입된 각 서비스의 물적 자원비용과 인적자원비용이 포함되었다.

1) 총 집행비용
2006년 한 해 동안 'J 공공도서관'을 운영하는 데 투입된 모든 예산을 의미한다.

2) 자료서비스
자료서비스를 운영·유지하기 위해 투입된 물적 자원비용으로 자료 구입비용(89,000,000원)을, 인적자원비용으로 수서 담당과 자료실에 근무하는 직원의 인건비용(179,138,416원)이 적용되었다.[6]

---

6) 종합자료실, 어린이 자료실, 유아 자료실 등 각 자료실에 근무하는 사서가 자료서비스와 참고서비스를 동시에 지원하고 있으므로 이들의 인적자원비용을 자료서비스와 참고서비스에서 50 : 50으로 나누어 적용하였음.

3) 시설서비스

도서관의 시설을 운영·유지하기 위해 투입된 물적 자원비용으로 개보수비용, 통신비, 수도·광열비, 공공요금 및 제세 비용(96,113,660원)을, 인적자원비용에 시설을 담당하는 직원의 인건비용(155,875,995원)이 적용되었다.

4) 참고서비스

참고서비스를 운영·유지하기 위한 인적자원에 자료실에서 근무하는 직원의 인건비용(111,249,265원)이 적용되었다. 단, 참고서비스는 물적 자원보다는 인적자원을 활용하여 제공하는 서비스이기 때문에 물적 자원에 투입된 비용은 여기서 배제되었다.

5) 교육 프로그램 서비스

도서관의 교육 프로그램을 운영·유지하기 위해 투입된 물적 자원비용으로 현수막, 홍보용 전단 비용(4,959,910원)을, 인적자원에 교육 프로그램을 담당하는 사서의 인건비와 시간강사비용(46,407,807원)이 적용되었고 그 내역은 <표 4>와 같다.

<표 4> 발생비용

	물적 자원비용(원)	인적자원비용(원)	합계(원)
총집행비용	667,039,360	471,946,992	1,138,986,352
자료제공 서비스	89,000,000	179,138,416	268,138,416
시설제공 서비스	96,113,660	155,875,995	251,989,655
참고 봉사 서비스	0	111,249,265	111,249,265
교육 프로그램 서비스	4,959,910	46,407,807	51,367,717

4.3.2 편익의 추정

'J 공공도서관'의 협조를 통해 2006년 한 해 동안의 이용통계를 근거로 편익을 추정하였다. 응답자에게 'J 공공도서관' 전체 서비스의 가치와 각각의 대표 서비스를 구분하여 지불의사금액을 작성하도록 요청하였다. 전체 서비스의 편익은 도서관에서 제공하는 전체 서비스의 가치에 대한 응답자의 평균 지불의사금액에 도서관 전체 이용자 수를 곱하여 추정되었다. 이때 기존의 가상가치평가법을 접한 이용자는 한 번 이용에 2,836원을 지불할 의사가 있다고 집계되어 총 편익이 3,365,330,892원으로 추정되었다. 반면 DM 포맷을 적용한 가상가치 평가법을 접한 응답자들은 한 번 이용에 804원을 지불할 의사가 있다고 집계되어 총 편익이 954,064,188원으로 추정되었다. 자료서비스의 편익 추정방법은 응답자들의 1회 자료이용 시 지불의사금액의 평균에 이용횟수인 대출·열람횟수를 곱해주었다. 기존의 가상가치평가법을 접한 응답자들은 평균 1,365원을 지불할 의사가 있는 것으로 집계되었고, 이에 이용횟수(열람횟수와 대출횟수)인 1,774,412(회)를 곱한 결과, 2,421,389,914(원)의 편익이 있는 것으로 추정되었다.

반면 DM 포맷을 적용한 가상가치평가법의 평균 지불의사금액은 88원으로 집계되어 편익이 156,148,256원인 것으로 추정되었다. 여기서 기존의 가상가치평가법과 DM 포맷을 적용한 가상가치평가법의 결과는 무려 15배 이상 차이가 나는 것으로 나타났다.

시설서비스의 편익은 도서관 시설에 대한 응답자들의 1회 시설이용 시 평균 지불의사금액에 실제 도서관 이용자 수를 곱하였다. 이때 기존의 가상가치평가법을 접한 응답자들은 1,437원을 지불할 의사가 있으며, 도서관 이용자 수(1,186,647명)를 곱한 결과 1,705,211,739원의 편익이 발생한 것으로 추정되었다. 한편 DM 포맷의 평균 지불의사금액은 157원이며, 여기에 도서관 이용자 수를 곱한 결과 186,303,579원 편익이 발생한 것으로 추정되었다. 전반적으로 DM 포맷을 적용한 가상가치평가법의 평균 지불의사금액은 기존의 가상가치평가법보다 낮게 나타났다. 그 이유는 아래와 같다.

첫째, DM 포맷을 적용한 가상가치평가법에 무의식적 긍정과 응답 거부를 감소시킬 수 있는 2가지 문항이 추가되었고, 둘째, 질문 2), 3)에서 '지불할 의사가 없다'라고 응답한 자 중 무의식적으로 질문 4)에서 제시한 1원 이상의 금액은 모두 0원으로 처리되었기 때문이라고 볼 수 있다. 즉 무의식 긍정 바이어스를 통제하였기 때문이다. 이러한 요인들로 인하여 평균 지불의사금액이 더욱 보수적으로 측정되었다고 볼 수 있다. 이 외 기존의 가상가치평가법과 DM 포맷을 적용한 가상가치평가법을 적용한 참고서비스의 편익이 약 17배 이상 차이가 났다. <표 5> 참조.

데이터 분석 시 응답자가 가상가치를 구체적인 금액 대신 범위를 설정한 경우에는 그 중간값을 책정하여 분석하였다. 예를 들어 응답자가 '1,500원~2,500원'으로 제시한 경우에는 '2,000원'으로 책정하였다. 몇몇 응답자의 경우 지불의사금액에 대한 답변 시 이용자들은 도서관이 공공재라고 생각하고 있어서 가치를 금액으로 측정하는 것에 대하여 매우 부정적인 반응을 드러냈다.

<표 5> 발생 편익

서비스 종류	방법론 A	방법론 B	비율 비교
전체 서비스	3,365,330,892	954,064,188	3.53 : 1

서비스 종류	방법론 A	방법론 B	비율 비교
자료 서비스	2,421,389,914	156,148,256	15.51 : 1
시설 서비스	1,705,211,739	186,303,579	9.15 : 1
참고 서비스	675,952,722	38,873,574	17.39 : 1
교육 프로그램 서비스	16,764,332	26,495,768	0.63 : 1

기존의 가상가치평가법과 DM 포맷을 적용한 가상가치평가법의 평균 지불의사금액을 Pearson Correlation의 Two-tailed test를 이용하여 상관관계를 알아보았다. <표 6>에서 보는 바와 같이 자료이용의 편익 상관계수가 -.349이며 유의지수가 .000, 시설제공서비스 역시 상관관계가, -.394이며 유의지수가 .000으로 나타나 음의 상관관계가 있는 것으로 나타났다. 이 외 3가지 측정 서비스의 결과 모두 가상가치평가법의 종류와 상관관계가 있는 것으로 나타났다. 즉, 대체로 DM 포맷을 적용한 가상가치평가법을 접한 응답자들이 기존의 가상가치평가법을 접한 응답자들보다 낮은 지불의사금액을 제시하였다. 결과적으로 2가지 가상가치평가법의 지불의사금액은 유의한 차이가 있는 것으로 나타났다.

<표 6> 방법론과 서비스별 지불의사와의 상관관계

		방법론	자료제공	시설제공	참고 봉사	교육 프로그램	전체 서비스
방법론	Pearson Correlation	1	-.349**	-.394**	-.313**	.185**	-.239**
	Sig. (2 tailed)		.000	.000	.000	.018	.001
	N	226	226	216	215	152	196

* Correlation is significant at the 0.05 level(2-tailed)
** Correlation is significant at the 0.05 level(2-tailed)

자료서비스 이용자를 대상으로 한 응답자 중 '가치가 있고 비용을 지불할 의사가 있다'라고 답한 경우는 6명(5.61%)이지만, '가치가 있으나 지불의사가 없다'라고 답한 응답자는 10배 이상인 70명(65.42%)으로 집계되었다. 시설제공서비스의 경우 '가치가 있고 비용을 지불할 의사가 있다'라고 답한 응답자는 14명(11.48%)이며, '가치는 있으나 비용을 지불할 의사는 없다'라고 답한 응답자는 4배 이상인 71명(58.20%)으로 집계되었다.

이 외 '가치가 있다고 생각하나, 상황에 따라 지불의사를 결정할 것이다'라고 답한 응답자는 자료서비스에서 23명(21.50%), 시설서비스에서 30명(24.59%)으로 집계되었다. 이는 기존의 가상가치평가법에서는 원하는 응답이 설문에 없거나 지불방법 또는 지불금액 때문에 모호한 상태에 있는 응답자들에게서 흔히 나타날 수 있는 응답 거부 바이어스가 감소한 경우라고 분석할 수 있다. <표 7> 참조

<표 7> 지불의사에 대한 응답자들의 의사 빈도

번호		자료 서비스(명)	시설 서비스(명)	참고 서비스(명)	교육 프로그램 서비스(명)
가치 판단 및 지불 여부	2-1. 가치가 있고 비용을 지불할 의사가 있다.	6(5.61%)	14(11.48%)	5(16.13%)	10(41.67%)
	2-2. 가치는 있으나 비용을 지불할 의사는 없다.	70(65.42%)	71(58.20%)	24(77/42%)	9(37.60%)
	2-3. 가치가 있다고 생각하나, 상황에 따라 지불의사를 결정할 것이다.	23(21.50%)	30(24.59%)	1(3.23%)	4(16.6%)
	2-4. 가치가 없으며 비용을 지불할 의사가 없다.	7(6.54%)	6(4.92%)	1(3.23%)	1(4.17%)
	무응답	1(0.93%)	1(0.82%)	0(%)	0(%)

번호		자료 서비스(명)	시설 서비스(명)	참고 서비스(명)	교육 프로그램 서비스(명)
지불 방법	3-1. 국가 예산이 부족한 경우 지불할 의사가 있다.	5(21.74%)	9(30.00%)	1(100%)	1(25%)
	3-2. 추가로 세금을 내지 않 으며 기존 세금으로 지원되 는 경우에만 지지한다.	8(34.79%)	8(26.67%)	0(0%)	1(25%)
	3-3. 적절한 비용이 제시된 다면 지불할 의사가 있다.	10(43.48%)	12(40.00%)	0(0%)	1(25%)
	무응답	0(0%)	1(3.33%)	0(0%)	1(25%)
금액	4. 가격 제시	104(97.20%)	116(95.08%)	31(100%)	21(87.5%)

4.3.3 경제성 분석

기존의 가상가치평가법과 DM 포맷을 적용한 가상가치평가법을 적용한 편익에 실제 발생한 비용을 나누어 경제성을 추정하였다. 기존의 가상가치평가법을 적용한 결과 대체로 경제성이 높게 추정되었다. DM 포맷을 적용한 가상가치평가법에서 모든 서비스의 측정 결과가 '1' 이하로 경제성이 없는 것으로 나타났다. 그 내용은 <표 8>과 같다. 전체 서비스의 편익을 제외한 결과, 기존의 가상가치평가법에서는 자료서비스가 경제성이 가장 높은 것으로 나타났고, DM 포맷을 적용한 가상가치평가법에서는 전체 서비스의 경제성이 가장 높은 것으로 나타났다.

<표 8> 경제성 분석

서비스 종류	방법론 A	방법론 B	비율
전체 서비스	2.95	0.84	3.53 : 1
자료 서비스	9.03	0.58	15.51 : 1
시설 서비스	6.77	0.74	9.15 : 1
참고 서비스	6.08	0.35	17.39 : 1

서비스 종류	방법론 A	방법론 B	비율
교육 프로그램 서비스	0.33	0.52	0.63 : 1

4.3.4 인구통계학적 분석

총 응답자를 인구통계학적 측면에서 분석한 결과는 <표 9>와 같다. 26세에서 34세 사이의 응답자가 62명(27.4%)으로 가장 많은 비중을 차지하고 있었고, 성별로는 여자 응답자가 128명(56%)으로 반수 이상인 것으로 나타났다. 직업 측면에서는 학생이 94명(41.6%)으로 가장 많은 수를 차지했다. 이때 신분이 "학생"이라고 표기된 응답자의 최종학력은 최종학력을 재학 이전 학력으로 인정하였다. 두 가지의 신분에 체크한 경우는 무효로 처리되었다.

<표 9> 인구통계학적 분석

번호	나이	성별	직업	최종학력
1	17세 이하 42명(18.6%)	남 90명(39.8%)	회사원 16명(7.1%)	초등학교 36명 (15.9%)
2	28세~25세 44명(19.5%)	여 128명(56.6%)	자영업 8명(3.5%)	중학교 7명 (3.1%)
3	26세~34세 62명(27.4%)	무응답 8명(3.5%)	학생 94명(41.6%)	고등학교 40명 (17.7%)
4	35세~44세 56명(24.8%)	-	주부 49명(21.7%)	대학교 131명 (58.0%)
5	45세~54세 14명(6.2%)	-	공무원 11명(4.9%)	대학원 이상 9명 (4.0%)
6	55세~64세 6명(2.7%)	-	기타 45명(19.9%)	무응답 3명 (1.3%)
7	65세 이상 2명(0.9%)	-	무응답 3명(1.3%)	-
8	무응답 0명(0%)	-	-	-

집단별로 지불의사비용의 상관관계에 대하여 살펴보았다. 나이로 구

분한 집단과 최종학력으로 구분한 집단이 자료제공, 시설제공을 포함한 4가지 서비스에서 모두 상관관계가 있는 것으로 나타났다. 성별로는 교육 프로그램 부분에서 상관관계가 있는 것으로 나타났고, 직업별로는 상관관계가 없는 것으로 나타났다. 특히 최종학력 집단과 서비스를 분석하였을 때 시설제공과 참고 봉사 서비스에서 학력이 높을수록 지불의사금액이 줄어드는 것으로 나타났다. <표 10> 참조

<표 10> 집단별 서비스 지불의사와의 상관관계

		자료이용	시설제공	참고 봉사	교육 프로그램	전체 서비스
나이	Pearson Correlation	-.155**	-.187**	-.233**	.182*	-.159*
	Sig. (2 tailed)	.022	.006	.004	.020	.026
	N	216	215	152	163	196
최종 학력	Pearson Correlation	-.192**	-.279**	-.292**	-.243**	-.176*
	Sig. (2 tailed)	.005	.000	.000	.002	.014
	N	213	212	151	162	194

* Correlation is significant at the 0.05 level(2-tailed)
** Correlation is significant at the 0.05 level(2-tailed)

5. 결론

가상가치평가법은 공공도서관의 가치를 정량적으로 평가하기 위한 거의 유일한 방법으로 인정되었다. 그런데도 응답자의 진실한 지불의사금액을 왜곡시키는 여러 가지 바이어스가 발생한다는 지적을 받아왔다. 여기에서 응답자의 지불의사금액 '0원'에는 서비스에 대하여 가치가 있다고 생각하나 제시한 지불방법 또는 제안된 지불 액수에 반대하는 응답자들이 포함되어 있다. 이러한 이유로 본 연구는 DM 포맷이 기존

의 가상가치평가법에서 지나치게 과대평가되는 결괏값을 보완하기 위하여 제안되었다. DM 포맷이 적용된 가상가치평가가 그렇지 않은 가상가치평가와의 지불의사금액의 차이, 그리고 우려되는 바이어스들이 감소하였는지에 대한 분석이 사례분석을 통하여 이루어졌다.

사례분석 결과 DM 포맷이 적용된 가상가치평가법이 기존의 가상가치평가법을 적용하였을 때보다 지불의사금액이 크게 낮게 나타났으며, 이는 DM 포맷이 응답자의 모호함을 해결함으로써 무의식 지불의사금액을 표현하는 응답자가 많이 감소한 것으로 분석되었다.

그러나 본 연구가 제안한 DM 포맷 역시 공공도서관의 가치평가를 위한 완벽한 도구가 될 수 없다. 왜냐하면, 응답자들은 여전히 비시장재의 가치를 정량적으로 평가하는 데 익숙하지 않으며 설문에서 사용되는 가상적인 상황이나 설정을 확실하게 이해하지 못하고 있기 때문이다. 따라서 더 정확하게 공공도서관의 가치를 평가할 수 있는 보완된 포맷의 개발이 시급한 시점이다. 또한, 본 연구에서는 평균 지불의사금액 추정 시 비이용자를 제외한 측정 서비스를 실제로 1회 이상 이용해본 자들만을 대상으로 실시하였다는 것이 한계점으로 지적되었다.

참고문헌

정혜경. 2005. "전문도서관 서비스의 경제적 가치평가를 위한 분석모형 개발", 정보관리학회지, 22(3): 147-162.

AabØ, Svanhild. 2005. "The Value of Public Libraries", http://www.ifla.org/IV/ifla71/Programme.htm.

Barron, Daniel D., Williams, Robert V., Bajjaly, Stephen, Arms, Jennifer, and Wilson, Steven. The Economic Impact of Public Libraries on South Carolina: a Study Prepared by the School of Library and Information Science: University of South Carolina.

Blamey, R.K., J.W. Bennett and M.D. Morrison. 1999. "Yea-Saying in Contingent Valuation Surveys", *Land Economics* 75(1): 126-141.

Champ, P.A., R.C. Bishop, T.C. Brown, and D.W. McCollum. 1997 "Using Donation Mechanisms to Value Nonuse Benefits From Public Goods", *Journal of Environmental Economics and Management* 33(2): 151-62.

Cummings, R.G., Harrison, G.W., and Rutstrom. 1995. "Homegrown Values and Hypothetical Surveys: Is the Dichotomous choice Approach Incentive-Compatible?" *American Economic Review* 85 (1): 260-66.

Griffiths, J.M. and King, D.W. 1993. "Special Libraries: Increasing the Information Edge." Washington, D.C.: Special Libraries Association.

Griffiths, J-M. and King, Donald W. 1994. "Libraries: the Undiscovered National Resources." in the Value and Impact of Information." London, Bowker-Saur. (British Library Research: Information Policy Issues): 79-116.

Holt, GE, Elliott, D. and Moore, A. 1999. "Placing a Value on Public Library Services", *Public Libraries* (March/April): 98-108.

Kanninen, B. 1995. "Bias in Discrete Response Contingent Valuation." *Journal of Environmental Economics and Management* 28:114-25.

Morris, A., Hawkins, M. and Sumsion, J. 2001. "The Economic Value of Public Libraries", The Council for Museums: Archives and Libraries.

Morris, A., Sumsion, J., and Hawkins, M. 2002. "Economic Value of Public Libraries in the UK", *Libri* (52): 78-87.

Navrud, S. 1992. 'Willingness to Pay for Preservation of Species: an Experiment with Actual Payments. In Pricing the European Environment, ed. S. Navrud. New York: Oxford University Press.

Noonan, D.S. 2003. "Contingent Valuation and Cultural Resources: a Meta-Analytic Review of the Literature", *Journal of Cultural Economics* (27): 159-176.

Opaluch, J.J. and Segerson, K. 1989. "Rational Roots of 'Irrational' Behavior: New Theories of Economic Decision-Making." *Northern Journal of Agricultural and Resource Economics* 18 (Oct.): 81-95.

Poll, Roswitha. 2003. "Measuring Impact and Outcome of Libraries." *Performance Measurement and Metrics* 4(1): 5-12.

Ready, R.C., J.C. Whitehead and G.C. Bloomquist (1995). Contingent Valuation When Respondents Are Ambivalent. *Journal of Environmental Economics and Management* 29: 181-196.

Seip, K. and Strand, J. 1992. "Willingness to Pay for Environmental Goods in Norway: a Contingent Valuation Study with Real Payment." *Environmental and Resource Economics* 12:191-208.

Viscusi, W.K., W.A. Magat and J. Huber, 1991. "Pricing Environmental Health Risks: Survey Assessments of Risk-Risk and Risk-Dollar Trade-Offs for Chronic Bronchitis." *Journal of Environmental Economics and Management* 21 (1): 32-51.

The Contingent Valuation Method in Public Libraries[7])

This study aims to present a new model measuring the economic value of public libraries, combining the dissonance minimizing (DM) and information bias minimizing (IBM) format in the contingent valuation (CV) surveys. The possible biases which are tied to the conventional CV surveys are reviewed. An empirical study is presented to compare the model with the conventional CVM and DM format. A cost-benefit analysis is used as a tool to determine if the benefit of public libraries outweighs the cost incurred in providing the services. The study conducts a case study in a public library to demonstrate how public libraries could apply the approach to their local studies.

---

7) 이 논문은 2008년 Journal of Librarianship and Information Science 40권 2호.(71~80쪽)에 게재되었음.

1. Introduction

1.1 Purpose of the study

Identifying the value of public libraries is critical to the survival and requisite to the strategic development of public libraries. How can the economic value or impact of public libraries be measured? The value has often been assessed in terms of both amount of use and performance measurement. However, neither of these methods is conducive to quantitative evaluation and do not equate the total benefits received by library users.

A number of recent papers have derived willingness to pay (WTP) in the CVM to elicit the monetary value of public library services. However, some studies (Loomis *et al.* 1996; Champ *et al.* 1997; Navrud, 1992) found the WTP value derived from the CVM to be a less than satisfactory predictor of actual value, concluding that the results exceeded those revealed in experimental or real-life markets.

One possible explanation for the unsatisfactory values is the presence of potential biases inherent to the design of the CV survey: yea-saying, protest answers and information bias, etc. Some of these biases overestimate while others underestimate actual WTP.

Recognizing the existence of such potential biases, several studies have provided new approaches in the CVM. Blamey *et al.* (1999) and Ready *et al.* (1995) proposed the dissonance minimizing (DM) format to minimize the possible yea-saying bias and proved that the DM was a more robust elicitation format, providing lower estimates of WTP than the dichotomous choice (DC) format. The DC format provides only one price out of a range of determined prices, and respondents are allowed to decide if their WTP is higher or lower than the price suggested.

This paper, therefore, raises the question of whether or not the DM format could substitute for assessing the economic value of public libraries by reducing any possible biases arising from the CVM. Throsby (2003) defines economic value as a "good or (preferably) money which comprises any direct use value of the cultural good or service in question and whatever non-market values it may give rise to."

And CVM involves directly asking people, in a hypothetical survey, how much they would be willing to pay for specific services. In this study, the economic value of public libraries means the mean WTP value of library services derived from CVM, with emphasis on its value to the user.

The main purpose of the study is to find a way of assessing the economic value of public libraries. This study proposes a new approach to combining the DM and IBM format in determining the economical value of public libraries using the CVM. As a result, this study lends guidance on how to execute a CV study for public library services. To this end, this study takes the following steps :

1) Presents a new approach (DM + IBM) to determine the economical value of public libraries based on previous research;

2) Designs survey questionnaires for the proposed model; and

3) Conducts a case study at the Jungrang Public Library (Korea) to demonstrate how the WTP value in the new model differs from those revealed in the conventional CVM and DM format + IBM format.

1.2 Potential biases discussed in the study

In our CV study, we focus on the yea-saying bias, protest answer bias and information bias among all biases, which may possibly occur in the process of execution as well as designing of a CV survey:

1) Yea-saying: Yea-saying is defined as the tendency to answer "yes" or "overestimating" when responding to CV questions as a result of expressing one's motivation instead of specifying a true preference. The yea-saying bias may be reduced in the DM format by allowing respondents to express their multiple attitudes.

2) Protest answers: A protest answer is defined as the tendency to refuse to answer at all since respondents oppose the payment vehicle, i.e. the use of a levy, but not actually the

program itself. Another possible source for protest answers may be respondents' ambivalence over trade-offs between money and changes in levels of a good (Ready *et al.*, 1995). The bias may be reduced in the DM format by allowing respondents to choose one of the categories in the follow-up question, intended to extract an absolute answer from the protest respondent.

3) Information bias: Respondents may not give valid and reliable answers to WTP questions since they are clearly unfamiliar with library services being valued and can not relate to the hypothetical situation (McFadden and Leonard, 1993; Boyle *et al.* 1993; Ready *et al.* 1995).

2. Literature Review

For the past two decades, the CVM has been widely used for valuing non-market goods developed in environmental economics, which is at the fore in CV technique development. In a well-known article on contingent donations to a public good in environmental economics, Champ *et al.* (1997) considers two experiments: 1) they ask respondents whether they would contribute k to the provision of the good, and 2) they ask a different set of respondents to contribute k towards the provision of the public good in question.

In the last decade, the CV method has been used to value various cultural goods, such as museums, theatres, and libraries (Noonan, 2003). There are a few previous CV studies in public libraries. Harless and Allen (1999) valued the reference service in a single library at Virginia. The study aimed to provide a better understanding of their total value, both use and non-use value. The 10 percent trimmed mean indicated that, on average, students were willing to pay $5.59 per semester to maintain the current hours of the reference desk.

Morris *et al.* (2001, 2002) estimated the proxy price for borrowing books in public libraries. Respondents were asked when they returned the books if they had benefited from them. Applying the WTP values, it was found that the value of borrowing the books amounted to about 7 to 8 percent of the purchase price of the book.

The St Louis Public Library (SLPL) Services Valuation Study team produced a guide, 'How to quantify the benefits of your library', complete with a very useful table of priced individual services. In applying the methodology, the research team used three cost-benefit analysis techniques: consumer surplus, cost of time, and contingent valuation. Based on a collected evaluation of all three methods, their final estimate showed a cost-benefit ratio of 1:4 (Holt *et al.*, 1999).

In a study of public libraries in Florida, McClure et al. (2001) requested to indicate in dollar terms the value to them of individual library programs and services. The total of these calculations was taken to equal the total benefits received by library users. Taxpayer investment was subtracted from total benefits to give a total return on investment. The key finding was a return of US$ 6.27 for every tax dollar invested.

In a similar study, commissioned by the Florida Department of State, State Library and Archives of Florida used several methods of which CV was one. This study found that overall Florida's public libraries returned $ 6.54 for every $1 invested (Florida, 2004). In the study of the British Library, the CV method was used to assess the value of the library, both the value enjoyed directly by users of the library and indirectly by UK citizens. The study showed a benefit-cost ratio of 4.4:1 (British Library, 2002).

However, there has been considerable controversy over whether the CV method adequately measures people's WTP for public goods. A number of recent papers have provided estimates of WTP derived in CVM surveys exceeding those revealed in experimental or real-life markets. Arrow, et al. (1993) discusses the drawbacks to the CV studies concerning the design of CV surveys, including yea-saying bias, embedding effect[8] and other biases.

Loomis, et al. (1996) reported the hypothetical WTP was twice that of actual WTP. In other studies, Champ, et al. (1997),

---

8) Respondents may not differentiate between the scales of a program. In order to remove the embedding effect, the split-sample survey and different scales of a program are required (Bonato, et al., 2001).

Duffield and Patterson (1991), and Navrud (1992) found the contingent value to be less than satisfactory predictors of actual contingent value. They concluded that hypothetical markets tended to overstate WTP for private as well as public goods. This is why the CVM has potential biases which concern the design of the CV survey such as yea-saying, protest answers, and information bias.

McFadden and Leonard (1993), Boyle *et al.* (1993), Ready *et al.* (1995), and Kanninen (1995) all said yea-saying in the CVM was a factor in the tendency to overestimate values. According to Kanninen's study (1995), when the CVM method was used, the portion of yea-sayers of all respondents was 20%.

The two main approaches to elicit WTP values are open-ended (OE)[9] and closed-ended (CE)[10] questions. OE questions are criticized as being too difficult for respondents leading to a large number of non-responses or protest zero responses (Johannesson *et al.*, 1991). Therefore the approach requires some kind of aid to make it easier for the respondent to answer the valuation.

In another approach, the CE question is a very popular elicitation technique for CV surveys since it is most similar to market transactions. However, it also has drawbacks in that the maximum WTP is not elicited directly, but only as a discrete indicator, which makes the CE questions a rather inefficient method.

---

9) In open-ended questions, respondents are simply requested to name their value for a public good.

10) In closed-ended questions, respondents are only asked whether or not they would pay a single price out of a range of predetermined prices.

One possible source for protest answers could be respondents' ambivalence over trade-offs between money and changes in levels of a good. If respondents are ambivalent, they might answer "no" even if they care for the good (Ready *et al.*, 1995). According to Blamey *et al.* (1999), some respondents may answer "no" or refuse to answer at all because they oppose the payment vehicle, i.e. the use of a levy, but not the program itself. Depending on how these protest answers are treated, substantial differences in estimated WTP can occur.

Some studies have provided modified CV formats to ascertain the actual value of a public good. Blamey *et al.* (1999) designed the dissonance minimizing (DM) format to remove protest answer bias from the survey sample. In the DM format designed by Blamey *et al.*, respondents are presented with up to five questions that distinguish those respondents who support the program from those who oppose it entirely. To test for possible answers against the payment vehicle, respondents who support the program but are not willing to pay the price are given three more statements.

The study did an empirical comparison of the DM format with other elicitation formats, the dichotomous choice (DC) format and ambivalence-reducing polychotomous choice (PC) format. The study affirmed that the DM would be a more robust elicitation format, providing lower estimates of WTP than the DC format.

AabØ (2005) applied two different CVM elicitation formats, the DM format and multiple bounded discrete choice data (MBDC) to correct for possible overestimation of value of the good in question. Given a pressed economic situation, one half of the respondents were asked their WTP to keep their local public library, while the other half were asked to indicate their WTA to compensate for their library to close down. Of the two groups of respondents, four additional subgroups were created in which two valuation questions were asked; one asked in one of the two CVM elicitation formats, the other open-ended.

The article determined the value of the Norwegian public libraries in monetary terms using the benefit-cost analysis and CVM. The WTP estimate was close to the average annual library costs per household in Norway, while the WTA estimate was five times higher. Based on a collected evaluation of both methods, their final estimate showed a cost-benefit ratio of 1:4. On the other hand, the information that respondents have regarding the hypothetical commodity is crucial for a CV survey, since they may not be very familiar with it.

Viscusi *et al.* (1991) and Krupnick and Cropper (1992) found that respondents who are not familiar with Alzheimer's disease (AD) can not give valid and reliable answers to WTP questions about AD. The study was designed to give respondents some information about AD and check whether they have or had experiences with AD, before asking the valuation question. Results demonstrated that the values between informed and uninformed respondents differed significantly.

If no library or information service were provided, people would have to obtain the information in some other way. The cost of their doing this by the next best method is the alternative cost of the service. Ready *et al.* (1995) proposes a set of options to minimize the ambivalence respondents feel when "forced to make difficult trade-offs between competing objectives" (p.182). Such ambivalence is held to result in protest or overestimating (yea-saying). Although modifications to survey instruments with a view to reducing information bias as well as protest answers bias would appear prospective, little progress has been made with regard to elicitation formats for CVM.

3. Methodology

A cost-benefit analysis is used as a tool to determine the economic value of public libraries if the benefits of public libraries outweigh the cost incurred in providing the services. The cost is based on the price of providing the services, and the benefit is measured by the estimated WTP value derived in CVM. To measure the benefit, respondents are asked to indicate how much they are willing to pay for the service. The total of the calculations is then taken to equal the total benefit received by library users.

The study used net benefit and the ratio of benefit to cost (B/C ratio) as economic analysis tools, which have often been used to evaluate investment alternatives. Net benefit is the total cost of input subtracted from the total benefits. To measure the ratio of benefit to cost, the benefit is divided by the cost. If B/C is positive, a prospective project is positive; if B/C is negative, then the project probably should be rejected.

The study also used open-ended questions in the survey. Closed-ended questions are vulnerable to biases associated with the price ranges used, which are derived from the bids that are chosen directly by the respondents, thereby influencing their valuation. According to Bonato *et al.* (2001), open-ended questions are better than closed-ended questions for directly eliciting maximum WTP.

This study explores the feasibility of using the DM format and presents a new approach measuring the economic value of public libraries, combining the DM and IBM format. An empirical comparison is done to compare the DM + IBM format with the conventional CVM and DM format.

3.1 Dissonance-minimizing (DM) format

In the previous studies, the DM format was proposed to reduce respondents' ambivalence when formulating their responses in CV surveys. The concept of ambivalence has much in common with the psychological phenomenon of cognitive dissonance studies. Reber (1985) defines cognitive dissonance as an "emotional state set up when two simultaneously held attitudes or cognitions are inconsistent or when there is a conflict between belief and overt behavior." In the DM model, we propose two questions based on the theory of Ready *et al.* (1995) and Blamey *et al.* (1999):

"Which of the following four statements most closely resembles your view?"

(1) I support the service and can afford payment.

(2) I support the service but can not afford payment.

(3) I support the service depending on the condition.

(4) I oppose the service regardless of the cost.

Allowing respondents to indicate which of the above categories most closely resembles their view is intended to reduce their multiple feelings. Choosing category e treated as negative responses. Those who choose category (3) are immediately asked to respond to a follow-up question. Respondents might overestimate the WTP value or might have refused to answer any of the WTP valuation questions because of the use of a levy but not (1) would be treated as a positive response, whereas choosing categories (2) or (4) would be because of the program itself if the DM format was not used in the CV survey. A follow-up question is added to distinguish those respondents who support the program from those who oppose it regardless of the payment vehicle as follows:

"Which of the following three statements most closely resembles your view?"

(1) I would pay a fee of any amount for the service if I were convinced that the government itself did not have enough public funds to pay for the service.

(2) I would pay a fee of any amount for the service only if it were funded out of existing taxes.

(3) I would pay if the suggested price seemed appropriate.

Respondents who chose (1) and (3) would be treated as a "yes" response and further asked to identify their WTP for the library service, whereas those who chose (2) would be treated as no response. The WTP value from the DM format is expected to be much lower than that derived from the conventional CVM format as a result of reduced yea-saying and protest answer bias. Early results demonstrated that the biases may be minimized with the use of the DM format by allowing respondents to express their multiple attitudes. The study presents the following hypothesis:

H1: The WTP value depending on the DM format is expected to be much lower than that of the conventional CVM.

3.2 Potential biases in the CM format

Without the use of the DM format in the conventional CVM, respondents tend to answer "yes" or refuse to answer any of the valuation questions. The DM question was designed to reduce the occurrence of yea-saying and protest answers, which are problems typically associated with conventional CVM questions.

However, it is also premature to label the DM format the perfect substitute for estimating the economic valuation of public libraries. Previous studies demonstrated that some biases are still to be expected in the DM format due to the lack of information about that which is being valued or the hypothetical question.

3.3 DM + IBM format

Based on the assumption that the information bias may also lead to the rejection of a significant number of valid responses, the study proposed a new modified CVM format measuring the economic value of public libraries, combining the DM and the information bias minimizing (IBM) format. The format was developed based on the concept that the more information one can acquire the better of a decision that can be made.

The new model makes the scenario as realistic as possible by providing respondents with the appropriate information and presenting alternative costs on the services being valued. We assume that use of the DM format gives more valid and reliable WTP values when it is accompanied by the appropriate information compared to when the respondent does not have the information at all.

If estimated WTP values derived in the DM format between informed and uninformed respondents differ significantly, information bias may be the problem. The study provides two questions for the IBM format: one is intended to give respondents information about the service being valued, and the other is to provide alternative options of the service in the real market. The example designed for the library material loan service in this study is as follows:

1) Information tip

"The Jungrang Public Library provides 120,000 titles to the public free of charge, including literature, non-literature, and other genres. The average purchasing price is 11,000 won for domestic books and 50,000 won for overseas books. The annual budget reaches 100 million won."

2) Alternative option

"Assume that there is no library to provide you library material loan service. Which alternative would you choose to replace this service?"

The alternative options are listed differently depending on how the library service is being valued. Options might include a bookstore, other public libraries, book loan stores, and other alternatives designed to elicit estimate WTP values for the library material loan service. The study presents the following hypotheses:

H2: If the WTP values derived in the DM format between informed and uninformed respondents differ significantly, information bias may be a problem.

H3: The WTP value derived in the DM + IBM format is expected to be higher than that for DM only.

3.4 WTP valuation question

The study checks whether survey participants have had any experience with the service before asking the valuation questions. The WTP question for library material loan service is as follows:

"Suppose that this library did not exist anymore. How much in fees would you be willing to pay for the item you loaned, taking into consideration the benefits of libraries to your life?"

The study calculates three WTPs for three formats (conventional CVM, DM, and DM + IBM). Suppose the mean WTP value of a service is 3,000 won, use frequency of the service is 1,500 won, and the cost of providing the service is 4,000,000 won. To obtain the total benefit (4,500,000 won) of the service, the mean WTP value, 3,000 won, is multiplied by use frequency of the service, 1,500 won. The cost of providing the service (4,000,000 won) is then divided by the benefit (4,500,000 won) to obtain the economic value of the service and B/C ratio of 1.125. (see Table 1) The calculation procedure to determine the economic value of a service is as follows:

1) Add all the respondents' WTP values for the service;
2) Divide the total values by the number of respondents to elicit the mean WTP value;
3) Multiply the mean WTP value by use frequency of the service to get the benefit; and
4) Then divide the cost of providing the service by the benefit

<Table 1> WTP value formulation for a service

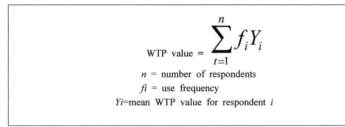

$$\text{WTP value} = \sum_{t=1}^{n} f_i Y_i$$

n = number of respondents
f_i = use frequency
Y_i=mean WTP value for respondent i

4. Case Study

The main purpose of the case study was to confirm how the new model (DM + IBM) produces different WTP values from the conventional CVM and DM format. The case study demonstrates how public libraries could apply the approach to their local studies and was developed by taking a random sample from the Jungrang Public Library in Seoul, Korea.

Located in the Jungrang district in the northeastern part of Seoul, the library focuses on the provision of information and life-long education opportunities. The library was opened in March 1999 and expanded in 2004 and contains a room for the handicapped and the elderly, infants, children, audio-visual activities, general services, and an electronic library. The establishment endeavors to provide a children-friendly environment and to carry out various cultural activities to promote reading among children. The library operates one branch establishment and supports the operation of 25 small lending libraries.

The survey was administered to 500 library visitors for a period of less than two months (Dec. 26, 2006 – Feb. 2, 2007). The survey collects data in the form of hypothetical questions aimed at eliciting WTP totals and mean values for the Jungrang Public Library. Respondents are asked to express their WTP in relation to given services used or received.

Individuals were randomly assigned to one of three types of survey formats corresponding with three elicitation formats: conventional CVM format (questionnaire *A*), DM format (questionnaire *B*) and a

proposed format to combine the DM and IBM formats (questionnaire
C) (see Table 2>.

<Table 2> Summary of Alternative Dependent Variables

Types	Description
Questionnaire A	Conventional CVM format
Questionnaire B	DM format (modified CVM format 1)
Questionnaire C	DM + IBM format (modified CVM format 2)

4.1 Results

A total of 500 questionnaires were distributed, and 399 were
returned for a response rate of about 80%. The fact that the DM +
IBM format removed protest respondents more effectively was
proved by the higher response rate (96%) than the DM format (84%)
in the case study. The response rate of the conventional CVM was
the lowest (52%) among the three formats (see Table 3).

<Table 3> Survey response rate

Types	Total surveyed	Returned	Valid response	Valid response rate
Questionnaire A	166	90	86	52%
Questionnaire B	167	148	140	84%
Questionnaire C	167	161	155	96%

The surveys were largely categorized into two sections: overall
value of the library and individual value of the main services. Costs
and use statistics were taken from the Korea Library Yearbook

(2006). The WTPs of the DM + IBM format were compared to those of the traditional CVM and DM formats for the Jungrang Public Library.

As shown in Table 4, the hypothetical WTP value derived in conventional CVM (2,836 won) was found to be more than three times that of the DM format (804 won), which proves 'Hypothesis 1' (The WTP value depending on the DM format is expected to be much lower than that of the conventional CVM.).

The DM format was designed to reduce yea-saying and protest answers bias by allowing respondents to express multiple attitudes. Those who responded with a conditional yes (I support the service depending on the condition) and then responded with categories 4-1 or 4-3 as shown in Table 5, are considered to have multiple feelings. On the other hand, if the CVM format was to be used, the respondents may not have had the appropriate answer category to fit their multiple feelings and might have unconsciously refused to answer or overestimate the WTP value.

A high proportion of those who responded with the DM questions (see Table 6) reflect a reduction of yea-saying or protest answers bias. When broken down by library service, facility use recorded the highest bias rate (24.59%), followed by material use (23.21%), literacy program (16.6%), and reference (3.23%). Thus, the result supported the theory that yea-saying bias and protest answer bias played an important role in the overestimation of values in the conventional CVM format.

On the other hand, the WTP values between the DM format (804 won) and the DM + IBM format (1,773 won) significantly differed. This outcome supports 'Hypothesis 2' (If the WTP values derived in the DM format between informed and uninformed respondents differ significantly, information bias may be a problem). We proved that one possible explanation for the underestimation of values in the DM format was the presence of information bias.

When broken down by library service, it is noted that with the DM + IBM format, the proportion of respondents that would pay for the services among those who had multiple attitudes increased by about 300% than those of the DM format only, excluding reference service (see Table 5). It also found that the estimated WTP value derived in the DM+IBM format (1,773 won) was more than two times that of the DM format (804 won) and supported 'Hypothesis 3' (The WTP value derived in the DM + IBM format is expected to be higher than that for DM only).

As shown in Table 4, the main services offered by the Jungrang Public Library are material use service, facility use service, reference service, and library literacy programs. In the DM + IBM approach, the overall economic value of the library material is 1.85 (B/C ratio). And when broken down by library service, material use service showed the highest economic value (B/C ratio of 3.52), followed by facility use (2.16), reference

(0.92), and literacy programs (0.69).

For example, the WTP value of the DM + IBM approach (1,773 won) was multiplied by the number of annual users (1,186,647) to ascertain the benefit, 2,103,925,131 won. The cost of providing the overall library service (1,138,986,352 won) was divided by the benefit (2,103,925,131 won) to get the overall economic value of the library (B/C ratio of 1.85). In the overall value of the library, the economic value of the DM format (0.84) was significantly lower than that of the CVM (2.95).

In terms of WTP values, a comparison by type of library service showed that literacy programs recorded the highest WTP value (13,083 won), followed by facility use service (339 won), material use (310 won), and reference service (128 won).

<Table 4> Comparison of overall economic value among 3 formats

(unit: Korean won)

Format		Overall	Material use	Facility use	Reference	Literacy program
Benefit (WTP)	CVM	2,836	1,365	1.437	2,417	12,052
	DM	804	88	157	139	19,048
	DM + IBM	1,773	310	339	128	13,083
Cost	Physical resource	1,138,986,352	89,000,000	96,113,660	0	4,959,910
	Personal resource		179,138,416	155,875,995	111,249,265	46,407,807
B/ C ratio (CVM: DM: DM +IBM)		2.95 : 0.84 : 1.85	15.51 : 1 : 3.52	9.15 : 1 : 2.16	17.39 : 1 : 0.92	0.63 : 1 : 0.69

<Table 5> Effect of DM question: Questionnaire *B* and Questionnaire *C*

Conditional yes: "I support the service depending on the condition"

Question	Format	Material use	Facility use	Reference	Literacy program
No. 1	DM	5 (4.7%)	9 (7.4%)	1 (3.2%)	1 (4.2%)
	DM + IBM	10 (8.1%)	12 (9.5%)	0 (0%)	1 (5.3%)
No. 3	DM	7 (6.5%)	10 (8.2%)	3 (9.7%)	2 (8.3%)
	DM + IBM	25 (20%)	28 (22%)	3 (7.5%)	4 (21%)

No. 1: I would pay a fee of any amount for the service if I were convinced
    that the government itself did not have enough public funds to pay for the service.
No. 3: I would pay if the suggested price seems appropriate

<Table 6> The Effect of DM question: Questionnaire *B*

Question	Material use	Facility use	Reference	Literacy program
No. 1-3 "I support the service depending on the condition."	23(21.50%)	30(24.59%)	1(3.23%)	4(16.6%)

5. Conclusion

Criticism of the CVM method has focused on the perceived overestimation of values. Various previous studies proved that the DM format reduced the occurrence of yea-saying and protest answer bias revealed in the CVM. The DM format in the study provided much lower estimates of WTP and a more appropriate function of protest answers when compared to the conventional CVM format. Little progress has been made in investigating whether or not the DM format could substitute for assessing the economic value of public libraries. The study aims to identify if the DM format is a satisfactory predictor of actual value. The study proposed an alternative format, the DM + IBM format − referred to as the information bias-minimizing (IBM) format.

The DM + IBM format was based on the notion that the DM format would be more effective in reducing yea-saying and protest answers bias as respondents are more familiar with the hypothetical situation and the library services that are being valued. And an empirical comparison is performed to compare the model with two existing formats: the conventional CVM and DM format. Estimates of median WTP range from as little as 804 won in the DM format to as much as 2,836 won with the conventional CVM format. Treating information bias and protest answers bias as valid (DM + CVM) produces an estimate median WTP that is 104% higher than the DM estimates.

Results affirmed the view that the DM + CVM was a more robust elicitation format than the DM format in the following aspects: First, the WTP value depending on the DM format is much lower than that of the conventional CVM format by removing the yea-saying and protest answer bias.

Secondly, it was clear that the WTP value derived in the DM + IBM format is more satisfactory than the DM format with only a reduction in the information bias.

The case study confirms how the proposed model, DM + IBM, could be applied to local studies. The proposed format enables a more qualitative analysis, providing a synergy effect that the DM format alone can not provide. Those results mean more respondents could provide real and valid WTP answers with the DM format or conventional CVM format.

However, the method has limitations, and the best results for CV surveys should be obtained by using use value (the usual benefit concept in library literature) and option value (the benefit to potential users of knowing they have the option of using the services). Further study is warranted in the area of measurement of economic value of public libraries by incorporating option value.

References

AabØ, Svanhild. (2005) 'Are Public Libraries Worth Their Price?', *New Library World* 106(1218/1219): 487-495.

Arrow, K., Solow, R., Portney, Paul R., Leamer, Edward E., Radner, Roy, and Schuman, Howard (1993) 'Report of the NOAA Panel on Contingent Valuation', *Federal Register*, 58: 4601-14.

British Library (2002) *Measuring Our Value*. United Kingdom: British Library. Available at: http://www.bk.uk (accessed 9 June 2007).

Blamey, R.K., J.W. Bennett and M.D. Morrison (1999) 'Yea-Saying in Contingent Valuation Surveys', *Land Economics* 75(1): 126-141.

Bonato, Dario, Nocera, Sandra, Telser, Harry (2001) The Contingent Valuation Method in Health Care: An Economic Evaluation of Alzheimer's Disease. Universitat Bern: Volkswirtschaftliches Institute.

Boyle, K.J., F.R. Johnson, D.W. McCollum, W.H. Desvousges, R.W. Dunford, and S.P. Hudson (1993) Valuing Public Goods: Discrete versus Continuous Contingent Valuation Responses. Department of Resource Economics, Workiing Paper, University of Maine.

Champ, P.A., R.C. Bishop, T.C. Brown, and D.W. McCollum (1997) 'Using Donation Mechanisms to Value Nonuse Benefits From Public Goods', *Journal of Environmental Economics and Management* 33(2): 151-62.

Duffield, J.W., and Patterson, D.A. (1991) Field Testing Existence Values: Comparison of Hypothetical and Cash Transaction Values. Paper presented at the annual meeting of the American Economic Association, New Orleans, LA.

Florida (2004) 'Taxpayer Return on Investment in Florida', available at: http://dis.dos.state.fl.us/bld/roi/publications.cfm (accessed 9 June 2007).

Harless and Allen (1999) 'Using the Contingent Valuation Method to Measure Patron Benefits of Reference Desk Service in an Academic Library', *College & Research Libraries* 60 (1): 56-69.

Holt, GE, Elliott, D. and Moore, A. (1999) 'Placing a Value on Public Library Services', *Public Libraries* (March/April): 98-108.

Kanninen, B. (1995) 'Bias in Discrete Response Contingent Valuation', *Journal of Environmental Economics and Management* 28: 114-25.

Krupnick, A.J. and Cropper, M.L. (1992) 'The Effect of Information on Health Risk Valuations', *Journal of Risk and Uncertainty* 5: 29-48.

Loomis, J., Brown T., Lucero, B., and Peterson, G. (1996) 'Improving Validity Experiments of Contingent Valuation Methods: Results of Efforts to Reduce the Disparity of Hypothetical and Actual Willingness to Pay', *Land Economics* 72 (Nov.): 450-61.

McClure, C. Fraser, B. Nelson, TW, and Robbins, JB. (2001) *Economic Benefits and Impacts from Public Libraries in the State of Florida*. Final Report to the State of Florida, Division of Library and Information Services. Florida State University Information Use Management and Policy Institute.

McFadden, D., and Leonard, G. (1993) *Issues in the Contingent Valuation of Environmental Goods: Methodology for Data Collection and Analysis*. In Contingent Valuation: A Critical Assessment, ed. J. Hausman.

Amsterdam: Elsevier.

Morris, A., Sumsion, J., and Hawkins, M. (2002) 'Economic Value of Public Libraries in the UK', *Libri* (52): 78-87.

Morris, A., Hawkins, M. and Sumsion, J. (2001) *The Economic Value of Public Libraries*. The Council for Museums: Archives and Libraries.

Navrud, S. (1992) *Willingness to Pay for Preservation of Species: An Experiment with Actual Payments*. In Pricing the European Environment, ed. S. Navrud. New York: Oxford University Press.

Noonan, D.S. (2003) 'Contingent Valuation and Cultural Resources: A Meta-Analytic Review of the Literature', *Journal of Cultural Economics* (27): 159-176.

Ready, R.C., J.C. Whitehead and G.C. Bloomquist (1995) Contingent Valuation When Respondents Are Ambivalent. *Journal of Environmental Economics and Management* 29: 181-196.

Throsby, D. (2003) 'Determining the Value of Cultural Goods: How much (or How Little) does Contingent Valuation Tell Us?' *Journal of Cultural Economics* (27): 275-285.

Reber, A.S. (1985) *The Penguin Dictionary of Psychology*. London: Penguin Books.

McFadden, D. and G. Leonard (1993). *Issues in the Contingent Valuation of Environmental Goods: Methodology for Data Collection and Analysis*. In Contingent Valuation: A Critical Assessment. Ed. J. Hausman. Amsterdam: Elsevier.

Viscusi, W.K., W.A. Magat and J. Huber (1991) 'Pricing Environmental Health Risks: Survey Assessments of Risk-Risk and Risk-Dollar Trade-Offs for Chronic Bronchitis', *Journal of Environmental Economics and Management* 21 (1): 32-51.

Assessing the Warm Glow Effect in Contingent Valuations for Public Libraries[11]

This article aims to present evidence of the warm glow effect in a public library setting. More specifically it tests whether individual respondents with different values for the warm glow component indeed report different values for their WTP. The data come from a contingent valuation survey conducted on randomly selected citizens of Korea, where the respondents are asked how much they are willing to pay for public library services. Results show that there is significant difference between traditional WTP and cold WTP, concluding that the traditional WTP value is not the real economic value of the public good.

---

11) 이 논문은 2010년 Journal of Librarianship and Information Science 42권 4호(236~244쪽)에 게재되었음 [공저: Lee, Soon-Jae, Jung, Eun-Joo].

1. Introduction

Contingent valuation (CV) is a nonmarket valuation method that is becoming increasingly popular in public libraries as well as in such industries as environmental goods and health. CV is a survey-based method in which respondents are asked to evaluate public library services, in general, by specifying the maximum amount they would be willing to pay to obtain the service. In 'contingent valuation', therefore, respondents are asked to state their willingness to pay (WTP) based on a specific hypothetical scenario and description of public libraries.

However, the CV method has been subject to much criticism because of the perceived overestimation of values. Criticism revolves mainly around the validity and reliability of the results when taking into account the effects of various biases and errors. One possible explanation for the overestimation of values is the presence of the warm glow effect. The warm glow effect is generally defined as a feeling of well-being or satisfaction generated by the act of giving.

Hausman (1993) argued that CV answers did not reflect real economic preferences due to the existence of the warm glow effect in CV surveys, and so such surveys should not be used as a nonmarket valuation method (Hausman, 1993). Prominent critics of CV hold that the real value of public goods would be more accurately assessed if the effect of warm glow motivation were removed from WTP (Kahneman and Knetsch, 1992; Champ, et al., 1997; Nunes and Schokkaert, 2003; Pouta, 2004).

Nonetheless, the negative position is debatable if it is possible to explain it by the existence of a warm glow component. Arrow (1951) supported the CV method, arguing that the warm glow effect was considered to be as a perfectly legitimate component, because it was not the essential aspect of economic preferences for public goods. Since then, the warm glow may be seen as a source of WTP in many CV studies.

There have been several studies presenting evidence on the significance of the warm glow effect in various fields. However, public libraries have overlooked identifying possible biases in CVM and, as a result, the relationship between the warm glow effect and WTP has not been systematically studied in a public library setting. The degree of the warm glow effect in CV may vary depending on the type of public goods to which the CV methods are applied.

This paper aims to present evidence of the warm glow effect in a public library setting. More specifically, this research tests whether individual respondents with different values for the warm glow component indeed report different values for their WTP. Finally this study will determine the actual WTP of the respondents, or if the warm glow effect can be considered a component of real WTP.

To this end, this study takes the following steps:

1. Conduct a survey to investigate if WTP responses in public libraries are affected by the warm glow effect;

2. Identify the degree to which the warm glow effect may be embedded in the CV surveys;

3. Examine if there is a significant difference between traditional WTP and "cold" WTP – that is, when taking out the effect of warm glow motivation; and

4. Determine whether or not the warm glow effect can be considered a component of real WTP.

2. Literature Review

Matthews (2002) has demonstrated that there are a number of different approaches to determine the value of a library and its services. Libraries may be interested in assessing the value of the library by asking users to estimate the real impact of the library in terms of accomplishments time savings, and money savings.

The contingent valuation method (CVM) has been considered a primary technique for assessing the value of nonmarket goods. Arrow, *et al.* (1993) supported that the method was the best approach for measuring both the direct and indirect benefits, and measured the value to the U.S. of legislation by using CVM.

Recognizing the value of CVM, the British Library (2004) commissioned a research study to estimate the economic impact of the Library on the UK economy. They used questionnaire including rigorous testing and analysis to estimate the value. The study found that the UK would lose £280 million of economic value per annum if the British Library did not exist.

However, a number of papers suggest that WTP derived in CVM tend to exceed that revealed in experimental or real-life markets. Several studies (Chung, 2008; Aabø, 2005; Champ, *et al.* 1997) have provided new approaches in CVM that also account for potential biases such as yea-saying, protest answers, and information bias.

One possible explanation for the overestimation of values is the presence of the warm glow effect. This theory of the warm glow effect first emerged in studies on contingent markets such as environmental goods and health. There have been very few attempts to account for biases in CVM such as warm glow in public libraries, calling for more studies in this area.

Becker (1974) and Andreoni (1989, 1990) argue warm glow as an important factor influencing a person's decision to make a donation to public goods. They also added that there were many other factors influencing this decision to privately provide public goods, such as social pressure, guilt, or sympathy.

Kahneman and Knetsch (1990) also reported that the warm glow bias was an important shortcoming of CVM. The study concluded that contingent valuation responses reflected the WTP in terms of the moral satisfaction derived from contributing to environmental goods. The responses were not a reflection of the economic value of these goods. The results of this study indicated that WTP could be predicted by levels of moral satisfaction, which increased with the size of the contribution.

In a similar study, Champ, *et al.* (1997) argued that the adoption of the WTP measure could never really escape the moral element. Their study confirmed the findings of Kahneman and Knetsch (1990) regarding the greater role of moral satisfaction versus economic value in contingent value responses. Accordingly, the study suggested that warm glow should be included as an interpretation of WTP for intangible public goods, such as a national park or a beach.

Hackl and Pruckner (2005) supported the view that the warm glow was a possible cause for biased WTP figures. This study presented an empirical framework to study the existence of warm glow in hypothetical WTP measures, but failed to indicate warm glow phenomena in WTP answers for the measurement of health-related Red Cross Services.

Chilton and Hutchinson (2000) carried out a controlled laboratory experiment to test how warm glow motives influence decisions regarding provision of a public good. Their research shows that the warm glow motive might be present in the majority of bids, although its presence did not always preclude a scope sensitivity test. Their study developed a behavioral framework to classify individual CV respondents in terms of the warm glow in their WTP responses. Chilton and Hutchinson (2000) found the existence of at least five possible behavioral categories for CV responses, depending on the type of underlying preferences and whether respondents were satiated or non-satiated with respect to the good.

Nunes and Schokkaert (2003) presented additional empirical evidence on the significance of the warm glow effect in WTP responses. The study designed a CV survey to measure the economic benefits of preventing commercial tourism development in the Alentejo Natural Park in Portugal, including a list of attitudinal items to investigate the warm glow effect. Although their results showed that cold WTP estimates were lower than the original estimates, they were cautious and recognized that since the scope and the adding-up effect with the cold measures were provisional, similar results would not be found in other samples with different questionnaires for other commodities.

Pouta (2004) supported the view that the warm glow effect had an important influence on the WTP answers. The study concluded that attitude and belief items in the questionnaire could influence people's decision of whether or not to donate, although warm glow was not statistically significant according to the Chi-Square test. And warm glow did not increase respondents' perceived confidence in their decisions. The six belief statements were elicited in a separate pilot study carried out by telephone interview, during which respondents were asked to rate their level of agreement or disagreement using a 7-point scale. The study also applied three types of attitudes toward the public good, policies dealing with the public good and paying for the public good. He also added that the degree of moral satisfaction in CV might be different depending on the type of public goods to which the method is applied.

Morin (2003) tested for the connection between a positive reaction to a social stimulus (I like this face) and an inference about the state of the world (I have seen this face before). And the study found that the attractiveness of a face increased the perceived familiarity regardless of prior exposure due to the warm glow effect elicited by attractive faces.

On the other hand, previous studies (Smith, 2000 & 2006; Hanley, *et al.*, 2003) suggest that different formats lead to significantly different WTP estimates. In particular, the format of the questionnaire is integral to reducing bias and improving the validity of WTP. Questionnaire format refers to the method by which the respondent is asked to provide their WTP. Four broad approaches have been used: open-ended, closed-ended, payment card, and bidding.

The opened-ended and closed-ended formats had been extensively developed and were recommended in environmental economics. The

National Oceanographic and Atmospheric Administration (NOAA) used the closed-ended format for the valuation of environmental benefits (Arrow, *et al.* 1993).

Smith (2000) questioned the tendency among healthcare CV studies to unilaterally adopt closed-ended formats given that healthcare surveys are generally more familiar than other environmental surveys. He added that environmental economics was mostly concerned with non-use valuation of large and unfamiliar commodities, such as wildlife, areas of natural beauty or air quality. In contrast, CV surveys in healthcare are valuing a good that is generally more familiar.

In recent years, however, there has been a move toward the payment card (PC) approach in health care and environmental literature. Kim and Byun (2003) showed that the estimated WTPs on Bukhansan National Park[12] based on the dichotomous choice format turned out to be higher than that of the PC format.

The PC method has been the single most frequently used questionnaire format, although there has been no theoretical justification for the superiority of one PC format to the other three approaches including the high-to-low, low-to-high, and random shuffle approaches. CV surveys are typically administered by one of two methods: face-to-face interview and telephone interview.

Smith (2006) used a general population sample of Australian

---

12) Bukhansan National Park, located in Seoul, is one of the major national parks in Korea.

respondents who were randomly allocated and surveyed in a face-to-face or telephone interview. The study found that there would be no difference in WTP within each questionnaire format across modes of administration: face-to-face or telephone. Additionally, he found that there was no significant difference in the WTP value between two different versions of the PC (high-to-low, low-to-high), but suggested further analysis on whether or not randomly shuffled versions could produce valid values.

3. Methodology

This study was designed to assess the role of the warm glow motive in reported WTP values and, more specifically, whether individual respondents with different levels of the warm glow component had different values for their WTP. The study would determine whether or not the warm glow effect could be considered a component of real WTP. The data come from a contingent valuation survey conducted on randomly selected citizens of Korea, where the respondents were asked how much they are willing to pay for public library services.

The respondents received one of the two different modes of survey administration: telephone interview and face-to-face interview, based on the strong justification that face-to-face interviews are by far the most appropriate mode of survey administration (Bateman, *et al.* 2002).

The survey was conducted at a suitable time and place for respondents between June 27 and August 23, 2008, beginning with a complete explanation of the purpose of the study prior to the beginning of the interview. Respondents in middle school ages or higher were randomly selected from among Korean residents during the sample collection period. Those under 14 were considered too young to complete the valuation questions, and therefore excluded from the survey.

In terms of questionnaire format, the study used the payment card (PC) method, which has been the single most frequently used questionnaire format, to improve the validity of WTP. Among several types of PC versions, the study incorporated the low-to-high approaches. Other PC versions consist of the high-to-low and random shuffle. In recent years, there has been no direct empirical comparison of these different PC versions (Smith, 2006).

3.1 Hypotheses

To measure the effect of the warm glow, we focus on the following points: 1) if respondents with different levels of satisfaction with public libraries and respondents in different socioeconomic characteristics, such as income, education and gender, report different values for their WTP and; 2) if respondents with different levels of warm glow motive report different values for their WTP; and 3) if there is a meaningful difference between cold WTP values and traditional WTP values.

This study surveyed public library users in Korea to test for three sets of research questions.

Hypothesis 1: There is a difference in WTP responses among those with different socioeconomic characteristics, such as income, education, and gender. And the higher the level of satisfaction with the public library's service, the higher the WTP.

Hypothesis 2: The higher the warm glow effect scores, the higher the WTP.

Hypothesis 3: There is significant difference in WTP between traditional WTP values and cold WTP values.

3.2 Survey design

In our survey, respondents were asked to assess the benefits of public libraries in Korea. The survey was restricted to one library system (public library) to control for differences in operational policies, library services, and others. The CV survey was composed of three sections: demographic factors, attitudinal questions, and WTP questions.

In the first section, respondents were asked to provide demographic information regarding gender, income, education, and their level of satisfaction with public libraries. This format was designed to determine if respondents with different satisfaction levels and socioeconomic characteristics had different WTP.

The second section introduced five attitudinal questions for respondents to answer using a five-point Likert-scale, with values ranging from 1 (for "I disagree strongly") to 5 (for "I agree strongly") to measure the influence of the warm glow effect in their WTP responses. Respondents were allowed to indicate one category that they felt most closely resembled their views. They were also allowed to check "I don't know" if they were unsure of their answer. This option effectively reduces the tendency of yea-saying and protest answer bias in the CV method.

The five questions concerning their beliefs and attitudes on the effects of the warm glow in their WTP responses are as follows:

1. I am willing to donate to fund-raising campaigns to promote public library services.

2. I like to contribute to a good cause on behalf of public libraries whenever I can afford it.

3. I respect those who voluntarily participate in fund-raising activities for the public library.

4. I get much satisfaction from donating to a fund-raising campaign in whatever form the donation may be.

5. I can not walk past a poor person or anyone who needs my help when I see him on the street.

The attitude statements were adopted from Nunes and Schokkaert (2003), which were formulated to capture the warm glow effect in CV surveys. The above five questions were items most associated with warm glow motives among the 17 attitudinal items suggested by the research. Among the five statements, three are intended to predict behavioral intentions toward public libraries, while the remaining two statements measure a person's warm glow motivation to give in general. We then analyzed the correlation between the individual's attitudinal scores and differences in WTP values.

In the third section, respondents were asked to provide their WTP, using the low-to-high version of the PC format. Before responding to the PC format, they were asked to indicate their willingness to accept a fee-based public library service using the following dichotomous question: "Are you willing to pay a fee for public library use?" Only those who answered 'yes' were allowed to provide WTP responses.

Respondents were then asked to assume the following scenario: the public library was about to be shut down because of a shortage in the operating budget. How much would they be willing to spend to save the library? The PC format was designed with a low-to-high ordered sequence of bids: 1,000, 3,000, 5,000, 7,000, 9,000, and 11,000 Korean won (KRW). The valuation would be excluded if the respondent's WTP were between the maximum amount he would vote for and the lowest amount he would not vote for. In other words, instead of asking respondents to indicate only the most they would be willing to pay to maintain the library's operations - as is done in traditional surveys - respondents were asked to choose among three possible options (Yes, No, Don't know) for every bid.

The study used a follow-up to the WTP questions about the respondent's level of certainty with respect to his/her response to the contingent valuation question. Smith (2006) added a question in the CV survey to confirm the degree of respondents' certainty in their WTP values. When respondents are 'sure' of their stated WTP, their WTP values are considered to be real WTP. When they are 'not sure' or 'don't know' about their stated WTP, their WTP values are considered inaccurate and excluded from total WTP value estimation. This use of a follow-up question to assess the respondent's level of certainty to the WTP question was expected to eliminate the effect of the warm glow motivation from their WTP.

4. Results

4.1 Demographic characteristics

The CV survey was conducted in mid-2008 to investigate the influence of warm glow effect in WTP responses. A random sample of 275 people was selected from the general population of Korea to complete the survey. A total of 231 were returned for a response rate of about 84%, with a valid response of 220 (about 95%). The survey was randomly administered face-to-face (199) and by telephone (32).

Table 1 shows that the frequency of library visits differed by the age of the respondent. The age group of the most frequent visitors was 19 or younger (37.66%), while the least frequent visitor age group was 50 or older (5.19%). About 52% of the respondents were college/university graduates, while 35% had a monthly income of more than KRW 1.5 million.

<Table 1. Demographic Statistics>

Classification		Number of respondent	Percent (%)	Cumulative (%)
Gender	Male	89	38.53	38.53
	Female	138	59.74	98.27
	No response	4	1.73	100
	Total	231(100%)		
Age	14-19	87	37.66	37.66
	20-29	45	19.48	57.14
	30-39	38	16.45	73.59
	40-49	35	15.15	88.74
	50 or older	12	5.19	93.94
	No response	14	6.06	100
	Total	231(100%)		
Academic background	Middle or High school	93	40.26	40.26
	College/University	119	51.52	91.77
	Graduate school	8	3.46	95.24

Classification		Number of respondent	Percent (%)	Cumulative (%)
	No response	11	4.76	100
	Total	231(100%)		
Monthly salary (KRW)	0	89	38.53	38.53
	Below 1.5 million	43	18.61	57.14
	1.5 - 3 million	56	24.24	81.39
	3 - 4.5 million	14	6.06	87.45
	Over 4.5 million	12	5.19	92.64
	No response	17	7.36	100.00
	Total	231(100%)		

The Pearson correlation was used to show the linear relationship between demographic factors and WTP. Table 2 indicates that WTP is positively related to academic background and income level. That is, we may expect that the higher the level of education or income, the higher the WTP. However, we find that WTP is not significantly correlated with gender and age, partially reinforcing the first hypothesis. The results indicate no significant relationship between WTP and the overall satisfaction level with public libraries. This finding indicates that the respondents' level of satisfaction with the public library does not affect the WTP level in CV surveys.

<Table 2. Pearson Correlations between Demographic Factors and WTP>

	Satisfaction	Gender	Age	Academic background	Income level
WTP	0.103	0.043	0.123	0.283**	0.159*

* indicates p-value <.05
** indicates p-value <.01

4.2 Effects of warm glow

4.2.1 Warm glow effect level and WTP for public libraries

A total of 163 respondents replied to the questions in Table 3, which were designed to identify the warm glow effect of the participants. The respondents reported the highest mean score, 4.03, for Question 3, followed by 3.35 and 3.33 for Questions 4 and 1, respectively.

<Table 3. Attitudinal Questions on Warm Glow Effect>

No	Questions	Likert score
1	I am willing to donate money for fund-raising campaigns to promote public library services	3.33
2	I am willing to pay additional taxes in the event of a budget deficiency to support public libraries.	3.29
3	I am likely to respect a friend who voluntarily participates in fund-raising activities for a public library.	4.03
4	I feel a sense of worth whenever I make a donation to a fund-raising campaign, whatever form the donation may be.	3.35
5	I can not refuse people who approach me on the street for help.	3.31

We classified the level of warm glow effect into three groups: high, medium, and low. The scale of the respondents' Likert scores is 4 (5 minus 1) and, when equally divided into high, medium and low, the coefficient is 1.3 (4 divided by 3). However, there is no respondent with a warm glow effect score of less than 1.5 and greater than 4.5 in the actual survey.

Therefore, the actual warm glow scale would be 3 (4.5 minus 1.5). The low level of warm glow ranges from 1.5 to 2.5, the medium level from 2.5 to 3.5, and the high level from 3.5 to 4.5.

Table 4 revealed that most respondents (90.2%) possessed high or medium levels of warm glow components in their WTP, while only 9.8% of the respondents showed a low level of warm glow motive in their WTP answers. The mean WTP was KRW 3,464 for all participants (n= 163), consisting of a sub-mean WTP of KRW 4,514 for high-level warm glow, KRW 4,514 for the medium-level, and KRW 2,056 for the low-level. As shown in Figure 1, the warm glow effect played an important role in the reported WTP values and, more specifically, three groups of respondents with different warm glow levels reported different values for their WTP. We hypothesized that respondents who had higher warm glow motive would show higher WTP than those who had lower warm glow motive. There is a significant relationship between the level of warm glow effect and mean WTP, supporting the second hypothesis.

<Table 4. Warm Glow Effect Level and WTP>

	Low (1.5~ 2.5)	Medium (2.5~3.5)	High (3.5~4.5)	Total
No. of Respondents (%)	16(9.8%)	71(43.6%)	76(46.6%)	163 (100%)
Mean WTP (KRW)	2,056	2,616	4,514	3,464

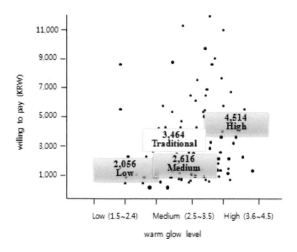

⟨Figure 1. Warm Glow Effect Level and WTP⟩

4.2.2 Cold WTP and traditional WTP[13)]

The Mann-Whitney U test was used to test the third hypothesis. As shown in Table 5, the Mann-Whitney U test of significance indicated no notable difference between cold WTP (KRW 2,056) and traditional WTP (KRW 3,464). According to the test, the difference between cold and traditional WTPs was significant at the 5% level. Table 5 reported the value of the Mann-Whitney U at 870. Data also indicated a definite pattern in the average WTP, with the whole group reporting higher WTP than the group with low warm glow, thus supporting the hypothesized relationship between the traditional and cold WTP.

---

13) 'Cold' WTP refers to a low level of a warm glow effect, whereas 'traditional' WTP refers to WTP consisting entirely of the warm glow effect.

<Table 5. Comparison between cold and traditional WTPs>

	Type	Respondents	Average order	Mean (KRW)	Standard error
WTP	Cold	16	3.0938	2,056	.670
	Traditional	163	4.7240	3,464	.843
	U = 870.000 (p =0.05*)				

The results also show that the warm glow effect played a major role in overvaluing the WTP. According to the formula in Figure 2, the 'real' WTP, namely 'cold' WTP, was KRW 2,056, and the proportion of real WTP in traditional WTP was calculated at 59.4% (in our case, 2,056÷ 3,464= 0.594). Around 40.6% of the reported WTP value is due to the warm glow effect, while the real WTP value is only 59.4% of the reported WTP value. This finding is surprising in that it has never been explored in previous studies.

The following illustrates an example. If a CV survey calculates the traditional WTP as KRW 10,000 for the service of a public library, the real (cold) WTP would be KRW 5,940 after removing the warm glow bias in the traditional WTP. We should consider the warm glow bias, valued at KRW 4,060, when evaluating the value of the library service. The formula in Figure 2 illustrates how the real WTP is generally calculated in a CV situation.

$$\text{Real WTP (\%)} = \left(\sum_{c=1}^{m} \frac{WTP_c}{m} \div \sum_{t=1}^{n} \frac{WTP_t}{n} \right) \times 100$$

$$\text{Where} \quad \sum_{c=1}^{m} \frac{WTP_c}{m} \sum_{c=1}^{m} \frac{WTP_c}{m} \quad : \text{cold WTP}$$

$$\sum_{t=1}^{n} \frac{WTP_t}{n} \sum_{t=1}^{n} \frac{WTP_t}{n} \quad : \text{traditional WTP}$$

m: number of respondents who belong to the group with low warm glow effect

n: total number of respondents in the CV survey (m ≤ n)

<Figure 2: Calculation of Real WTP>

The follow-up question was designed to identify the respondent's level of certainty regarding their WTP responses. As Table 6 shows, the proportion of those who were unsure was 13.5% (22/163), while all of the respondents (22/22) registered a warm glow effect. Those who indicated 'don't know' amounted to 25.8% (42/163), and 88.1% (37/42) showed a warm glow effect to reduce overestimation. Of those who reported that they were 'sure' of their WTP response, 88.9% (88/99) still showed a medium- or high-level warm glow effect in their WTP valuation.

Most of the respondents who were sure of their WTP response appeared to be unaware of how deeply their stated WTP reflected warm glow motive. This finding supports the fact that respondents were involved in warm glow motives in their WTP valuation regardless of the certainty of their responses. We confirmed that although respondents were sure of their stated WTP, we could not consider this real WTP based only on their certainty. This finding points to the existence of some deficiencies in previous studies (e.g., Smith, 2006).

<Table 6. Respondents' Confidence Level and Warm Glow Effect>

No.	Confidence Level	Warm Glow Level	No. of Respondents	Mean WTP (KRW)
1	Unsure	Low	0	-
		Medium	16	1,821
		High	6	3.234
2	Don't know	Low	5	2,250
		Medium	12	3,141
		High	25	5,784
3	Sure	Low	11	1,862
		Medium	43	2,887
		High	45	4,546

4.3 Validity test

Two elements in the survey were used to ensure greater internal validity of the final WTP values. First, respondents were allowed to choose among three different responses: "yes", "no", and "don't know" as opposed to being offered only the yes/no response alternatives. Where respondents indicated 'don't know', it would be worth exploring if these were 'true' or 'protest answers'. Second, the study used a low-to-high format based on the theory that the random or low-to-high formats were more representative of an individual's actual WTP than the high-to-low format. Boyle

(1985) suggested that the high-to-low format might be subject to 'starting point bias', leading to an artificially inflated WTP. Smith (2006) performed a 'validity test' and concluded that the random PC format appeared to closely resemble actual WTP. Third, we calculated Cronbach's alpha (α)[14] to check the reliability of the measures for warm glow level and WTP responses. As shown in Table 6, the value of Cronbach's α was 0.730, indicating that the factors comprising the research model possessed high reliability. Kerlinger and Lee (2000) proposed that Cronbach's α of greater than 0.70 indicated high validity.

<Table 7. Results of Cronbach's α >

	Factor	Cronbach's α
WTP	Warm glow level	0.730

5. Conclusion

The contingent valuation (CV) is a survey-based method in which respondents are asked to state their willingness to pay (WTP) in a specific hypothetical scenario. The CV survey method is a widely used technique for valuing non-market goods,

---

14) The standardized Cronbach's α can be defined as $\alpha = \dfrac{N \cdot \bar{r}}{(1 + (N - 1) \cdot \bar{r})}$

Where N is the number of components (items or testlets) and $\bar{r}$ is the average of all (Pearson) correlation coefficients between the components.

including public library services. However, the CV method has been heavily criticized for perceived overestimation of values, i.e., the values do not reflect real economic preference because of the existence of the warm glow effect in CV surveys. This paper aims to investigate the significance of the existence of the warm glow effect in the valuation of public libraries. To identify the significance of the warm glow effect, this study introduced a list of attitudinal items. In addition, we tried to determine if demographic factors would affect WTP responses for public libraries. This study surveyed public library users in Korea to test for three sets of research questions.

We found that the users' overall satisfaction with public libraries was not significantly related to their WTP responses. However, some socioeconomic factors, such as income and education, were positively related to WTP, while gender and age had no significant bearing on WTP valuation. People with higher income and education are more willing to pay for public library services. As expected, people with high warm glow motives had high WTP values. The study confirmed the presence of a significant warm glow effect in the WTP responses and concluded that the traditional WTP value was not the real economic value of the goods. Results showed that cold WTP estimates are much lower than traditional WTP. It can be assumed that traditional WTP values contain the warm glow effect.

Our findings support that warm glow effects exist significantly in CV for public libraries, indicating that when conducting valuations for public libraries using a CV survey, so-called warm glow bias must be excluded for an accurate estimation. This study could also be broadly applied to estimate the economic value of other public goods. Contrary to previous studies, our study confirmed that even people who are confident that their stated WTP was free of the warm glow effect are still susceptible to warm glow, potentially misleading the valuation procedure.

References

Aabø, Svanhild (2005) *Value of Public Libraries: a Methodological Discussion and Empirical Study Applying the Contingent Valuation Method*, Faculty of Humanities.

Andreoni, J. (1989) 'Giving with Impure Altruism: Applications to Charity and Ricardian Equivalence', *Journal of Political Economy* 97 (6): 1447-58.

Andreoni, J. (1990) 'Impure Altruism and Donations to Public Goods: a Theory of Warm-Glow Giving', *Economic Journal* 100 (401): 464-77.

Arrow, Kenneth J. (1951). *Social Choice and Individual Values*. Wiley, New York.

Arrow, Kenneth J., Solow, Robert, Portney, Paul R., Leamer, Edward E., Radner, Roy and Schuman, Howard (1993) *Report of the NOAA Panel on Contingent Valuation*, Federal Register, 58, Washington DC.

Bateman, I., Carson, R.T. and Day, B. (2002) *Economic Valuation with Stated Preference Techniques: a Manual*, 89-111, Edward Elgar Publishing, Camberley, UK.

Becker, Gary S. (1974) 'A theory of social interactions', *Journal of Political Economy* 82 (Nov./Dec.): 1063-93.

British Library (2004) *British Library: Measuring Our Value.*

Champ, Patricia A., Bishop, Richard C., Brown, Thomas C. and McCollum, Daniel W. (1997) 'Using Donation Mechanisms to Value Nonuse Benefits from Public Goods', *Journa of Environmental Economics and Management* 33 (2): 151-62.

Corneille, O., Monin, B. and Players, G.. (2005) 'Is Positivity a Cue or a Response Option? Warm Glow vs. Evaluative Matching in the Familiarity for Attractive and Not-So-Attractive Faces', *Journal of Experimental Social Psychology* 41 (4): 431-37.

Chung, Hye-Kyung (2008) 'The Contingent Valuation Method in Public Libraries', *Journal of Librarianship and Information Science* 40 (2): 71-80.

Hackl, Franz and Pruckner, Gerald J. (2005) 'Warm Glow, Free-Riding and Vehicle Neutrality in a Health-Related Contingent Valuation Study', *Health Economics* 14 (3): 293-306.

Hausman, J. (ed.) (1993) *Contingent Valuation: a Critical Assessment*, North-Holland, New York.

Hanley, Nick, Ryan, Mandy and Wright, Robert (2003) 'Estimating the Monetary Value of Health Care: Lessons from Environmental Economics', *Health Economics* 12 (1): 3-16.

Kahneman, D. and Knetsch, J. (1992) 'Valuing Public Goods: the Purchase of Moral Satisfaction', *Journal of Environmental Economics and Management* 22 (1): 57-70.

Kim, J. and Byun, W. (2003) 'A Comparison of the WTPs according to the CVM Question Formats', *Journal of Korean Forestry Society* 92(3): 270-275.

Matthews, Joseph R. (2002) *The Bottom Line: Determining and Communicating the Value of the Special Library, Libraries Unlimited*, Westport, Conn.

Nunes, Paulo A.L.D. (2002) *The Contingent Valuation of Natural Parks: Assessing the Warm Glow Propensity Factor, in: New Horizons in Environmental Economics Series*, Edward Elgar Publishing, Camberley, UK.

Nunes, Paulo A.L.D. and Schokkaert, Erik (2003) 'Identifying the Warm Glow Effect in Contingent Valuation', *Journal of Environmental Economics and Management* 45 (2): 231-45.

Portugal, Frank H. (2000) *Valuing Information Intangibles: Measuring the Bottom-Line contribution of Librarians and Information Professionals,* Special Libraries Association, Washington, DC.

Pouta, Eija (2004) 'Attitude and Belief Questions as a Source of Context Effect in a Contingent valuation survey', *Journal of Economic Psychology* 25 (2): 229-42.

Smith, Richard D. (2000) 'The Discrete Choice Willingness-To-Pay Question Format in Health Economics: Should We Adopt Environmental Guidelines? *Medical Decision Marking* 20 (2): 194-204.

Smith, Richard D. (2006) 'It's Not Just What You Do, It's The Way That You Do It: the Effect of Different Payment Card Formats and Survey Administration on Willingness To Pay for Health Gain', *Health Economics* 15 (3): 281-93.

Welsh, M. P. and Poe, G. L. (1998) 'Elicitation Effects in Contingent Valuation: Comparisons to a Multiple Bounded Discrete Choice Approach', *Journal of Environmental Economics and Management* 36 (2): 170-85.

Analyzing Altruistic Motivations in Public Library Valuation using Contingent Valuation Method[15)]

Altruism is recognized as a significant component of *willingness to pay* (WTP) estimates when using *contingent valuation method* (CVM). The argument of whether all values that are motivated by altruism can be considered as real value has been discussed in various fields. In order to derive the real WTP value for public library valuation, an attempt was made to decompose an individual's total WTP into two categories: *local* versus *global* and *paternalistic* versus *non-paternalistic*. A contingent valuation survey was conducted to demonstrate how altruistic motivations affect WTP estimates for public libraries. Approximately 22 percent of the WTP value was found to be excluded from the total WTP value, because they are motivated by local and non-paternalistic altruistic attitudes. The results suggest that in a WTP study using the contingent valuation method, one must design a survey questionnaire taking into account two different aspects of altruistic motivation with a comprehensive view.

---

15) 이 논문은 2012년 Library & Information Science Research 34권 1호(72~78쪽)에 게재되었음
[공저: Lee, Soon-Jae].

1. Introduction

The *contingent valuation method* (CVM) is a survey-based technique generally accepted as a meaningful tool used to estimate the value of various nonmarket goods, including libraries and museums. More than 40 projects have been reported as applying CVM as a way to measure the value of public library services (Chung et al., 2009). The values of public goods in CVM are broadly categorized into two attitudes: pure self-interest and altruism. In general, the altruistic values are divided into two categories: *global* versus *local* and *paternalistic* versus *non-paternalistic*. Global altruism is projected toward those outside of one's direct family members, and local altruism toward members of one's own family. Similarly, paternalistic altruism is based on specific public goods being valued, while non-paternalistic altruism is not attached to any particular public goods being valued, and is often referred to as "pure altruism."

The question of whether *willingness to pay* (WTP) motivated by altruism should be included as benefits has been discussed in the literature of welfare economics (Aabø & Audunson, 2002; Brady, 2008; Johannsson, 1992; Margolis, 1982; Milgrom, 1993; Ray, 1987). In the standard neo-classical model, value is understood as the personal benefits each individual receives from the public project. It implies that the amount people are willing to pay for a public project is independent of the benefits others receive. Milgrom (1993) indicated that counting one person's WTP for another's happiness in a benefit-cost calculation leads to false conclusions, due to double or triple counting of the beneficiary's benefits. Several studies (e.g., Bergstrom, 1982; Jacobsson et al., 2007; Johannson, 1992; Jones-Lee, 1991; Ray, 1987) took a different view, however. They argued that Milgrom's view was too broad to derive accurate WTP values. Thus, it becomes necessary to discriminate between different aspects of altruistic values, and determine the validity of their inclusion in the public goods valuation analysis.

Jones-Lee (1991), based on the results in Bergstrom (1982), insisted that one could include altruism in willingness to pay if, and only if, altruism was exclusively safety-focused. In estimating values of statistical lives, Jacobsson et al. (2007) suggested that policymakers ignore neutral altruism, although the policymakers include paternalistic altruism that focuses on others' safety. Aabø and Strand (2004) appear to be the first to address the issue of altruism in the field of public libraries. In a practical application of the WTP approach, they made a distinction between local and global altruism, but they did not attempt to distinguish between paternalistic and non-paternalistic altruism.

In the field of public library valuation, very few empirical studies have dealt with the two aspects of altruistic values in a comprehensive manner, even though it is of great importance in analyzing WTP values in public goods valuation. This research introduces a new approach to integrate two categories of altruistic motivations (local versus global, non-paternalistic versus paternalistic) in order to evaluate the role of altruism in public library valuation.

2. Problem Statement

Contingent valuation method (CVM) is generally accepted as a meaningful method to cover the nonuse value, as well as the use value of various nonmarket goods. Altruistic motivation, a major component of nonuse value in contingent valuation (CV) surveys for public goods valuation, presented some fundamental problems of interpretation in the economics literature (Bergstrom, 1982; Johansson, 1992; Milgrom, 1993; Ray, 1987; Rodriguez & Leon, 2003).

Existing literature reviews address the necessity to analyze the role of altruism when using CVM (e.g., Bergstrom, 1982; Johannson, 1992; Milgrom, 1993; Ray, 1987), as the altruistic value is an important factor of overestimated WTP values in the conventional CVM format. There are very few studies that actually conduct CV surveys with a complete understanding of the role of altruism. Without good answers to altruistic motivations, the CVM is in serious trouble as part of a decision-making procedure.

The form of altruism has roughly been classified into two different categories: local versus global altruism, and non-paternalistic versus paternalistic altruism. Researchers have agreed that altruism arising from local and non-paternalistic motivations should be excluded from the total value, due to problems of double counting (Aabø & Strand, 2004; Brady, 2008; Jacobsson et al., 2007; Johansson, 1994; Jones-Lee, 1991, 1992).

Nonetheless, little research has addressed this issue in valuation projects of public libraries. Aabø and Strand (2004) found that values arising from global altruism compose a significant share of the public library's total value. It is not sufficient to conclude the WTP value of the library by only including one dimension of altruism, however, since the other dimension of altruism, paternalistic versus non-paternalistic, is not taken into account in the valuation.

Thus, there is a need to extend the work of Aabø and Strand (2004) by analyzing the two categories of altruistic motivation to derive the true WTP in public library valuation. The attempt to make a distinction between paternalistic and non-paternalistic altruism needs to be made operational in the public library setting. There are many questions, such as "Do traditional CVM results include altruistic motivations? And if so, "What proportion of altruistic value should be excluded from the real WTP?" The research questions are 1) what proportion of global altruism is arising from paternalistic and non-paternalistic altruism, respectively, and 2) how do these altruisms affect the true public library value?

This research contributes to the task of identifying how the value of the public library is affected by altruism, and what fraction of altruistic motivation should be excluded when using the CVM. In addition, the CV survey conducted demonstrates how local public libraries should apply this approach to their valuation projects.

3. Literature Review

The *total value* of a public library is defined as the sum of *use value* (direct use value) and *nonuse value* (indirect use value). Use value is the value derived from *present use value* ("I want to use the library regularly"). Nonuse value is the value derived from nonusers who have no direct use of the library.

In general, altruistic motivations are classified into two different categories to incorporate the altruistic motivations as a reasonable benefit: global versus local and non-paternalistic versus paternalistic (e.g., Aabø & Strand; 2004; Bergstrom, 1982; Johansson, 1994; Jones-Lee, 1991, 1992). The first question about altruism is whether it is motivated by local or global altruism.

Strand (2004a) divided altruism into three value components: pure self-interest, interest towards one's close family members, and altruism towards all others. An important issue was whether the two latter parts should be included in the real value of public goods. The study found that about 30 percent of total value of statistical lives is found to be motivated by pure self-interest, 50 percent by concerns for close family members, and about 20 percent by altruistic concerns. He suggested that the concept of close family members may include those not sharing a common household budget.

In the field of public libraries, Aabø and Strand (2004) defined local altruism as the sum of values arising from pure self-interest and close families, and therefore excluded them from the total WTP value. This definition implies that the values arising from global altruism, directed towards others rather than the respondents' close family members, can be included as part of the overall social value of public libraries.

Whether global altruism is arising from paternalistic or non-paternalistic motives, the second category has been discussed in economics in order to derive accurate values of public goods. Paternalistic altruism has been studied by Jones-Lee (1991) and Johansson (1994), while non-paternalistic altruism has been discussed by Lazo, et al. (1997) and Strand (2004b) in the context of value of statistical lives.

Results from recent research in economics prove suggest that values motivated by global and paternalistic altruism should be included in proper public goods valuation, whereas values arising from local and pure altruism typically ought to be excluded (Bergstrom, 1982; Johansson, 1994; Jones-Lee, 1991, 1992). It implies that one should include its WTP only if altruism is directed towards others rather than close family members, and only if the WTP is exclusively safety-focused.

This is why double counting can occur when WTP values based on non-paternalistic motivations are included to the WTP estimates. Jones-Lee (1991) demonstrated that the values base on non-paternalistic motivations should be excluded from the total WTP estimates in the valuation of statistical lives if the altruism is not entirely safety focused, due to the likelihood of double or triple counting the beneficiary's benefits.

Empirical evidence on the value of altruism was provided by Viscusi, et al. (1988) for health risks, and by Johanesson, et al. (1996) for the value of safety. Eight years later, Rodriguez and Leon (2004) investigated the hypothesis of paternalistic altruism by utilizing a choice experiment technique. They found that altruistic preferences were relevant for evaluating welfare measures if one was concerned with those goods affecting the welfare of others.

Aabø and Strand (2004) addressed the value of public libraries in terms of the specific context of WTP assessments. They found that 40% of the library's total value is motivated by nonuse value, and 15% to 30% of total value is motivated by global altruism in nonuse value. They argued that altruism should be included in public library valuation, if and only if, it is global.

4. Methodology

4.1. Contingent valuation method

The contingent valuation method is used to assess the intangible economic analysis of public library valuation. It is a survey methodology developed to assign value to nonmarket goods. Respondents are asked to understand their value of constructed changes in the provision of particular goods, and state their maximum willingness to pay for the improvement (or alternatively, their minimum compensations for the worsening) that this change implies for them.

In this study, respondents were requested to assume financial crisis over the country, and reflecting the budgetary structure of public libraries, the maintenance of public libraries was forced to be paid for on voluntary basis by residents. To avoid the shutdown of public libraries, only those respondents with a positive WTP were allowed to voluntarily choose the maximum amount of monthly fees they would be willing to pay.

4.2. Survey design and implementation

4.2.1. Sample

The survey was conducted in person in March 2010. A total of 300 questionnaires were prepared for random distribution to passengers at the Jamsil subway station, located in the southeastern ward of Seoul. From the distributed questionnaires, the study was based on the data obtained with a choice experiment survey in Jamsil of Seoul. The city, with a population of approximately 11 million inhabitants, was chosen, because it represents roughly a quarter of the entire South Korean population. Jamsil is also one of the main business centers of Seoul, as it is the hub for the main subway line, Line 2, and many connecting bus routes pass through as well. This busy crossroads gave researchers access to various population groups in terms of age, occupation, and levels of education.

4.2.2. Mode of survey administration

Researchers approached approximately 300 people at the Meeting Plaza, located at the intersection of Jamsil metro station and a large shopping center, and 200 agreed to take the survey. A gift certificate valued at 5,000 Korean won was given to those who participated in the survey.

A number of people spent several minutes in a face-to-face interview. In-person interviews were preferred, based on strong justifications that the mode was by far the most appropriate mode of survey administration (Bateman, et al., 2002). Some respondents agreed to participate but were not available at the time because of time or space constraints, and they were e-mailed the questionnaire. The purpose of the survey was thoroughly explained in the e-mails, and prior to the interviews.

4.2.3. WTP question format

The survey used the payment card (PC) format, where respondents were requested to review an ordered sequence of bids and value each price. Respondents also had the option of selecting "not sure", in addition to "yes" or "no", which allowed them to express ambivalence, and make less of a commitment (Welsh & Poe, 1998).

The respondents' WTP was then placed in between the minimum and maximum amount they voted for. Furthermore, in order to avoid starting point bias, respondents were randomly given one of two different versions of the PC questionnaire formats, either the high-to-low or the low-to-high listings. According to Smith (2006), the high-to-low version results in significantly higher values than the low-to-high version. In each case, the values on the cards ranged from 1,000 to 15,000 Korean won[16]. The range was derived from the pretest—conducted in January 2010 to improve the internal validity of WTP values—in which no one gave a value of over 15,000 Korean won.

4.2.4. Survey design

The questionnaire, revised based on the results of the pretest, consisted of three sections. The first section was composed of three parts relating to demographic issues, respondents' levels of satisfaction,

---

16) In 2010, approximately 1,200 Korean won was equivalent to U.S. $1.

and perceptions toward public libraries. The demographic details included gender, age, education level, and occupation.

The second section was designed to estimate the respondents' total WTP. Respondents were requested to express their WTP estimates in a hypothetical situation. To avoid the closure of public libraries, only those respondents with a positive WTP were allowed to voluntarily choose the maximum amount of monthly fees they would be willing to pay; they were given eight different price ranges.

The third section was designed to distinguish between altruistic motivations that ought to have been included or excluded from WTP values. Respondents were requested to allocate a percentage to each type of motivation, based on their subjective measures of how each motivation affects their WTP valuations.

Those respondents that stated a positive (+) value on altruistic motivation were requested to move on to the next item. These respondents were then requested to designate a certain percentage to a list of statements relating to the two different motivations: local and global altruisms.

- *Local altruism*: I am willing to pay for the operation of public library, since I (and my close family) may need to use it. (Close family is defined as those who share a common budget and a single decision maker in the household.)
- *Global altruism*: I am willing to pay for the operation of public library, since the public library promotes national pride and has bequest value.

Only those respondents who gave a positive value on global altruism proceeded to the next item. In addition, local altruists who were 100% motivated by self-interest were removed from the sample because of the risk of double counting, based on the concept that altruism should be included in public library valuation if, and only if, it is global. The next items were designed to distinguish whether the respondents' WTP values are derived from paternalistic or non-paternalistic motivations.

- *non-paternalistic altruism*: I am willing to pay, since public libraries are similar to other cultural facilities (such as museums and stadiums), and thus will increase the overall welfare and happiness of the community.
- *Paternalistic altruism*: I am willing to pay, since public libraries contribute specifically to heightening the cultural level of the community as a direct result of utilizing the facility and its resources.

Only those who gave a positive value on paternalistic altruism statements were included in the public library valuations, based on the assumption that increased altruism does not change the true WTP for the public library value when their altruism is non-paternalistic. Figure 1 illustrates the composition of different dimensions of altruism.

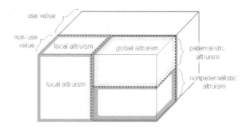

〈Figure 1〉 Public library valuations and
dimensions of altruism

4.2.5. Validity

Three elements were used in the survey to ensure greater validity of
the final WTP values. First, two different PC formats, a low-to-high
and a high-to-low listing of values, were used to avoid starting point
bias that might have occurred if either one was adopted. Smith (2006)
found that the high-to-low PC format produced significantly higher
results, compared to other formats such as the low-to-high and
shuffled formats, because of starting point bias.

Second, when stating their WTP from the PC, respondents
were allowed to express their level of certainty. This implied that
the respondents were allowed to express their level of uncertainty
in their WTP valuation, in addition to the yes or no response,
while the conservative survey considered only the definite yes or
no responses. Third, once an initial WTP amount had been stated,
the respondents were then asked a series of follow-up questions
to clarify whether they were absolutely certain that it was the
amount they would be willing to pay. It was designed to reduce

the ambivalence of respondents and enhance the internal validity of WTP values.

5. Findings

5.1 Description of survey data

Table 1 summarizes the characteristics of the sample. A total of 200 people responded to survey, with only one invalid response. Specifically, the face-to-face interview sample accounted for roughly three-fourths (147 respondents) of the sample, while the e-mail survey accounted for the remaining one-fourth (53 respondents). Of the valid respondents, 51.8% were female, and 98.5% of the respondents were between the age of 20 and 50. Also, 92% of the respondents held diplomas from undergraduate or graduate school; roughly half of the respondents were office workers, while 11.2% were unemployed. Notably, 70.4% of respondents had visited a public library at least once in the last year, and more than 40% used the library at least once a month. While it might appear that the survey was overrepresented by frequent library users, according to the 2008 Public Library Statistic, Koreans visited the public library 4.18 times—that is, once every three month—in 2010 ("Citizens used the public library more than 4 times last year", 2010). The respondents reflect this statistic.

Ten questions were provided to measure the satisfaction level, willingness-to-pay, and altruistic motivation with regards to public library valuation. The mean score of the overall satisfaction level with public libraries was 2.86 out of 5, as represented in Table 2, indicating that respondents were fairly satisfied with the public library service.[17] Respondents were willing to pay up to 6,712 Korean won monthly on average as a contribution to the operating expenses of the public library.

⟨Table 1⟩ Descriptive statistics for socioeconomic variables

		Frequency	Percent (%)
Gender	Male	96	48.2
	Female	103	51.8
Age	Teens	2	1.0
	20's	57	28.6
	30's	64	32.2
	40's	38	19.1
	50's	37	18.6
	60's or older	1	0.5
Education	Middle school	1	0.5
	High school	5	7.5
	College	126	63.3
	Graduate school	57	28.6
Occupation	Student (college + graduate)	20	10.2
	Housewife	11	5.6
	Office worker	93	47.4
	Manufacturing worker	26	13.3
	Professional	8	4.1
	Self-employed	16	8.2
	Unemployed	22	11.2

---

17) The 5-point Likert scale was used as follows: 1=strongly agree, 2=agree, 3=neutral, 4=disagree, 5=strongly disagree. 30.7% of the respondents were satisfied with the overall library service, while 17.2% were unsatisfied.

		Frequency	Percent (%)
Library visit	2-3 times a week	14	7.0
	Once a week	24	12.1
	1-3 times a month	45	22.6
	1-6 times a year	57	28.6
	Once a few years	43	21.6
	Almost no use	16	8.0

When using the low-to-high format, the mean WTP was 6,135 Korean won, while 7,167 Korean won when using the high-to-low format. A summary of responses to these questions using the two different versions of PC questionnaire formats is described in Table 2. There is no significant difference between the WTP values of the high-to-low and low-to-high formats.[18]

Just over a quarter, 26.8%, of the total public library value was found to be derived from altruistic motivations. The false altruistic motivation, which was excluded from the value of the public library, accounted for 21.54% of total value, while the true altruistic motivation arising from global and paternalistic motivation, which was included in the total value of the public library, accounted for 5.26%. This implies that approximately 1,799 Korean won is motivated by altruistic motivations, and only 353 Korean won among this value can be properly included in the real library value.

⟨Table 2⟩ Descriptive statistics for other variables

Variables		N	Mean
Overall satisfaction of public library		186	2.86
WTP (KRW)	Total	118	6,712

---

18) The difference between the mean WTP values using different formats was not significant (p = 0.190).

Variables		N	Mean
Overall satisfaction of public library		186	2.86
Altruism (%)	Low-to-high	52	6,135
	High-to-low	66	7,167
	Total altruism	117	26.80
	False altruism1)	117	21.54
	True altruism2)	117	5.26

1) False altruism refers to the proportion of altruistic motivation that should be excluded from library valuation.

2) True altruism refers to the proportion of altruistic motivation that should be included in library valuation,

5.2 Relationship among socioeconomic variables, WTP, and altruistic motivation

Table 3 reports the relationship among socioeconomic variables, WTP, and altruistic motivations. According to the correlation matrix, socioeconomic characteristics such as gender, age, education, and occupation, were not significantly related to the level of altruistic motivation. It was found that age was positively related to the WTP amount with Pearson's r of 0.272 ($p = 0.003$), indicating that older people were more willing to pay a higher amount than younger people. Also, education level was marginally positively related to the WTP amount, with Pearson's r of 0.159 ($p = 0.086$), implying that well-educated people were most likely to pay a higher price for public library operations.

On the other hand, the frequency of library visits and satisfaction levels toward the public library was positively related to the level of altruistic motivation with Pearson's r of 0.260 ($p = 0.000$). The amount of WTP was somewhat positively related to the level of altruistic motivation, with Pearson's r of 0.122, but the relationship was not significant. The level of false altruistic motivation that should be excluded from the proper library valuation, however, was positively related to the level of total altruistic motivation, with Pearson's r of 0.717 ($p = 0.000$), that is, the higher the level of total altruistic motivation, the higher the level of false altruistic motivation.

⟨Table 3⟩ Correlation matrix of socioeconomic variables, WTP, and altruistic motivations

	Gender	Age	Education	Occupation	Frequency of visit	Satisfaction level	WTP	Total altruism	False Altruism
Gender	1								
	.								
	199								
Age	-.307**	1							
	.000	.							
	199	199							
Education	-.201**	.582**	1						
	.004	.000	.						
	199	199	199						
Occupation	.148*	.057	.104	1					
	.039	.429	.145	.					
	196	196	196	196					
Frequency of visit	-.240**	.363**	.303**	-.147*	1				
	.001	.000	.000	.041	.				
	198	198	198	195	199				
Satisfaction level	-.101	.225**	.170*	-.021	.260**	1			
	.170	.002	.021	.776	.000	.			
	185	185	185	182	185	186			
WTP	-.098	.272**	.159	.033	-.023	.074	1		
	.293	.003	.086	.725	.802	.445	.		
	118	118	118	116	117	109	118		

	Gender	Age	Education	Occupation	Frequency of visit	Satisfaction level	WTP	Total altruism	False Altruism
Total altruism	-.001	-.026	-.060	.078	.043	-.056	.122	1	
	.983	.716	.399	.280	.547	.451	.190	.	
	199	199	199	196	199	186	118	200	
False altruism	.122	.050	.062	.003	.210*	.124	.025	.717**	1
	.191	.592	.508	.975	.024	.197	.792	.000	.
	116	116	116	113	116	109	113	117	117

** Correlation is significant at 0.01 level (2-tailed).
* Correlation is significant at 0.05 level (2-tailed).

5.3 Measurement of different altruistic values

The nonuse value of the public library contains altruism, which accounted for 26.8% of the total library value. This altruistic motivation can be classified into local and global altruism, and each type can be further classified into paternalistic and non-paternalistic altruism (see Table 4). Of the 26.8%, global altruism accounted for 13.7% and local altruism 13.1%. Furthermore, of the 13.7% of global altruism, paternalistic altruism accounted for 5.2%, and non-paternalistic altruism 8.5%.

Therefore, 5.2% of the public library value arising from true altruism should be included in the total library value. However, false altruism, the sum of local altruism (13.1%) and non-paternalistic altruism (8.5%), should be excluded from library valuation. This means that 21.6% of the public library value was overestimated in its traditional WTP value.

Total value (100%): WTP			
Use value	Nonuse value(26.8%)		
	Local altruism	Global altruism(13.7%)	
73.2%	13.1%	Paternalistic altruism	Nonpaternalistic Altruism
		5.2%	8.5%
	False altruism	True altruism	False altruism

Eighty percent of the respondents were confident of their valuation, whereas only 1.8% was unsure. Such high level of respondents' certainty ensures the validity of the WTP values. Also, the use of two different PC formats, low-to-high listing (44%) and high-to-low listing (56%), decreases the starting point bias, thereby further enhancing the overall validity of the WTP values.

6. Discussion

The results support the argument of several studies (e.g., Aabø & Strand, 2004; Bergstrom, 1982; Jones-Lee, 1991, 1992) that it is improper to completely remove or exclude altruism as a whole from the public goods valuation analysis, as altruism is further composed of different dimensions of altruistic values.

Prior studies suggest the different dimensions of altruism: local versus global altruism, and paternalistic versus non-paternalistic altruism. In order to identify the specific altruistic values that need to be included or excluded in public library valuation, altruistic values are measured based on the following equations (1), (2), and (3):

$$\text{Altruism} = \text{Altruism}^{local} + \text{Altruism}^{global} \text{ or } \text{Altruism}^{paternalistic}$$
$$+ \text{Altruism}^{non\text{-}paternalistic}$$
$$\text{Altruism}^{local} = \text{Altruism}^{local}_{paternalistic} + \text{Altruism}^{local}_{nonaternalistic}$$
$$\text{Altruism}^{global} = \text{Altruism}^{global}_{paternalistic} + \text{Altruism}^{global}_{non\text{-}paternalistic} \quad (1)$$
$$\text{Altruism}^{true} = \text{Altruism}^{global \cap paternalistic} \quad (2)$$
$$\text{Altruism}^{false} = \text{Altruism} - \text{Altruism}^{true} = \text{Altruism}^{local}$$
$$+ \text{Altruism}^{global \cap non\text{-}paternalistic} \quad (3)$$

Altruism consists of local and global altruism, say some studies (e.g., Aabø & Strand, 2004) or paternalistic and non-paternalistic altruism, say other studies (e.g., Bergstrom, 1982, Jones-Lee, 1991, 1992). In previous studies, the two different dimensions were assumed to be mutually exclusive. However, this study suggests integrating the two dimensions of altruistic motivation.

In this WTP survey, those who possess global altruistic motivation are classified as paternalistic or non-paternalistic. Among the 200 respondents, 118 expressed their willingness to pay a monthly operating expense to finance the public library, and 105 of those 118 possessed global altruism: "I think that the value of public libraries are beneficial for the community residents".

Among the 105 respondents with global altruism, non-paternalistic altruism, such as, "I expressed willingness to pay because public libraries were considered public good, such as museums, for the community", accounted for 62 percent, while paternalistic altruism, "I expressed willingness to pay for the object of public libraries", accounted for the remaining 38%.

The proportion of paternalistic (or "pure") altruism should be included in the public library value because it is "true" altruism inherent in the human nature. However, the proportion of non-paternalistic altruism, as well as local altruism, is "false" altruism and should be excluded from the library value. This proportion accounts for 8.5% of WTP value in library valuation, and the "false" altruism as a whole accounts for 21.6% of total value.

In the meantime, there are some limitations to this study. The survey sample was collected from the passengers of the Seoul metropolitan subway station, which was chosen because of the easy access to various population groups. The risk of lacking geographic diversity, and not reflecting the possible difference in altruistic attitudes of small cities or rural area residents, however, clearly exists.

Furthermore, due to the use of nonprobability sampling, generalizations beyond the context of the study are difficult to infer, and the result of the altruistic behaviors shown in the study may not reflect that of the general population. Also, some altruistic behaviors may have been differently shaped by specific types of people or culture, which may possibly affect the WTP value of the public library differently across various countries.

The discussion of altruism naturally leads to the topic of charitable donations, as the two are directly related. Koreans often claim that Korea is a nation of sympathy, while criticizing the West for its selfishness and individualism., Ironically, however, it is evident that donation is a significant part of life to Americans, while Koreans tend to be less generous with such contributions. According to AAFCR (2003)'s report, Giving USA, 89% of households in USA have made a donation to charitable organizations, while 43% of Koreans have never donated a penny in their lives.

Several studies have concluded that higher-income households donate higher amounts than lower-income households (Bekkers & Wiepking, 2007; Lyons & Nivison-Smith, 2006). Bekkers and Wiepking (2007) conducted a survey on characteristics of individuals and households that were involved in giving, and identified eight important factors mainly driving the act of giving, including income.

However, this issue has never been applied to specific nonmarket goods, such as public libraries, in order to compare the difference between various countries. There is a need for future research to study whether people in higher-GNP countries like the United States and Norway tend to have stronger altruism in public library valuation than those in relatively lower-GNP countries like

Korea, and whether there is a difference in paternalistic and non-paternalistic altruism across countries.

For future research, it is suggested that CVM studies incorporate the difference in cultures across various countries, which evidently cause the difference in charitable donations, to the overall total valuation of the public library. Such studies will overcome the limitations from conducting a sample in a rather restricted area, and will represent a more accurate valuation of the influence of altruism on public goods.

7. Conclusion

Contingent valuation studies on public libraries have been conducted across countries, and altruism in the context of WTP assessment of public goods is one of the central issues in this stream of literature. This research attempted a new approach to integrate two different dimensions of altruistic motivations (local versus global and non-paternalistic versus paternalistic) in a comprehensive mode, thereby measuring the relative importance of four different altruistic motives for public library valuation.

This is the first study that attempted to measure global altruism in two different segments in valuing public libraries. This research extends Aabø and Strand's (2004) by integrating another dimension of altruism (paternalistic versus non-paternalistic), finding that global altruism in nonuse value, 13.7% of total library value, is composed of paternalistic (5.2%) and non-paternalistic altruism (8.5%), and suggests the portion of non-paternalistic altruism be excluded from public library valuation.

The fact that previous CVM studies on public library valuation failed to deal with this issue implies the overestimation of library values. Thus, when designing questionnaires for CVM surveys, the altruistic value based on self-interest ought to be excluded, as it causes a double counting problem. Also, the questionnaire should be designed to exclude the portion that respondents evaluate as general public goods, rather than the specific value of the public library itself.

This study supports the argument of previous research that altruism is composed of two different dimensions (local versus global and paternalistic versus non-paternalistic). Findings suggest, however, that the two aspects do not exist exclusively, but coexist and are closely integrated.

It is inappropriate to include the full value motivated by people's global altruistic attitude in their real WTP, as a significant portion (8.5% out of 13.7%) of those people were willing to pay regardless of whether the object was a public library. Thus, for a more accurate evaluation of the public library, this portion of global altruism ought to be excluded from the real WTP.

References

Aabø, S., & Audunson, R. (2002). Rational choice and valuation of public libraries: Can economic models for evaluating non-market goods be applied to public libraries? *Journal of Librarianship and Information Science, 34*(1), 5-15.

Aabø, S., & Strand, J. (2004). Public library valuation, nonuse values, and altruistic motivations. *Library & Information Science Research, 26*(3), 351-372.

AAFCR (2003). *Giving USA: The annual report on philanthropy for the year 2003.* Indianapolis, IN: AAFRC Trust for Philanthropy.

Bateman, I. J., Carson, R. T., Day, B., Hanemman, M., & Hanley, N., et al. (2002). *Economic valuation with stated preference techniques: A manual.* (248-295). UK: Edward Elgar Pub.

Bekkers, R., & Wiepking, P. (2007). Generosity and philanthropy: A literature review. Retrieved from http:// http://ssrn.com/abstract=1015507

Bergstrom, T. C. (1982). When is a man's life worth more than his human capital? In M.W. Jones-Lee (Ed.): *The value of life and safety.* Amsterdam: North-Holland.

Brady, K. L. (2008). Safety-focused altruism: valuing the lives of others (Master's thesis). Utah State University, Logan, Utah.

Chung, H. K., Ko, Y. M., Shim, W. S., & Pyo, S. H. (2009). An exploratory meta-analysis of library economic valuation studies. *Journal of the Korean Society for Library and Information Science, 43*(4), 117-137.

Citizens used the public library more than 4 times last year. (2010). Herald Media. 3. 31.

Holt, G. E., Elliot, D., & Moore, A. (1999). Placing a value on public library services. *Public Libraries,* 38(2), 98-108.

Jacobsson, F., Johannesson, M., & Borgquist, L. (2007). Is altruism paternalistic? *Economics Journal, 117*(520), 761-781.

Johanesson, M., Johansson, P. O., & O'Conor, R. M. (1996). The value of private safety versus the value of public safety. *Journal of Risk and Uncertainty, 13*(3), 263-275.

Johansson, P. O. (1992). Altruism in cost-benefit analysis. *Environmental and Resource Economics, 2*(6), 605-613.

Johansson, P. O. (1994). Altruism and the value of statistical life: Empirical implications. *Journal of Health Economics, 13*(1), 111-118.

Jones-Lee, M. W. (1991). Altruism and the value of other people's safety. *Journal of Risk and Uncertainty, 4*(2), 213-219.

Jones-Lee, M. W. (1992). Paternalistic altruism and the value on statistical life. *Economic Journal, 13*(1), 80-90.

Lazo, J. K., McClelland, G. H., & Schulze, W. D. (1997). Economic theory and psychology of non-use values. *Land Economics, 18,* 255-270.

Margolis, H. (1984). *Selfishness, altruism, and rationality: A theory of social choice.* Chicago: University of Chicago Press.

Milgrom, P. (1993). Is sympathy an economic value? Philosophy, economics, and the contingent valuation method. In J. A. Hausman (Ed.): *Contingent Valuation.* Amsterdam: North-Holland.

Navrud, S., & Strand, J. (2002). Social costs and benefits of preserving and restoring the Nidaros Cathedral. In S. Navrud, & R.C. Ready (Eds.), *Valuing cultural heritage* (pp. 31-39). Cheltenham, UK: Elgar Publishing.

Noonan, D. (2002). *Contingent valuation studies in the arts and culture: an annotated bibliography*. Chicago, Il.: The Cultural Policy Center at the University of Chicago. Retrieved from http://cultrapolicy.uchicago.edu/publications.html.

Ojea, E., & Loureiro, M. L. (2007). Altruistic, egoistic and biospheric values in willingness to pay (WTP) for wildlife. *Ecological Economics, 63*(4), 807-814.

Pollicino, M., & Maddison, D. (2001). Valuing the benefits of cleaning Lincoln Cathedral. *Journal of Cultural Economics, 25*(2), 131-148.

Ray, D. (1987). non-paternalistic intergenerational altruism. *Journal of Economic Theory, 41*(1), 112-132.

Rodriguez, M. X. & Leon, C. J. (2003). Altruism and the economic values of environmental and social policies. *Environmental and Resource Economics, 28*(2), 233-249.

Schenk, R. E. (1987). Altruism as a source of self-interested behavior. *Public Choice, 53*(2), 187-192.

Smith, R. D. (2006). It's not just what you do, it's the way that you do it: The effect of different payment card formats and survey administration on willingness to pay for health gain. *Health Economics, 15*(3), 281-93.

Strand, J. (2004a). *Public- and private-good values of statistical lives: results from a combined choice-experiment and contingent-valuation survey.* (Working paper.) Oslo, Norway: University of Oslo. Retrieved from http://folk.uio.no/jostrand/lifepaper02.pdf

Strand, J. (2004b). *Public-good valuation and intrafamily allocation.* (CESifo Working Paper, No. 1351). Oslo, Norway: University of Oslo. Retrieved from http://www.ifo.de/pls/guestci/download/CESifo%20Working%20Papers%202004/CESifo%20Working%20Papers%20December%202004/cesifo1_wp1351.pdf

Viscusi, W. K., Magat, W. A., & Forrest, A. (1988). Altruistic and private valuations of risk reduction. *Journal of Policy Analysis and Management, 7*(2), 227-245.

Willis, K. (1993). *Paying for heritage.* Newcastle, UK: Economic and Social Research Council, Countryside Change Initiative.

정혜경

미국 오하이오 주의 켄트주립대학교에서 문헌정보학석사(MLS) 학위를 취득한 후, 노스
캐롤라이나 주의 가드너웹 대학교 중앙도서관에서 자료조직 책임사서로 3년여 동안 재
직하였다. 한국으로 돌아와서는 한국외국어대학교 외국학종합연구센터 연구원 겸 사서
로 근무하다가, 지난 20여 년 동안 KDI 국제정책대학원 정보자료 실장, 경제협력센터
실장, 개발자료 팀장 등으로 재임하고 있다. 2004년 성균관대학교에서 문헌정보학 분
야 박사학위를 취득하였으며, 이후 성균관대·명지대·이화여대 등에서 자료조직과 기
록관리 분야 강의를 해왔다. 석사과정부터 약 30편에 가까운 학술논문과 저서『디지털
아카이빙의 경제성 분석』등이 있다.

도서관과 경제성 분석

초판인쇄 2020년 7월 31일
초판발행 2020년 7월 31일

지은이 정혜경
펴낸이 채종준
펴낸곳 한국학술정보㈜
주소 경기도 파주시 회동길 230(문발동)
전화 031) 908-3181(대표)
팩스 031) 908-3189
홈페이지 http://ebook.kstudy.com
전자우편 출판사업부 publish@kstudy.com
등록 제일산-115호(2000. 6. 19)

ISBN 979-11-6603-031-4 93010